CHRISTIAN SPIRITUALITY

Themes from the Tradition

LAWRENCE S. CUNNINGHAM
AND
KEITH J. EGAN

PAULIST PRESS
New York • Mahwah, N.J.

Acknowledgments
The excerpt from "The Dry Salvages" in *Four Quartets*, copyright 1941 by T. S. Eliot and renewed 1969 by Esme Valerie Eliot, is reprinted by permission of Harcourt Brace & Company and Faber and Faber Ltd. The excerpt from "Song: If you seek…" is reprinted from *The Collected Poems of Thomas Merton*, published by New Directions, © 1961–1971, 1976, 1977 by the Trustees of the Merton Legacy Trust.

Cover design by Tim McKeen.

Library of Congress Cataloging-in-Publication Data

Cunningham, Lawrence.
    Christian spirituality : themes from the tradition / Lawrence S. Cunningham and Keith J. Egan.
        p.   cm.
    Includes bibliographical references and index.
    ISBN 0-8091-3660-0
    1. Spiritual life—Christianity. I. Egan, Keith J., 1930–   . II. Title.
BV4501.2.C856 1996
248—dc20   96-24740
                                                                       CIP

Published by Paulist Press
997 Macarthur Boulevard
Mahwah, New Jersey 07430

Printed and bound in the
United States of America

Contents

For
Cecilia Cunningham
and
Connie Egan

Introduction

*T*he idea for this book emerged from our common experience of teaching a course on Christian spirituality for MA/MDiv and senior undergraduate students from Saint Mary's College and the University of Notre Dame. That course focused on some classical texts from the Catholic tradition but, as we worked at a close reading of those texts, it was soon apparent that we had to expend much energy doing reflective work on some of the themes that ran through the writings of various authors. We subsequently taught an intensive summer school graduate course on the writings of Thomas Merton and Saint John of the Cross which added further stimulation to our thinking. The influence of these two spiritual masters are reflected thoroughout these chapters.

This present book, then, pays homage to those classic authors and others within the tradition whom we lacked time to consider but who are represented in these pages. Our experience with the classics very much determined what we wanted to say and how we came to pick the chapter topics. We hope that these pages will send our readers to the classics themselves.

This work makes no pretense of being a systematic treatment of spirituality. Our intention is simply to reflect on some major classical themes in spirituality while providing, through the suggested readings and exercises appended to the end of each chapter, some clues for further study and research. In our chapters we have tried to blend both historical surveys and contemporary reflection. Thus, for example, we draw heavily on traditional topics like solitude or friendship or asceticism from the classical sources but have attempted to show how these themes, traditional in the history of the tradition, have a contemporary pertinence.

We have attempted to pitch our writing to a specific audience: persons interested in Christian spirituality who would like both some historical context and actual reflection on the historical

1

materials. To aid in that aim we have alternated heavily historical chapters with more reflective ones. We envision the book being used, for example, in a formal classroom setting (supplemented, where appropriate, by some primary texts) or by an individual or small group for non-formal learning. We hope that the book reflects our common desire to read texts and to reflect on them in a sapiential fashion.

Each author took primary responsibility for a given chapter. We would exchange drafts for critique. Drafts were then rewritten. Finally, we took all of the chapters and spread them out on a long table to determine the order in which they should be put in the book. We then each reread the entire manuscript several times and met once again to see where there were problems, duplications, and so on.

This exercise in mutual criticism was accompanied by some "ground rules" which we set for ourselves. We would use the RSV/NRSV for scriptural quotations. Even though we were in debt to continental scholarship (who can write on spirituality seriously without access to the *Dictionnaire de spiritualité*?) we did not, with rare exceptions, put any foreign language bibliographical citations into our footnotes. We annotated some books at the end of each chapter for further reading. To the best of our ability we used gender inclusive language but did observe the older conventions when citing earlier authors.

The decision to limit the book to ten chapters has behind it a pedagogical reason and has no mystical significance. We felt that to add further to the book might make it too bulky for an introductory course taught in the space of one semester. We think that the chapters have a natural progression so that one topic gets amplified in the next. The controlling motif of the entire work is that Christian spirituality is best construed as a way of life as disciples of Jesus Christ in the Spirit. We see that way or journey as an open-ended, not yet finished, process. The decision to close the book with a chapter on the eucharist symbolizes our conviction that the many aspects of eucharistic theology enhance the insight of Vatican II that the liturgy is the apex of the Christian life. In the eucharist we can learn about the presence of Christ, the community that emerges from that presence, the virtue of hospitality understood as fundamental for ecclesiology, and the need to serve the world in justice and compassion.

Many of the ideas in this work have been tested out in the classrooms of Saint Mary's College and the University of Notre Dame as well at various places where we have been invited to speak. We are grateful to all of those whom we have met on our intellectual and spiritual journey; we can only pray that we have done justice to their insights, encouragement, and criticisms.

Keith J. Egan wishes, in particular, to thank the Lilly Fellows Program for the Humanities and the Arts housed at Valparaiso University who provided him space and time for research and writing during his sabbatical; much of his work on this book was done in that most agreeable setting. He also acknowledges the support of Saint Mary's College in giving him sabbatical leave. Lawrence S. Cunningham is much in debt to the University of Notre Dame for making the life of its faculty such a hospitable place within which to teach and write. We both express our thanks to the editorial staff of Paulist Press for their confidence in contracting for this work and their patience as we brought it to a final conclusion.

We dedicate these pages to Connie Egan and Cecilia Cunningham—our companions on the way.

1

Christian Spirituality

Introduction

*I*n 1958, in his private journal, Thomas Merton, not for the first time, reflected on the tension between his vocation as a monk and his role as a writer who had gained a certain amount of public fame. He recalled that as a young monk he had decided to give up writing in order to go "upward" into a "higher spirituality." He soon saw that this was a false step, that there was nothing wrong or contradictory about being both an authentic monk and a writer. To oppose these two roles was to have a false sense of the relationship between nature and grace.

What is striking about Merton's reflection is his use of the word "spirituality." Merton seems to have understood the word as somehow connected to otherworldliness, asceticism, disconnected from ordinary human tasks like writing. It had a pejorative ring to it.

Merton did not always use the word "spirituality" in this fashion, but when he did, he was calling on a tradition that had a history behind it. The word "spirituality" was first used in the seventeenth century in a negative fashion to describe elite forms of subjective religious practice.[1] It was a negative term when used of religious experience.

That is surely not the case today. Indeed, the word "spirituality" is today employed to describe everything from New Age practices and therapies to overcome addictions (such as Twelve Step programs like Alcoholics Anonymous) to forms of oriental meditation, prayer groups, and retreats in the desert. Books on spirituality

---

1. It is also the case that in this same period the word "mysticism" takes on the shading that the word popularly has today; see Michel de Certeau, *The Mystic Fable*, Vol. 1 (Chicago: University of Chicago Press, 1992) 94 et passim.

appear regularly from Christians, Jews, and Muslims. The word is used in so many ways that there has sprung up a whole literature attempting to define what the term means. The root from which the word "spirituality" springs is the Latin noun *spiritus* which means, as is evident, "spirit." In that sense, at least, we can say that spirituality signifies something connected with spirit, as opposed to— what? The body? The earthly? The material?

When the founding editors of the multi-volumed encyclopedia of world spirituality attempted to define spirituality, they knew that they had to provide a wide enough description to do justice to the widely divergent forms of religions they hoped to survey. The editors settled on this description: "...that inner dimension of the person called by certain traditions 'the spirit.' This spiritual core is the deepest center of the person. It is here that the person experiences ultimate reality...."[2]

That description seems terribly general but it will suffice for our purposes. Many words (e.g. "religion") are immediately understood by most people (we know generally what the word "religion" means) but are extremely hard to define with precision. Nonetheless, "religion," like "spirituality," as a general term is understood to have enough general characteristics—what the philosopher Ludwig Wittgenstein called "family resemblances"—to permit us to use the term with some assurance.

In this book "spirituality" refers to that dimension or dimensions of human experience which provide the spiritual aspect of our lives by enriching and giving "thickness" to our ordinary existence.

Christian Spirituality

Joann Wolski Conn has wisely noted that while the definition of spirituality may be generic, there are no generic spiritualities.[3] Spirituality quite rightly refers to our religious experience, but that experience is always rooted in a particularity: Jewish or Islamic or Christian or something else.

---

2. Preface to *World Spirituality: An Encyclopedic History of the Religious Quest*, general editor: Ewert Cousins (New York: Crossroad, 1985–).

3. Joann Wolski Conn. "Towards Spiritual Maturity," in *Freeing Theology: The Essential of Theology in Feminist Perspective,* edited by Catherine Mowry LaCugna (San Francisco: Harper/Collins, 1993) 237.

In this volume we intend to speak of *Christian* spirituality, and, to make the matter more particular, that spirituality which finds its expression in the Catholic tradition. We do not mean Catholic in any narrowly confessional fashion. We designate our approach as Christian and Catholic only to be clear about where our own roots are and what we know best. We also hope that these pages will indicate that we have drawn strongly on Anglican, Orthodox, and Reformed traditions in order to do justice to the insights these traditions have given us.

What is Christian spirituality?

Many authors have attempted to provide a definition or description in answer to that question.[4] It is obvious that the answer must engage the adjective *Christian*—our spirituality must have something to do with Jesus Christ. It is equally obvious that in the two millennia of the history of Christianity there have been—and continue to be—wildly different ways in which people have engaged Jesus. It is also clear that our answer must somehow do justice to the word "spirit." We will argue later on that it would be more precise to speak of Christian spiritualities rather than spirituality.

It will suffice for now if we simply say that Christian spirituality is the lived encounter with Jesus Christ in the Spirit. In that sense, Christian spirituality is concerned not so much with the doctrines of Christianity as with the ways those teachings shape us as individuals who are part of the Christian community who live in the larger world.

There is another issue: it is clear that we have behind us a whole tradition that has shaped us as Christians—what the bible has beautifully called a "whole cloud of witnesses" (Heb 12:1). In order to understand our spirituality we also need to have some sense of what has gone before us, how that "before us" has shaped us, and what we can apply to our lives today in both positive and negative ways.

That sense of a tradition brings with it one other question: how to study our common spiritual tradition. These are all issues upon which we will reflect in this chapter.

The Study of Christian Spirituality

The contemporary liberation theologian, Gustavo Gutiérrez, provides a handy schema for understanding the background and

---

4. In the appendix at the end of this chapter we provide a representative sample of such descriptions.

development of Christian spirituality. He distinguishes three stages in the formation of a Christian spiritual tradition which may be outlined in this fashion:

(1) Certain persons in the past have had a powerful religious experience as they lived their Christian faith. This experience may have been triggered by a conversion experience or a shattering event in their life or a state of awareness derived from their practice of prayer or preaching or daily living. These experiences gave them a new insight into the life of the Spirit or a new way of understanding God's word or a different approach in their desire to follow Jesus.

(2) They or people close to them reflect upon the experience and attempt to express it any one of a different number of ways: through their writing; through artistic expressions; in the formation of followers; by the composition of prayers; by preaching and teaching; by the founding of a new kind of Christian community, etc. Some of these insights may have such a lasting impression that new "schools" of spirituality are founded like that of the Franciscans or Cistercians or Jesuits. Indeed, the tradition speaks to us of spiritualities that have developed for quite specific communities or "types" within the church. A quick scan of the literature would reveal mission spiritualities, feminist spiritualities, and so on.

(3) These experiences and the traditions founded from them then enter into the broad Christian tradition. In the words of Gutiérrez, they "are not the end of the line...they are offered to the ecclesial community as a new way of being Christian."[5] Such traditions are built upon and drawn from or modified by subsequent generations of Christians.

The three stage analysis of Gutiérrez is not unlike that recently proposed by the Canadian scholar, Walter Principe, who proposes a similar three stage approach to the study of spirituality:

(1) The first level is the *real* or *existential* quality of a Christian's life as "influenced by the Holy Spirit or Spirit of God incorporating the person of Jesus Christ as Head, through whom he or she has access to the Father in a life of faith, hope, and service."

(2) The formulation of a *teaching* about the lived reality by transforming it into a formal theological system or a more practical, and less formal, orientation toward life.

---

5. Gustavo Gutiérrez, *We Drink from Our Own Wells* (Maryknoll: Orbis, 1983) 52-53. This is also the analysis of spirituality given in the *Catechism of the Catholic Church* #2684.

(3) The study by scholars about the first and second stages (especially the second) from a theological, historical, or comparative perspective.[6]

If we take the hints provided by these scholars, it seems clear that when we discuss Christian spirituality we must pay attention to Christian *experience*, how that experience gets *articulated*, and how we are to understand it both for its own sake and for whatever it might teach us about our own spiritual journey. Of necessity, then, the study of spirituality will call upon a number of disciplines: religious psychology, history, theology, cultural analysis, and so on.

The Contours of Christian Spirituality

In one sense this entire book will attempt to trace the outline or contours of Christian spirituality. Nonetheless, as a preliminary exploration we might make some broad generalizations, based on the word of God, that can serve as markers for what will follow in subsequent chapters.

(1) Christian spirituality presupposes a *way of life* and not an abstract philosophy or a code of beliefs. To be a Christian is to live in a certain way. In the New Testament the idea that to be a follower of Jesus is to enter on a way is a fundamental motif.

In a number of places in the Acts of the Apostles (9:2; 19:9; 19:23; 22:4; 24:14) we see that the term "The Way" was one of the oldest designations for being a Christian. Early Christians were called "followers of the way."

In the gospels we also see the concept of the way (in Greek: *hodos*) used to describe being a follower of Jesus. Mark's gospel has a wonderful scene set outside Jericho as Jesus makes his final journey to Jerusalem. He meets and cures the blind man, Bartimaeus, who "received his sight and followed him on the way" (Mk 10:52). Matthew has Jesus saying that his followers should follow him through the narrow gate since the "way is hard that leads to life" (Mt 7:13-14). Even in a late work like the epistle to the Hebrews we are told that Christ the high priest permits us entrance into the heavenly temple by "a new and living way he opened for us" (Heb 10:10).

---

6. Walter Principe, "Toward Defining Spirituality," *Sciences Religieuses/Studies in Religion* 12/2 (1983) 127-41. This essay is also extremely helpful for its history of the development of the word "spirituality."

Finally, we have the affirmation, in John's gospel, that the way of the Christian is rooted in Christ who says "I am the way..." (Jn 14:6).

We have evidence in the history of early Christianity that to choose the Christian life was to choose a way. The metaphor of the two ways occurs in the Hebrew bible (Dt 30:19; Jer 21:8) and was common in the Dead Sea community of the Jewish Essenes at Qumran. It also occurs as an introduction to an early second century church document called "The Teaching of the Twelve Apostles" (the *Didache*) which begins with this stark observation: "There are two ways, one of life and the other of death; and between the two ways there is a vast difference." Other early Christian writers like the author of the *Epistle of Barnabas* will contrast the way of light and the way of darkness.

To describe the Christian life as a way is to say implicitly that our life has a *direction* and a *goal* and that being on the way means that we are not *there yet*; we have not reached the goal.

To say that the Christian life has a direction is another way of saying something strongly emphasized at the Second Vatican Council: the Christian people are a pilgrim people, and our life, with all its burdens and joys, has a direction that begins in God and ends with God when all things are summed up in Christ.

To set out on this way, almost by definition, means that we have not yet arrived at our goal. In the context of Christian spirituality it means that our journey is as yet incomplete, tentative, but forward looking. To be on the way is not yet to be perfect. The Second Vatican Council expressed this "not yet" in powerful words: "For even now on this earth the Church is marked with a genuine though imperfect holiness. However, until there is a new heaven and a new earth...(cf. 2 Pet 3:13), the pilgrim Church in her sacraments and institutions, which pertain to this present time, takes on the appearance of the passing world. She herself dwells among creatures who groan and travail in pain until now and await the revelation of the [children] of God (cf. Rom 8:19-22)."[7]

(2) This Christian way of life is a life of *discipleship*. The word "disciple" (Greek: *mathetes*) occurs over two hundred and sixty times in the New Testament. Nearly seventy times in the gospels the word "disciple" is linked to the verb "to follow" (Greek: *akolouthein*). Discipleship is such a richly complicated concept in

---

7. Dogmatic Constitution on the Church, #48, in *The Documents of Vatican II,* edited by Abbott and Gallagher (New York: America Press, 1966).

the New Testament that it might be useful to unpack it a bit by setting out some of the notions connected to discipleship:

- One becomes a disciple by being called by Jesus (Mk 1:17). In other words, discipleship comes from the initiative of Jesus. One does not merely "sign up." One is called. To be a disciple is to respond to grace.
- The gospel call of Jesus cuts across both social lines (e.g. "tax collectors and sinners"—Mk 2:15) and sexual ones (Lk 8:2). Ritual purity and religious obedience were not primary criteria.
- The response to the call of Jesus demanded a radically changed life that would risk possessions, security, and home in order to be with him (Mk 3:14). The ultimate demand of discipleship finds its fullest expression in the cross.
- The relationship of Jesus to his disciples is a pedagogical one (teacher in relation to pupil) but it is also more than that. To be a disciple is not merely to learn the teaching of Jesus but to adhere to him as a person. Jesus does not say that we should follow his teaching; we are called to follow him. The modern Christian martyr, Dietrich Bonhoeffer, has put the matter clearly in a classic work: "Discipleship means adherence to Christ, and because Christ is the object of this adherence, it must take the form of discipleship....Christianity without the living Christ is inevitably Christianity without discipleship, and Christianity without discipleship is always Christianity without Christ."[8]
- To be a disciple of Jesus permits us to share in his ministry. The disciples were to share in his style of life (Mt 8:20) but they were also called upon to heal the sick, exorcise the demonic, and proclaim the kingdom of God (Mk 6:7-13; Lk 10:2-12).
- In the final analysis, to be a disciple is to exercise sacrifical love after the manner of Jesus. Disciples must share with one another (Lk 6:30). The disciple is to be a servant (Greek: *diakonos*) to the extent that he or she is willing to take the last place in order to serve as Jesus himself has served (Mk 9:35). The ultimate test of this love is to give as Jesus himself gave on the cross. That final form of love is summed up in the command of Jesus: "Love one another as I have loved you. No one has greater love than this, to lay down one's life for another" (Jn 15:12-13).

---

8. *The Cost of Discipleship*, rev. ed. (New York: Macmillan, 1963) 63-64.

To this point we have described Christian spirituality as a way of discipleship. Let us underscore how central this description is for the Christian life. Johannes Metz has argued that this way is the *only* way to know Christ in any authentic fashion. Merely reading about Jesus or practicing some of his characteristic virtues is not enough. Metz writes: "Every attempt to know him [i.e. Christ], to understand him, is therefore always a journey, a following. It is only by following and imitating him that we know whom we are dealing with. Following Christ is therefore not just a subsequent application of the church's Christology to our life; the practice of following Christ is itself a central part of Christology....In this sense every Christology is subject to the primacy of practice."[9]

(3) The call to the way of discipleship is a call to belong to a *community*. While the gospels tell us that Jesus called many disciples on an individual basis, the actual living out of discipleship was in the community that went on the way with Jesus. There is nothing in the New Testament to suggest that being a Christian was a purely individual calling. Each person must make a personal response to the call of Jesus, but answering that call implies (or better: demands) that we join into that body of believers who witness to saving acts of the Lord in his life, death, and resurrection.

In the post-resurrection understanding of discipleship the theme of entering into the life, death, and resurrection of Christ is symbolized by baptism which is, at the same time, an initiation into the community of believers and an initiation into the body of Christ: "For just as the body is one and has many members, and all the members of the body, though many, are one body, so it is with Christ. For by one Spirit we were all baptized into one body—Jews or Greeks, slaves or free—and all were made to drink of one Spirit" (1 Cor 12:12-13).[10]

(4) The way of discipleship in community finds its highest expression in the sharing of the *eucharist*. It is in "the breaking of the bread" that Christ is recognized (Lk 24:30-31). It is in that gath-

---

9. Johannes B. Metz, *Followers of Christ* (New York: Paulist, 1978) 39-40. Two other books which treat discipleship in depth are: Dietrich Bonhoeffer, *The Cost of Discipleship,* rev. ed. (New York: Macmillan, 1963) and Fernando Segovia, ed., *Discipleship in the New Testament* (Philadelphia: Fortress, 1985).

10. For a fuller explication of the relationship of discipleship to ecclesiology, see Avery Dulles, *A Church To Believe In: Discipleship and the Dynamics of Freedom* (New York: Crossroad, 1982).

ered community when the word is preached and the bread broken that the memory of the life, death, and resurrection of Christ is remembered, re-called, re-enacted, and proclaimed. Luke provides a quick profile of this community of disciples: "And they devoted themselves to the teaching of the apostles and fellowship (Greek: *koinonia*), to the breaking of the bread and to prayers" (Acts 2:42).

We would like to emphasize this final point of the gathered community which celebrates the word and the eucharist in order to underscore the point that the spirituality of the Christian, while it makes strong individual demands on a person, is not fully captured in individual life. Authentic Christian spirituality must have an ecclesial character to it. Among the many meanings of the eucharist is its significance in shaping the community which affirms Jesus as Lord. Christian disciples gather to share in the Lord's supper in order to re-enact his saving acts in time and place and to affirm a communality of purpose. Indeed, one could say that one way to understand the missionary nature of the church is to say that as disciples of Jesus our task is to invite others to share at this table.

(5) Next, we affirm that someone sets out on the way of discipleship in the eucharistic community of believers *in the Spirit*. This brings us full circle to our term *spiritu*ality.

We insist on this point because it is all too easy to glide over the fact that the Christian faith is a trinitarian one. The Christian law of prayer (the so-called *lex orandi*) insists that we pray to God the Father through Jesus Christ in the Holy Spirit. It would be a tragic misshaping of the Christian faith to ignore that fact. It is all too easy to caricature the Christian mystical tradition as urging us simply to seek God as if God were some kind of timeless abstraction rather than a dynamic living personal God who is revealed by the Father through the Son in the Holy Spirit.

The New Testament makes clear that we know God best by looking at Jesus who reveals the Father to us in the Spirit. Luke Timothy Johnson makes this point so powerfully that we do not hesitate to quote him fully:

> Distinctive to Christian spirituality is the conviction that the Spirit has been made available, indeed powerfully present in the world, through the resurrection of Jesus. Jesus was, Paul tells us, "designated Son of God in power according to the Spirit of holiness by his resurrection from the dead" and therefore it is "through him that we have received grace and apostleship" (Rom 1:5). In contrast to Adam who became a "living being," says Paul,

Jesus by his resurrection became "life-giving spirit" (1 Cor 15:45). Jesus is not only the source of the Spirit. Jesus provides as well the shape of the Spirit's work. The pattern of transformation is given in the life and death of the messiah himself. The work of sanctification is therefore the work of replicating in the lives of Christians the messianic pattern enacted by God in Jesus.[11]

(6) Finally, any authentic Christian spirituality must reach out to everyone without respect to class, gender, or social condition. While there are many forms of Christian living that seek close bonds among its members (e.g. in the monastic life), it is incompatible for any group or individual to become so closed off to the needs of the world as to reflect either indifference or isolation from the sufferings, aspirations, and hopes of humanity. That would seem to be the clear meaning of the scriptures in its missionary call to teach the whole world and the Matthean insistence (Mt 25) that to find Christ one must find him in the hungry, thirsty, naked and imprisoned of the world. To turn Christian spirituality into a personal vehicle for therapy or as a shield from the exigent realities around us is to deform the heart of the message of Christ.

The Tradition of Christian Spirituality

Anyone who looks at the long history of Christianity in even a cursory manner recognizes that there are a bewildering number of ways in which people have attempted to live out the Christian life. In the name of the gospel, persons have formed communities to flesh out the call of radical discipleship, but these communities may have quite different emphases (e.g. some are aggressively missionary while others withdraw into a life of contemplation). Great saints have sought God through the exericse of the intellectual life or the life of charity or the following of Christ in radical poverty. People have sought to express quite particular forms of Christian spirituality based on the actual historical and existential situations in which they find themselves. Thus, for example, we find feminist spiritualities or spiritualities focused on the family or on the laity as well as spiritualities derived from the great spiritual masters/mistresses of the past.

Finally, no authentic Catholic spirituality can remain indifferent

11. Luke Timothy Johnson, *Faith's Freedom: A Classic Spirituality for Contemporary Christians* (Minneapolis: Fortress/Augsburg, 1990) 29.

to the insights of other Christian traditions or to the spiritual
search that characterizes the other religious traditions of the world.
An authentic Catholic spirituality must be, in other words, both
ecumenically and interreligiously open. That is the clear teaching
of the Second Vatican Council.

We will have many opportunities in the course of this book to
provide historical context for our consideration of particular aspects
of Christian spirituality. At this stage, however, we might again set
out some general considerations that stand behind any authentic
Christian spirituality both generally and in its particulars.

We might begin with what, at first blush, seems to be a paradox:
all Christian spirituality must root itself in the revealed word of
God, but in the word of God there is no single coherent spirituality
but, rather, many spiritualities. We will have many occasions later
in this book to notice what appear to be tensions within the gospel:
the tension between the desert and the city; the tension between
being in the world and shunning the world; the tension between
prayer and action, between theologies of the cross and theologies of
the resurrection, etc.

We will also note that entire ways of being Christian have been
based on a "canon within a canon" which is to say that there is a
certain angle of reading the gospel which emphasizes one particular strain within in it. There have been "monastic" readings of the
gospel and "missionary" ones. This complexity means that the bible
provides us with a catholicity of choices within the general framework of the scriptures. As one recent scholar has written: "We can
no longer expect to extract the spirituality of the New Testament,
but have every chance of detecting many."[12]

One good way to understand the relationship of the bible to the
Christian life is to think of the bible not so much as a text to be read
(although it is surely that) but as a text to be performed. After all,
is that not part of our common Christian experience? When we bap-
tize, celebrate the eucharist, enter into Sunday worship, serve the
poor through various activities, attempt to follow Christ in the living out of virtue, etc.—are not all those gestures and activities ways
of performing what we find in the word of God?

Frances Young has developed a rather fruitful analogy from
music to articulate the "performative" character of the bible:

---

12. Cheslyn Jones. "The New Testament," in *The Study of Spirituality,*
edited by C. Jones, G. Wainwright, and E. Yarnold (New York: Oxford
University Press, 1986) 60.

The biblical canon, then, is as it were the reportoire, inherited, given, to be performed. Selections are performed day by day and week by week in the liturgy. Exegetes, like musicians, need the discipline of rehearsing the score, trying out new ways of inter- pretation, researching the possibilities of meaning, grappling with the "physical" or "historical" restraints of the language, preparing for performance with appropriate ornamentation, Within their work, there will be bad performances and false inter- pretations....But all preachers and congregations are the per- formers and the hearers on whose inspiration the communication of the Word of God depends. The Word is both "incarnate" in a time-bound text and yet eternal, transcending the limits of human language and culture. Amateurs and professionals have a go with varying degrees of skill, fostering an audience which will be able to recognize the truly masterly performance. But any good performance has an authenticity of its own...."[13]

If Frances Young is correct—and her analogy is very appealing— some practical consequences may be drawn from it. When we read a particular spiritual master or mistress we might ask of the work: What text is being performed? What is the particular emphasis and from what books of the bible does this writer most commonly go to to shape his or her understanding of the Christian life?

We can obviously ask the same questions of the liturgy. At given seasons we might ask why these texts were chosen and what their "performance" says to us? Why do we read the prophets at Advent and how do we participate in their yearning? Why do we read the creation narratives on the eve of Easter and how do we understand ourselves as part of the "new creation" which they propose?

At a more personal level, we might turn the question back on ourselves: Where do we find our spiritual nourishment in the word of God? To put the question in a simpler fashion: What is our text? Conversely, we may ask which parts of the bible must upset and repel us? And for what reason?

We never hear the word of God in an abstract setting or apart from the gritty realities of our own social and personal life. The word of God always comes to us within the thickness of ordinary life. Those words take on significance and can be interpreted only against the background of such experience.Thus, for example, we might draw great aid from the reading of a given "classic" in our common spiri-

---

13. Frances Young, *Virtuoso Theology* (Cleveland: Pilgrim, 1992) 25.

tual tradition but it is useful to know that such a text comes from, say, a monastic or mendicant milieu of a different age with prescriptions for living that are hardly applicable for our own time.

Walter Principe has provided some fine guidelines for our encounter with such texts.[14] Basically, he writes that we must question the text: What is the text's view of God (king, friend, ineffable, etc.)? How do the persons of Jesus and the Spirit become revealed in this text, if at all? What does this text urge on us in our way to God? What virtues are stressed? What is its view of the world and of history? Questions like these, Principe writes, can provide us with a window into the imaginary world of the author(s). To these questions, we can also reverse the process and ask: What is not being talked about? What is being presupposed? How are these texts helpful for or antagonistic to a holistic anthropology?

As we query texts from the past it is crucial to be sensitive to the cultural situation of these texts. Such sensitivity permits us to read in a manner that allows us to disentangle what is peculiar to a given time but not useful for our own and, equally, frees us from the temptation to a kind of spiritual fundamentalism.

A few words may be in order about both of these points.

If we pick up a text like Thérèse of Lisieux's *The Story of a Soul* the contemporary reader might well be put off by what appears to be a sentimental and saccharine approach to the saint's devotional life reflected in her choice of language and the rules of her religious community. What one must do is to contextualize the milieu of late nineteenth century Catholic piety in such a way to read *behind* and *beyond* those accidental elements. Only then would it be possible to grasp her compelling doctrine of finding God in the ordinary, her solidarity with the poor and forgotten, and her heroic courage in the face of doubt, illness, and disappointment.

We could multiply examples of this need to contextualize. One does not need to live in an actual desert, weave baskets and live in a cave in order to learn from the spiritual teachings of the early desert fathers and mothers. Monastic spirituality may teach us much about the following of Christ without demanding that we join monastic communities, just as liberationist spiritualities might provide us with new insights while not turning us into activists.

The second form of naiveté with respect to our study of the spiritual tradition is the temptation to a simple-minded fundamental-

---

14. Walter Principe, "Theological Trends: Pluralism in Christian Spirituality," *The Way* 32 (1992) 54 61.

ism. In our context, fundamentalism signifies nothing more than a crass literalism which attempts to imitate at a very superficial level. To follow the poor life of St. Francis of Assisi, for instance, does not mean that one must acquire sandals, a brown religious habit, and a rope for the waist. Such garb may well have been peasant wear in the thirteenth century but today such a costume might symbolize religion and not poverty.

Contemporary Christian Spirituality

A final clarification about Christian spirituality demands some attention to what we might call "the signs of the times." Another way of saying that is to ask what we have learned from the culture in which we live and the errors we have detected in the past. Such "signs of the times" act as guiding principles as we investigate specific topics in this work.

In the first place, authentic Christian spirituality must be *holistic*. Such a spirituality will recognize explicitly that we are human persons and not merely souls imprisoned in bodies. The radical disjunction between the "spiritual" and the "human" has been the source of much harm in the past. Contemporary spiritual writers are unanimous in their rejection of the idea that spirituality is simply concerned with "interiority." Such a disjunction fails to integrate in the Christian way of life crucial elements of sane living: friendship, sexuality, health, family ties, and so on. Contemporary spirituality "is not limited to a concern with the interior life but seeks an integration of all aspects of human life and experience."[15]

One way of understanding how holistic our understanding of the Christian way is would be to ask how well a given spirituality helps us develop as human persons. Anyone who has read in the history of spirituality knows that a misbegotten approach to the spiritual life can bring about enormous danger to a person. It can feed on passive-aggressive tendencies; it can be an instrument for self-punishment or wielded as a form of control over another.

The greatest spiritual directors in the Christian tradition have always recognized this, whether it be a St. Francis of Assisi who forbade his friars to perform outlandish penances or a St. Teresa of Avila who prayed to be kept free from gloomy saints. It is perhaps

---

15. Philip Sheldrake, *Spirituality and History* (New York: Crossroad, 1992) 50.

best summed up in a story that comes from the early desert ascetics. A monk once complained that a brother fell asleep during the night vigils. The old abba replied that when he saw a brother nod off he let him rest his head on his lap to get a decent sleep. To paraphrase the old scholastic saying: Christian spirituality should not destroy a person's humanity; it should perfect it.

Christian spirituality, secondly, cannot be limited to an exclusively individualistic "care of the soul." We have already noted that the way of Christian discipleship is found in community. The old aphorism that defines the spiritual journey as *Solus cum Solo* ("Alone with the One") is truncated and inaedquate. Contemporary spiritual writers unanimously insist that what we do as followers of Jesus must include a concern not only with our immediate community but with humanity as a whole. Indeed, one might say that this is the deepest meaning of *catholic* spirituality: a discipleship that concerns the universal (catholic) needs of the world. Our common way of discipleship, as we have already noted, is best understood as being part of the pilgrim people of God. After all, that charity by which we love God and others is, as Paul famously notes "a more excellent *way*..." (1 Cor 13:1).

In that sense, at least, there is no gap between action and contemplation, between being in the world and outside the world, between solitude and community. Those are all spiritual demands which must be kept in balanced tension. In this regard we might call as a witness one of the most austere spiritual writers and mystics of the Christian tradition, the fourteenth century German Dominican, Meister Eckhart. Speaking to the young members of a Dominican community Eckhart gave this piece of advice: "I have said before: if a man were in ecstasy, as St. Paul was, and knew that some sick man needed him to give him a bit of soup, I should think it far better if you would abandon your ecstasy out of love and show greater love in caring for the other in need."[16]

Christian spirituality, thirdly, must hold in balance a sense of the transcendent as well as a sense of the immanent. To concern oneself only with the transcendent is to fall into some of the errors described above: flight from the world of humanity, reduction of spirituality to oneself in relationship to God, a tendency to self-absorption.

---

16. "Counsels on Discernment," in *Meister Eckhart: The Essential Sermons,* edited by Edmund Colledge and Bernard McGinn (New York: Paulist, 1981) 258.

By contrast, to focus too exclusively on the horizontal plane of life, with no reference to the ultimate reality of God as revealed in Christ, is to reduce spirituality to the merely therapeutic. That our Christian way should be holistic is something we have already affirmed, but faith is not only about our well-being; it goads us to go beyond and beneath our experience to that ultimate ground which is God.

Authentic spirituality, then, demands that we locate ourselves consciously in the world around us (and even beyond us) while, simultaneously, accepting that this is not all there is. This balance between the "now" and the "not yet"—between our immanent sense of God as more intimate to us than we are to ourselves (the phrase is Augustine's) and the reality of a transcendent God as Other—is the deepest task of the Christian. It is, as T. S. Eliot once wrote, the "intersection of the timeless moment."

Finally, any authentic Christian spirituality must include an element of discernment. Discernment, in this context, means that spiritual critical faculty by which we judge what is worthy and what is peripheral, what is useful and what is noxious. Such judgments cannot rest in experience alone no matter how deep and satisfying that experience might be. Our experience must be tempered or judged with the same aids by which we form conscience: through sound teaching, through the aid of the larger community, by the tradition of the spiritual masters/mistresses of the past.

Michael Buckley wisely writes that to use only that criterion (of personal experience) is a temptation "only under the persuasion that the intensity of experience absolves one from discretion, critical reflection, and the doctrinal content of Christian faith, giving a priority over the unspeakable Mystery that approaches human beings through experience and transferring the religious guidance of a single person or of an entire community to an unchangeable subjectivity, to sentimentality, or superstitious or excited enthusiasms."[17]

It is difficult to describe fully the "how" of discernment when it comes to the Christian life but some generalizations are obvious. A sound spirituality should rest on a sound theology so that what we do is not divorced from our critical grasp of what we believe. There is no particular merit in being an ignorant Christian but there is much danger in cultivating ignorance as part of a "spiritual" strategy. It is

---

17. "Discernment of Spirits," in *The New Dictionary of Catholic Spirituality,* edited by Michael Downey (Collegeville: Liturgical Press, 1993) 274-75.

worthwhile noting that there is today an intense desire to bring theology and spirituality into closer harmony.

If our way of being a disciple of Jesus is one that finds its natural home in community (as we have insisted), then part of our discernment about the authentic character of our Christian life must come from the experience, the wisdom, the counsel, and the inherited tradition of the community. As Bernard of Clairvaux noted centuries ago: the people who are their own spiritual directors have fools for disciples.[18] This standing within a tradition teaches us from the experience of the past and, simultaneously, we add to that tradition.

Further Reading

Christian Spirituality Bulletin [Publication of the Society for the Study of Christian Spirituality; this is an invaluable resource for current trends in research in the field.]

Downey, Michael, ed. *The New Dictionary of Christian Spirituality* (Collegeville: Liturgical Press, 1993). [Indispensable reference work with articles by noted scholars in the field.]

Gutiérrez, Gustavo. *We Drink from Our Own Wells* (Maryknoll: Orbis, 1984). [An excellent, biblically rooted, approach to spirituality from a liberationist perspective.]

Johnson, Luke Timothy. *Faith's Freedom: A Classic Spirituality for Contemporary Christians* (Minneapolis: Fortress/Augsburg, 1990). [An introduction to Christian spirituality by a noted biblical scholar.]

Principe, Walter. "Towards Defining Spirituality," *Sciences Religieuses/Studies in Religion* 12/2 (1983) 127-141. [A thorough study of the origin and development of the concept of spirituality in the Christian tradition.]

Exercises

(1) We have provided in an appendix a sampling of definitions and descriptions of Christian spirituality. Attempt a full description of your

---

18. From *Epistula* #87: *Qui se sibi magistrum constituit stulto se discipulum subdit.*

own that would do justice to the interplay of doctrine, ethics, and the life of prayer.

(2) There are many spiritualities in the Christian tradition. Each tends to "privilege" certain emphases in scripture. Make a list of biblical passages which you would consider to be at the heart of any authentic Christian spirituality. Ask a friend to do a similar list. Compare the two lists.

(3) In this chapter we have emphasized the notion of discipleship *as a constitutive element of Christian spirituality. Try to describe your concept of being a disciple of Jesus keyed to your own state of life (e.g. as an unmarried young person in school, as a mature person in the workforce, etc.).*

Appendix:
Some Definitions/Descriptions of Christian Spirituality

"My spirituality is my Christian living as guided by the Holy Spirit....Each [spirituality] is a living out of the Christian life under the inspiration of the Holy Spirit, through the gifts the indwelling spirit produces in us for our own personal sanctification and our contribution to the life of the community."
Walter Burghardt, S.J., "Characteristics of Social Justice Spirituality," *Origins* 24/9 (July 21, 1994) 159.

"A spirituality or a spiritual direction is a certain, symbolic way of hearing and living the Gospel. This 'Way' is conditioned by a period, a 'fertilized soil' the particular influence of a specific milieu. It can be incarnated in a clearly identified group of human beings and can continue, historically, enriched or impoverished....In this way, a 'spiritual tradition' or a 'school' of spirituality comes to be.
There are a number of elements that describe a school of spirituality:
1) The most noteworthy characteristic is a given number of emphases or constants regarding one or another aspect of Christian Faith or Life in the Spirit....
2) Each spiritual school or tradition is characterized by a certain way of praying and a specific understanding of mission....
3) Schools of spirituality nearly always have their own pedagogical methods, implicit or explicit....

4) Each school has its *preferred biblical texts* that call for close attention.

5) Finally, schools of spirituality are rooted in *an intense spiritual experience*....In general, the experience that gives birth to a new spiritual school is twofold: the experience of the personal interior life of the founder and the experience of spiritual formation of the first disciples, but successfully achieved in a new form."

Raymond Deville, *The French School of Spirituality: An Introduction and Reader* (Pittsburgh: Duquesne University Press, 1994) 153-54.

"The term spirituality refers to the Spirit at work in persons 1) within a culture 2) in relation to a tradition, 3) in memory of Jesus Christ, 4) in the light of contemporary events, hopes, sufferings and promises, 5) in efforts to combine elements of action and contemplation, 6) with respect to charism and community, 7) as expressed and authenticated in praxis."

Michael Downey, "Jean Vanier: Recovering the Heart," *Spirituality Today* 38 (Winter 1986) 339-40.

"Christian spirituality is the daily, communal, lived expression of one's ultimate beliefs, characterized by openness to the self-transcending love of God, self, neighbor, and world through Jesus Christ and in the power of the Holy Spirit."

Elizabeth Dreyer, "Christian Spirituality," *The Harper/Collins Encyclopedia of Catholicism,* ed. Richard McBrien (San Francisco: Harper/Collins, 1995).

"A way of being a Christian, that has as its foundation an advance through death, sin, and slavery, in accordance with the Spirit, who is the life-giving power that sets the human person free....Christian spirituality consists in embracing the liberated body and thus being able to say 'Abba—Father!' and to enter into comradely communion with others."

Gustavo Gutiérrez, *We Drink from Our Own Wells* (Maryknoll: Orbis, 1984) 70.

"One of the essential features of biblical spirituality is the importance of the community, the church. Another is integrating one's life in the world with one's relationship with God. A third, among many, is the personal interaction with God through all sorts of prayer. Christian spirituality includes more than an introspective search for psychological health; ideally it integrates relationships to God and creation with those to self and others."

Bradley C. Holt, *Thirsty For God: A Brief History of Christian Spirituality* (Minneapolis: Augsburg, 1993) 3.

"Spirituality is a lived experience, the effort to apply relevant elements in the deposit of Christian faith to the guidance of men and women toward their spiritual growth, the progressive development of their persons which flowers into a proportionately increased insight and joy in the beatific vision."

Introduction to *Ignatius of Loyola: Spiritual Exercises and Selected Works,* edited by George Ganss, S.J. (New York: Paulist, 1991) 61.

"The specific *Christian* spirituality, then, is one that is centered on the experience of God as saviour through Jesus. We acknowledge that the gift of life, of peace, of reconciliation, and of righteousness, comes from the crucified and resurrected Messiah. And in the messianic pattern enacted by Jesus' life and death, we recognize as well the model for our own acceptance of that gift. In every situation, our instinct is to 'look to Jesus' (Heb 12:2). From beginning to end, the form of spirituality is the imitation of Christ."

Luke Timothy Johnson, *Faith's Freedom: A Classic Spiritualty for Contemporary Christians* (Minneapolis: Fortress/Augsburg, 1990) 28.

"Spirituality has to do with our experiencing of God and with the transformation of our consciousness and our lives as outcomes of that experience. Since God is in principle available to everyone, spirituality is not exclusively Christian.

Christian spirituality is life in the Holy Spirit who incorporates the Christian into the Body of Jesus Christ, through whom the Christian has access to God the Creator in a life of faith, hope, love, and service. It is *visionary, sacramental, relational,* and *transformational.*"

Richard McBrien, *Catholicism*, new edition (San Francisco: Harper/Collins, 1994) 1058.

"Literally, spirituality means life in God's Spirit and a living relationship with God's Spirit. Talk about Eastern or African spirituality unfortunately blurs this precise sense of the word and reduces it again to 'religiousness.' In a strict Christian sense, the word has to mean what Paul calls the new life *'en pneumati.'*"

Jurgen Moltmann, *The Spirit of Life* (Minneapolis: Fortress, 1992) 83.

"A process of being conformed to the image of Christ for the sake of others."

M. Robert Mulholland, Jr. *Invitation to a Journey: A Road Map for Spiritual Formation* (Downers Grove: IVP Press, 1993) 15.

"There are three major factors combined together in the living unity of the Christian religion: doctrine, worship and deeds....The strength of the Christian religion lies in this complex structure embracing the whole of human life."

John Macquarrie, *Paths in Spirituality*, 2nd edition (Harrisburg: Morehouse, 1992) 11.

"In its fundamental sense, spirituality is concerned with the shaping, empowering and maturing of the 'spiritual person' (1 Cor 2:14-15)—that is, the person alive to and responsive to God in the world, as opposed to the person who merely exists within and responds to the world."

Alister McGrath, *Evangelicalism and The Future of Christianity* (Downers Grove: IVP, 1995) 125.

"Christian Spirituality is the lived experience of the Christian belief in both its general and more specialized forms....It is possible to distinguish spirituality from doctrine in that it concentrates not on faith itself but on the reaction that faith arouses in religious consciousness and practice. It can likewise be distinguished from Christian ethics in that it treats not all human actions in their relation to God but those acts in which the relation to God is immediate and explicit."

Introduction to *Christian Spirituality: Origins to the Twelfth Century,* edited by Bernard McGinn et al. (New York: Crossroad, 1985) xv-xvi.

"Spirituality is understood to be the way of life of a people, a movement by the Spirit of God, and the grounding of one's identity as a Christian in every circumstance of life. It is the struggle to live the totality of one's personal and communitarian life in keeping with the Gospel; spirituality is the orientation and perspective of all

the dimensions of a person's life in the following of Jesus and in continuous dialogue with the Father."
National Pastoral Plan for Hispanic Ministry (Washington, D.C.: United States Catholic Conference, 1987) 7.

" 'Spirituality' refers to the unfolding, day by day, of that fundamental decision to become or to remain a Christian which we make at baptism, repeat at confirmation, and renew each time we receive the eucharist...."
William Reiser, S.J., *Looking for a God To Pray To: Christian Spirituality in Transition* (New York: Paulist, 1994) 2.

"A distinctive Christian spirituality focuses on God's self-giving in Christ, animated by the Holy Spirit. Spirituality refers to a *lived* experience and a disciplined life of prayer and action, but it cannot be conceived apart from the specific theological beliefs that are ingredients in the forms of life that manifest authentic Christian faith. Love of God and neighbor are at the heart of all Christian prayer and action."
Don E. Saliers, "Spirituality," in *A New Handbook of Christian Theology,* edited by Donald Musser and Joseph Price (Nashville: Abingdon, 1992) 460.

"Christian spirituality, then, is personal participation in the mystery of Christ begun in faith, sealed by baptism into the death and resurrection of Jesus Christ, nourished by the sharing of the Lord's Supper, which the community celebrated regularly in memory of Him who was truly present wherever his followers gathered, and was expressed by a simple life of universal love that bore witness to life in the Spirit and attracted others to faith."
Sandra Schneiders, "Scripture and Spirituality," in *Christian Spirituality: Origins to the Twelfth Century,* edited by Bernard McGinn et al. (New York: Crossroad, 1985) 2.

"A friend once described spirituality to me as 'theology on two feet.' In other words, spirituality (at least in a Christian context) is a useful term to describe how, individually and collectively, we personally appropriate the traditional Christian beliefs about God, humanity, and the world and express them in terms of our basic attitudes, life-style, and activity. On a personal level, spiritualty is how we stand before God in the context of our everyday lives. For Christians, this involves two complementary dimensions: our tradition and our experience of the culture and the world in which we live, by which we are influenced, and to which we respond. The question of how these two dimensions relate to each other is a complex one."

Philip Sheldrake, *Images of Holiness: Explorations in Contemporary Spirituality*. (Notre Dame: Ave Maria, 1988) 2.

"I would suggest that what the word 'spirituality' seeks to express is the conscious human response to God that is both personal and ecclesial. In short: 'life in the Spirit.'"

Philip Sheldrake, *Spirituality and History* (New York: Crossroad, 1992) 37.

"Spirituality as associated with breath suggests two things. First, spirituality in this sense is an animating life principle. Second, the spirit is the human person in his or her devotional aspect. Thus in the biblical sense the "spiritual person" is one attracted to and in communion with the reality within and beyond the visible one. She or he is attracted to 'things of the spirit.' Spirituality in this sense is the practice of religion. What a person does with what that person believes is 'spirituality.'...Spirituality is what the early Christians did to put into practice what they believed. It was what they did to respond to a world filled with the presence of God and the risen Christ."

Bonnie Thurston, *Spiritual Life in the Early Church* (Minneapolis: Augsburg/Fortress, 1993) 2-3.

"And if 'spirituality' can be given any coherent meaning, perhaps it is to be understood in terms of this task: each believer making his or her own that engagement with the questioning of the heart of faith which is so evident in the classical documents of Christian belief....The questioning involved here is not our interrogation of the data, but its interrogation of us....And the greatness of the Christian saints lies in their readiness to be questioned, judged, stripped naked, and left speechless by that which lies at the center of their faith."

Rowan Williams, *The Wound of Knowledge: Christian Spirituality from the New Testament to St. John of the Cross* (Boston: Cowley, 1991) 1.

"God's presence in Christ, in the body of believers who unite in his name and teaching and in each person not only as disciples but as a human being...."

Richard Woods,"Spirituality (Christian), "History of," in *The New Dictionary of Catholic Spirituality,* edited by Michael Downey (Collegeville: Liturgical Press, 1993) *sub voce.*

2

Hearers and Doers
of the Word

Introduction

*I*t would seem obvious that any authentic Christian spirituality
must take into account the bible as a fundamental source for
being a disciple of Jesus. The church, in its official self-understand-
ing, asserts that it has always venerated the sacred scriptures as
much as it has venerated the body of the Lord. The church's liturgy,
after all, frames itself around word and eucharist. As the Second
Vatican Council stated, the church has never failed to present to the
faithful the bread of life from the one table of the word of God and
the body of Christ.[1] Yves Congar puts the matter clearly and emphatically: "In the case of the Written Word, Scripture is actually there,
rather like the Eucharist. There is, in other words, a 'real presence'
of the Word. Like the Eucharist, too, it calls for a 'spiritual eating'
involving the intervention of charity and therefore of the Holy
Spirit."[2]

At the same time, Christianity is not a "religion of the book" in
any narrow or constricted sense of the term. It does not venerate a
"written and dead" word but the incarnate and living word.[3]
Furthermore, Catholic spirituality insists that the scriptures are to
be read within the context of the believing community which first
produced them. While the church is at the service of the word of

---

1. Paraphrased from the *Catechism of the Catholic Church* #104. The
catechism here glosses the Dogmatic Constitution on Revelation (*Dei
Verbum*) from the Second Vatican Council; see: VI.22.

2. Yves Congar, *The Word and the Spirit* (New York: Harper and Row,
1986) 25.

3. *Catechism* #108.

God it has never thought of the scriptures as outside the life of the community. The relationship between the word and its reception in the living tradition has been brilliantly, even audaciously, described by a contemporary theologian in these words:

> The depths and richness of the revelation of God in Christ is being slowly brought into actuality by the interaction of the Christ-Event, carried forward in tradition, with the ever expanding and deepening human experience in history. Surely we have a wider and more profound appreciation of the meaning of Christ for human history two thousand years after his coming than did the first generations of Christians....In short, the Christ-event is not a radio signal that is strongest at the point of transmission and gets weaker as it gets geographically and chronologically farther from the tower.[4]

The deep paradox that we confront is this: The human words of the bible, written in particular places at a particular time by persons who were of that time and place, somehow reveal to us the awe-ful mystery of God in Christ: the divine word through human words. We might truly say by way of analogy that the scriptures are like Christ: incarnate in time and place yet transcendent; visible and tactile yet spiritual and beyond; or, as the patristic tradition often said, a *sacrament*—a visible sign of an invisible grace. Just as the believer must look at Christ through the eyes of faith to understand fully, so one must come to the scriptures open to the grace of God who will illumine the text as the text illumines us.

The question is: *How* do we encounter Christ in the scriptures? That is not an idle question. Do we simply "read" the bible? Where does that leave those many in the world who do not read? Do we "hear" the bible by way of someone else who tells us what it means? To whom should we listen (a casual cruise through the religious channels on television leads us to suspect that not everyone is telling us the whole story)? Do we open the bible at random or select certain passages or begin at the beginning or...what?

---

4. Sandra M. Schneiders, *The Revelatory Text: Interpreting the New Testament as Sacred Scripture* (San Francisco: HarperCollins, 1991) 75-76. Her point is clear. The New Testament writers tolerate, for example, slavery even though after centuries of discernment we have all learned as Christians (through bitter experience) that human slavery is morally intolerable.

Those questions frame the discussion of this chapter. In the background of our discussion is the conviction that we "listen" to the bible from within the community that received and nourished it—the assembly of believers considered historically and actually. We also stipulate that reading the scriptures is not a one way street. We direct our hearts and minds to the word but, in faith, the word speaks back to us. In other words: we read and are read. The encounter with God's word is always a dialogue.

One final note of introduction: this chapter does not pretend to be an introduction to the study of the bible. Our focus is on the relationship of the word of God to the Christian journey of discipleship. We will confront the bible, in these pages, as a primary source for the Christian life and not as only a classic text to be studied.

The Word of God in Community

Father John Shea, the contemporary theologian and storyteller, has a wonderfully pithy summary of ecclesiology:

> *Gather the people.*
> *Tell the story.*
> *Break the bread.*

In that little tercet Shea has summed up the New Testament idea of the church—the assembly or gathering (which is what the New Testament Greek word *ekklesia* means) who meet together to retell the saving acts of Jesus Christ and to re-enact his passion, death, and resurrection in the eucharistic meal which the New Testament frequently calls the "breaking of the bread."

Long before there was a completed "New Testament" (understood as the twenty-four books which make up that portion of the bible) Christians gathered together to tell the story of what Jesus accomplished. In a real sense the New Testament grew out of the community's response to the story which was told in the Christian assembly. One ancient form of that story is embedded in what is known as the apostolic proclamation (kerygma); this kerygma is a kind of shorthand creed of what the earliest Christians believed about Jesus whom they called the Christ.

This ancient proclamation, which is the heart of the *gospel* (good news), consists of these affirmations: Jesus of Nazareth was the fulfillment of the scriptures. He did mighty deeds and taught mighty words. He was crucified, he died, and he was raised from the dead by the power of God. We, who are his followers, proclaim this as the truth.[5]

In essence, that is ideally what we do when we gather at the weekly liturgy with some degree of preparation and attention. We listen to the readings which speak about the prophetic yearning for the savior in the Old Testament readings, respond to those readings with the same prayers and hymns which Jesus himself knew (e.g. the psalms), and then stand to hear of the saving deeds of Jesus who is the Christ. In other words, by our *gathering* and our *listening* and our *responding* to the good news we affirm that Jesus *alive* is our Lord and savior. We enter into the story of Jesus as it has been told from the beginnings of the church.

In the liturgy we *listen* to the scriptural readings and we *respond* in prayers drawn from the scriptures. We also *perform* the scriptures as we noted in a previous chapter. The very act of gathering together for worship is a performance based on the New Testament understanding of *ekklesia* (i.e. a "gathering together"). Initiation rites like baptism and the eucharistic liturgy and sacraments of ministry are, after all, the carrying out or performing (through ritual) of what is found in the scriptures. Even smaller gestures like the ritual kiss of peace are performative acts drawn from the scriptures.

The performance of the word of God is not limited to what we do ritually *within* the liturgy. The proper response to what we proclaim, listen, and perform is meant to "spill over" from worship into a way of living that is consonant with, and a continuation of, those formal moments of gathered worship. Thus, for example, the sharing of the one bread and the one cup at the liturgy constitutes ritually what is the goal of human life: the unity of all people, redeemed by Christ, who are *companions* (i.e. bread-sharers). It is for that reason that authentic Christian spirituality links common worship (liturgy) with the works of charity as well as the desire for, and commitment to, social justice.

The core of the liturgy is the celebration of the eucharist on Sunday.[6] Yet Sunday is part of the great cycle of the liturgical year which grew over the centuries into a complex whole by which

---

5. Various formulations of this kerygma may be found in Acts 2:22-36, 3:17ff, 10:34-43, etc.

6. Sunday is the "foundation and nucleus of the whole liturgical year," teaches the Second Vatican Council: Constitution on the Sacred Liturgy #106.

Christians experienced panoramically the unfolding mystery of Christ.[7] Thus, with the changing of the seasons, we are able to move from the longing for the savior expressed in Advent through Christ's birth and public manifestation (in the Christmas/Epiphany season) and through the penitential season of Lent until we enter into the passion, death, and resurrection of Christ. In the season after Pentecost (the "birthday" of the church) we listen to the word of God until the season begins again in Advent. Thus, the liturgy presents to us the mysteries of Christ as an unfolding proclamation over the liturgical year crystallized in the moments of gathering when we assemble on Sunday.

By way of summary: when we "go to church" on Sunday we do what Christians have done since the earliest day: We listen to the word of God; we act it out; we attempt to translate what we have heard into a way of life. This encounter is the most fundamental and crucial way in which we hear the word of God, not as pure individuals but as part of a people who "tell the story" to each other and to anyone else who will listen. In a real sense, being a Christian means to enter into the story which tells us about Jesus the Christ in the Spirit and to respond to that story both as individuals and as part of the local and worldwide community.

It should be obvious from the above that many of the things we do as Christians—from evangelization to acts of charity or the works of justice—are different ways of fleshing out the word of God through concrete acts, gestures, and performances.

The Word of God and Public Prayer

The prayer life of early Christians (i.e. before the fourth century) is only imperfectly understood. Whether there was formal pattern of prayer in the assembly is debated. One thing, however, is quite clear: Christians prayed outside the regular liturgy, e.g. before meals, during Lenten services, at the time of religious instruction, at regular times (at morning, noon, and evening or at the third, sixth, and ninth hour). Even when Christians prayed privately, they were expected to have the whole Christian people in mind; as the third century North African bishop, Cyprian of Carthage, said:

---

7. For a brief description of this historical evolution, see Peter Cobb's "The History of the Christian Year," in *The Study of Liturgy,* edited by C. Jones et al., rev. ed. (New York: Oxford University Press, 1992) 455-71.

"Our prayer is public and common; and when we pray, we pray not for one but for the whole people, because we the whole people are one." [8]

Not suprisingly, Cyprian's words appear in his commentary on the Lord's Prayer which came to the Christian community, after all, as an answer Jesus gave to those who asked him how to pray (Lk 11:1). Early in the second century an anonymous church order called *The Didache* not only singles out the Lord's Prayer but recommends that it be said three times a day.

The use of the Lord's Prayer did not exhaust the possibilities of the bible as a prayerbook for the church. Christians accepted from the Old Testament the collection of hymns and prayers known as the book of Psalms (called the "psalter") and incorporated those hymns into its own liturgy. The psalter also became the heart of the formal prayer of the church which is to this day in use in monasteries and other religious houses who recite the "divine Office" or by individuals or groups who pray the "hours" of the common prayer of the church at such services as vespers in the evening.

It is difficult to overestimate the role of the psalter as a shaping force in Christian prayer. Pope John Paul II has written, in response to a question about his own prayer: "The Book of Psalms is irreplaceable."[9] It is central to the formal liturgy; it is called on to be a resource for informal prayer groups and forms a rich source of devotionalism for Christians of every denomination. This attitude toward the psalms was made, somewhat breathlessly, by the great fourth century bishop and theologian, Athanasius of Alexandria:

> For I believe that the whole of human existence, for both the disposition of the soul and the movements of thoughts, has been measured out and encompassed by the words of the psalter. And nothing beyond these is found among men. For whether there was necessity of repentance or confession, or tribulation and trial befell us, or being plotted against or if someone has become sorrowful and disturbed and suffered something...or one wants to sing praises and give thanks to the Lord—for any such eventuality he has instruction in the divine psalms. Let one therefore select things said in them of these circumstances and reciting

---

8. *Commentary on the Lord's Prayer* (chapter #8). For a concise discussion of the "problem" of early Christian prayer, see Paul Bradshaw, "The Divine Office: The First Three Centuries," in *The Study of Liturgy* 399-403.

9. In *Crossing the Threshold of Hope* (New York: Knopf, 1994) 17.

what has been written as concerning him, and, being affected by the writings, lift them up to the Lord.[10]

We should also note, by way of conclusion, that many of the "constructed" prayers found either in the liturgy or in private devotion draw deeply on the scriptures. Commonly used prayers are often compilations of scriptural verses (e.g. the "Hail Mary") or echo biblical sentiments (e.g. "Glory be..."). Such prayers take on new and deep meaning when they are relearned from our encounter with them in the study of the scriptures. We shall focus more intently on these prayer formulas in a subsequent chapter.

Bible Study

Christians have always affirmed the bible as the word of God and, as such, they have used the bible not only in formal or informal settings for prayer and worship but also as a resource to study and from which to learn how to lead a fully Christian life. Because the bible was considered to be inspired by God's Spirit it was natural enough for readers to accept that everything in the scriptures spoke of God even when the bible seems to be merely relating ordinary and banal things.

One of St. Augustine's great insights was (as he tells us in the *Confessions*) to learn, as St. Paul put it, that the "letter kills but the spirit gives life"—i.e. that the bible has a deep meaning which stands behind the literal text which was accessible to the most profound mind but equally available to the barely literate person:

...and it seemed to me all the more right that the authority of Scripture should be respected and accepted with the purest faith, because while all can read it with ease, it also has a deeper meaning in which its great secrets are locked away. Its plain language and simple style make it accessible to everyone, and yet it absorbs the attention of the learned.[11]

---

10. "A Letter to Marcellinus," in *Athanasius,* edited by Robert C. Gregg (New York: Paulist, 1980) 126-27. For a study of the impact of the psalms on Jewish and Christian piety, see William L. Holladay, *The Psalms Through Three Thousand Years* (Minneapolis: Augsburg/Fortress, 1993).

11. *The Confessions,* Book VI, Chapter 5 (Pine-Coffin translation).

How the bible has been taught, interpreted, and studied is an enormously complex subject into which we cannot stray in our brief book. What we can do is to set out some general observations that would be useful for those who are committed to both the study and living of Christian spirituality.

(1) The bible is not a book but a collection of books written over a long period of time, containing many quite different types of literature (e.g. narratives, laws, collections of poetry, chronicles, proverbs, gospels, letters, etc.). While one must know what one is reading (one reads a law code like the book of Leviticus differently than a volume of poetry like the psalter) the Christian tradition, in its liturgical and spiritual tradition, has always read the bible as a whole.

By reading the bible "whole" we mean both that one part of the bible may shed light on another, and, more importantly, as a total "message" the bible, Old Testament and New, tells the story of God's revelation to humankind as that revelation was given to the people of Israel and continued in the person of Jesus the Jew: "In many and various ways God spoke of old to our ancestors through the prophets; but in these last days he has spoken to us by a Son, whom he appointed the heir of all things, through whom also he created the world" (Heb 1:1-2).

(2) Because the bible is God's word, we are always "reaching up" for its ultimate meaning. That the bible has a clear meaning (often called the "literal" sense) is obvious, but the full significance of that meaning is never fully appreciated "once and forever" at any moment in history.[12] Not to understand that fact is to create enormous difficulties for oneself and, paradoxically, to freeze the interpretation of the bible into a limited and cramped understanding of the text.

An example might clarify this point. The New Testament tells us that at the last supper Jesus took bread, blessed and broke it, and said, "This is my body." The early Christians accepted that in the eucharistic bread Christ was truly present, that what they dealt with was not ordinary bread. Nonetheless, it took over a thousand years for the church (at least in the west) to develop a theory about

---

12. This fact is not fully appreciated by so-called "fundamentalists" who "read" scripture as if we cannot always strive for a deeper, more nuanced, understanding. The Catholic tradition has never committed itself to what is now called "fundamentalism"—a way of reading scripture which has a very short history in Christianity.

how Christ was present in the eucharist by appealing to a model called "transsubstantiation." The New Testament tells us that Christ is present; later reflection on that text attempts an explanation of the "how" of that presence.[13] The point is that the Christian tradition reflected long over the eucharistic narratives of consecration seeking to learn more and understand better. This reflection on scripture is, at heart, what authentic theology really is. The plain truth is that much of the early development of the doctrines about the Trinity and the divinity of Christ—to name the most burning issues of early Christian debate—were attempts to plumb the meaning of the witness of the scriptures.

Even today Christians struggle (as they will struggle in the future) about how to understand the demands of the scriptures as they live out their Christian life: What does it mean to be a disciple of Jesus? We have already seen a broad sketch of discipleship in our opening chapter, but we must always ask more: How does the concept of discipleship "fit" into the life of a young person in the world of business? of a peasant farmer in Central America? of an executive for a multinational corporation? of a soldier? of a housewife? etc.

Every age is called upon to wrestle not with only a reading of a "text" but with how that text is to be understood in terms of being lived out and "made flesh." The way people over the past two millennia have attempted to live out what they have encountered in God's word can be fairly called the history of the Christian tradition. There is much truth in the observation of the Protestant theologian Gerhard Eboling that the history of Christianity is basically the history of the interpretation of the bible.

(3) How we understand the scriptures depends very much on where we encounter them and with what openness we are capable in that encounter. This has been the great insight of the liberation theologians. When we encounter the bible, say, among the poor, phrases and motifs which tend otherwise to be "spiritualized" take on a new actuality. When we pray "Give us this day our daily bread" it does matter whether we utter that petition in a suburban parish

---

13. The debates about the eucharist at the reformation were not mainly over the presence of Christ in the eucharist but *how* to understand that presence. Similarly, the western church teaches that Christ is present *when* the words of institution are recited; the Orthodox tradition insists that Christ is present when the Holy Spirit is invoked in the liturgy. Both traditions, however, accept that Christ is truly present.

or in a third world slum. Only when we are alert to where we are and from what perspective we listen to the word of God does it take on power and actuality.

Lectio Divina

St. Benedict, in his *Rule* (chapter #48), stipulates that monks should have regular periods for manual work and for "prayerful reading" (*lectio divina*—literally, "divine reading"). The same section of the *Rule* stipulates when that reading is to take place, rules for being sure that it does take place, and the injunction that on Sunday the whole community should be engaged in reading (apart from those who have necessary tasks to perform).

Lectio does not mean technical biblical study (which is the task of the professional biblical commentator) or the mere scanning of the text for the sake of information or the "story." It means a close, prayerful, openness to the text so that one both reads the text and, in patient expectation, is open to the text speaking back to the person. A medieval monk, the Carthusian solitary, Guigo II, developed a kind of plan for such reading. Guigo argued that one first reads, which leads one to think about (i.e. meditate on) the significance of the text; that process in turn leads a person to respond in prayer, and that prayer, in turn, should point to the gift of the quiet stillness in the presence of God (contemplation).

These four stages should not be conceived in any mechanical manner. One does not move lockstep through the steps. Guigo himself conceived of this approach to reading the word of God as an interdependent and holistic enterprise: "Reading without meditation is sterile; meditation without reading is liable to error; prayer without meditation is lukewarm, meditation without prayer is unfruitful, prayer when it is fervent wins contemplation...."[14]

The practice of *lectio* was essentially a monastic one but in more recent time it has been seen as an enormously rich resource for

---

14. Guigo II, *The Ladder of Monks and Twelve Meditations* (Kalamazoo: Cistercian Publications, 1978) 82. On the enormous impact this practice had on the development of monastic culture, see the classic work of Jean Leclercq, *The Love of Learning and the Desire for God* (New York: Fordham, 1961). Michael Casey's "Seven Principles of Lectio Divina," in his *The Undivided Heart* (Petersham: St. Bede's Publications, 1994) 4-9 is a very useful and practical guide to *lectio*.

everyone in the church. With a renewed interest in a biblically based spirituality, it was inevitable that such a rich resource would be recovered and adapted for the needs of all who are serious about the spiritual journey. One new element to the traditional "stages" suggested by Guigo is apparent in contemporary writers on the life of prayer. With an intense desire to root the Christian life of virtue and service in a deep encounter with the scriptures, contemporary writers have tried to link scriptural *lectio* to one's situation in the world.

Carlo Martini, a noted Jesuit biblical scholar who became cardinal-archbishop of Milan, has made the practice of *lectio* a centerpiece of his apostolate in his diocese. He regularly gives meditations on the scriptures to groups of people either in person or over the radio.[15] He has modified the old monastic practice of *lectio* to the need for a well educated and active Christian life. In a recent book[16] Martini says that parallel to the four stages suggested by Guigo one should also seek from the prayerful readings of scripture a sense of hope and courage (*consolatio*) which leads one to life choices (*discretio*) motivating the will (*deliberatio*) to a course of activity (*actio*) either for a present situation or as a life choice.

The Protestant spiritual writer, M. Robert Mulholland, has an even simpler step beyond that of Guigo; he calls it *incarnatio*—that is to say, the "fleshing out" of the text as it shapes our own being and our way of being in the world.[17] Other writers (e.g. William H. Shannon) simply call this next step "action" (*actio*).

Whatever terminology is added to round out Guigo's schema, the point is clear enough: the act of prayerful reading of the word of God has a certain parallel to our participation in the liturgy. It is a privileged and special moment to enter into communion with God by being nourished by his presence, but that moment of nourishment is not the end of the Christian life. Just as we leave the liturgical assembly, so also we must, of necessity, break off from our

---

15. His conviction about the necessity of biblical prayer and reading has been stated forcefully: "I am convinced that for a Christian today it is difficult, if not impossible, to keep one's faith without nourishing oneself through the listening to scripture personally as well as with others." Quoted in Michael Paul Gallagher's *Letters on Prayer* (London: Darton, Longman and Todd, 1994) 39.

16. Introduction to *The Joy of the Gospel* (Collegeville: Liturgical Press, 1994).

17. In *Invitation to a Journey: A Road Map for Spiritual Formation* (Downers Grove: IVP, 1993) 105.

reading in order to go about the rounds of daily life, living what we
have read.

There is another point. Reading need not always be understood
in an active sense as if we were only talking about the act of reading. The old tradition, rooted in Benedict and made explicit in
Guigo, insists that *lectio* can also be done by prayerful *listening*. We
hear the word of God proclaimed on a regular basis in the liturgy.
The question is: Do we listen? One practical form of *lectio* would be
to take a certain phrase from the liturgy that strikes us powerfully
as we hear it (e.g. "Lamb of God...have mercy on us" or "Glory to
God in the highest," etc.) and make it part of our ordinary prayer
during the week, reciting it, for example, as an introduction to
grace before meals or as part of our evening prayer.

A number of laudable things happen from such a practice. First,
it is a way of prolonging the public liturgy by extending prayer
through the week (when the words come up again in the following
liturgy they are reinforced and "thickened" in our heart). Secondly,
it trains us to take vaguely familiar phrases and attend to them for
the power that they possess but which we may have not noticed
because of the routine of recitation.[18] Finally, it allows us to remove
language from a familiar setting (e.g. our parish church) and redis-
cover it in a new setting whether privately in our home or somewhere in "non-churchy" surroundings.

Reading the Bible Whole

There are many approaches to biblical study, and all of them help
us to deepen our knowledge of God's word. We must never despise the
professional biblical scholars nor fear their work. We need people
who can accurately provide us the best text of the biblical materials
and the translations that remain faithful to the text and meaning of
the text. Furthermore, there is an ongoing need to detect the hidden
nuances, barely understood structures, interdependences, literary
forms, and cultural backgrounds of the texts we consider as part of
our bible. This level of scholarship is not only mandated but required
by the Second Vatican Council's Dogmatic Constitution on Revelation

---

18. This practice might also lead us into something close to the discipline of "centering prayer" by which we deeply consider a word (or a few
words) and then let go of the word in order to be still in the presence of God;
see the chapter on meditation and contemplation.

(*Dei Verbum* 3:12-13) which essentially repeated the mind of Pius XII's 1943 *Divino Afflante Spiritu* on the renewal of biblical studies.

Catholics should hardly need to be reminded of the need for biblical scholarship except for the fact that there is always (and perhaps more so today) a tendency toward a certain kind of non-historical biblical fundamentalism which, if indulged, blocks a mature and profound encounter with the word of God (which, as we have already stated and the church teaches, is written in human words). One thing, however, is clear: the Catholic tradition never reads the scriptures only from a literalistic or "fundamentalist" perspective. The tradition testifies that there is always more to be learned beneath the text.

This temptation to a fundamentalistic reading of scripture is a persistent one. Early in this chapter we saw that St. Augustine, as a young person seeking the truth, was "turned off" by the bible since he thought it a tissue of badly written fables. It was only when he heard the profound meditations of St. Ambrose in Milan that he got a first glimpse of the endless depths of revelation.

We can distinguish our approach to the scriptures by saying that there is a "scholarly" way of reading and a "sapiential" way. Such a distinction, of course, does not mean a radical separation. We need the "scholarly" way in order to read with maturity while we read "sapientially" in order to encounter the wisdom which the bible teaches. In that latter reading we must read the bible whole.

What does reading the bible whole mean?

In the first place it means that, like the earliest Christian community, we read all the scriptures as pointing to, and finding their completion in, Christ: "In many and various ways God spoke of old to our ancestors by the prophets; but in these last days he has spoken to us by a Son, whom God has appointed the heir to all things, through whom God also created the world. He [i.e. the Son] reflects the glory of God and bears the very stamp of God's nature, upholding the universe by the power of God's word" (Heb 1:1-3).

To say that all the scriptures lead to Christ does not mean that what is in the Old Testament is valuable only relative to Christ. God chose a people, entered a covenant with that people, raised up prophets from among them, inspired them to write the psalter, and gave them the spirit of wisdom. We read, for example, the book of Exodus to acknowledge what God has done for Israel. We pray the psalms at the liturgy because Jesus gave us the example as one who himself prayed the psalms. We try to understand Jesus as a source of wisdom because the Old Testament teaches us about wisdom. We cannot understand the "new creation" through Christ unless we root that notion in the very concept of creation. In short, we read the bible as a seamless web rather than, in the pejorative sense of the term, "old" as opposed to "new." Reading the bible whole demands that we enter into the world of the chosen people from whom Jesus comes.[19]

Secondly, we read the bible whole both as individuals who attempt to follow the way of discipleship and as a community. We read the psalms or the great prophets not only as part of the worship of the church but because we believe that the prophets teach us directly about who and what we are as Christians. The late literary critic Northrup Frye once said (in his book *The Great Code*) that the bible is endlessly self-referential.

What Frye meant was that almost anything one reads in the New Testament takes on a fuller meaning (or better: cannot be understood!) unless it is read against the background from which it comes. Simple words or titles in the gospels (e.g. shepherd, way, truth, life, light, etc.) are only transparent to us when we see those words or titles against the long tradition which gives them their full meaning in the context of the gospel story.

That practice of reading the bible whole is an ancient one. Already in the earliest New Testament literature Paul appealed frequently, in his letters to the churches of Rome, Corinth, and Galatia, to the events and personages of the Old Testament in order to make sense of his conversion to Jesus. He "reads" the figure of Adam and Abraham both in their own terms and as he now experiences them as a follower of the new way of Jesus Christ. What Paul does in his letters is what we do today as we read the bible as the story of salvation revealed to the chosen people who give us Jesus whom we call the Christ.

It may not be out of place here to note that one ancient tradition in the Christian spiritual tradition is *lectio continua,* or reading the entire bible straight through. This may appear as a daunting task but it is a wonderful practice for those seriously committed to a biblical spirituality. Some great theologians (e.g. Yves Congar) have told us that when they are concerned with a specific great issue in theology they have read through the entire bible to watch for a cer-

---

19. The temptation to erase the Judaic roots of our common faith is a very old heresy; this temptation to "forget" the Jewishness of Jesus is something to be resisted at every turn. It is unfair to read the New Testament as if it cancels out the Old.

tain theme or idea. Recent editions of the bible have provided aids[20] to help the person who might be fearful about entering on such an enterprise.

Reading the Bible in Part

We have affirmed that as a Christian people we are obliged to read the bible as a whole. We now must specify something that may seem like a paradox: no single person or group of persons has ever managed to encompass all that the bible in general or the New Testament in particular has to say into their life and teaching. Every attempt, personal and social, to live a "New Testament life" is always partial. The reason for this is simple: the New Testament focuses on Jesus the Christ but it proposes not one way of following Jesus but many ways, just as parts of the New Testament emphasize one aspect of Jesus while not highlighting another. (John's gospel emphasizes the divine and pre-existent features of the Word before the incarnation while large patches of the synoptics emphasize Jesus as an itinerant preacher, miracle worker, etc. These various "portraits" are part of a larger, and not always harmonious, whole.)

The fact that we read the bible "in part" while seeking the whole is crucial for an understanding of the history of Christian spirituality. What that history tells us, in fact, is that in every age someone sees something in the scriptures that provides a clue about how to live as a disciple of the Lord. One could argue, for example, that persons have attached themselves to a certain text or series of texts and from them formed a style of Christian living that says, in effect: Here is a new and different way of being a Christian. The monastic tradition, for instance, loved those portions of the Acts of the Apostles that emphasized a community that shared goods and lived a life of prayer and worship. Others, while not denying the validity of the monastic impulse, focused on Jesus as an itinerant preacher who lived "on the road" in poverty preaching to the poor. Thus, in a famous phrase of G. K. Chesterton, the Benedictine and Franciscan models of Christian life complemented each other: "What Benedict stored, Francis scattered." Others, at various times, became missionaries in obedience to the mandate of Jesus to "teach all nations," while still others imitated Jesus in his hidden life at

---

20. For example, *The Catholic Study Bible* (Oxford University Press).

Nazareth or were obedient to his command to feed the poor, clothe the naked, etc.[21]

In a similar fashion we can look at prayers, devotional practices, Christian art, and other manifestations of Christian practice to note how different aspects of the gospel get a particular emphasis: the hieratic and stylized Byzantine mosaics of a judging Christ call on a reading and a sensibility quite different from late medieval artworks on the crucifixion of Jesus. One is not more correct than the other; it is better to say that each "sees" the gospel through a particular lens or attempts to capture a particular emphasis.

The same is true of other, larger, realities like entire theological "systems" within Christianity. The liberation theologies today bring a certain sensibility, forged in the synoptic gospels and the book of Exodus, that is quite different from, say, the broodingly beautiful work of Hans Urs von Balthasar with its enormous debt to the Johannine vision of the exalted Christ. What is true today is true also in the past: the "sensibility" of Thomas Aquinas is demonstrably different from that of his Franciscan counterpart, St. Bonaventure, even though they taught in the same university and died, two months apart, in the same year (1274).

There are some practical conclusions that we can draw from the above observations. First, we must understand that our encounter with the word of God is not ever "final" and totally realized and has never been fully realized. That fact brings with it a practical hint when we study spiritual writings or the lives of those who have made their mark on the spiritual tradition. We can always make these queries: From where in the scriptures do they draw their inspiration? What models and titles do they highlight (and, conversely, which ones do they slight or ignore)? How do they illumine our own sense of reading and listening to the scriptures? [22]

Secondly, we can query ourselves, and the questions are simple ones: What is our text/texts? Are we "commandment" persons or "beatitude" persons? Is our image of the Christ we follow that of judge or shepherd or friend or crucified one or transfigured one? What must we learn from other images/texts that lead us into a

---

21. Some typologies from the Catholic tradition as deriving from scriptural models is explored in Lawrence S. Cunningham, *The Catholic Heritage* (New York: Crossroad, 1983).

22. Asking questions of a text in spirituality has been wonderfully described in Walter Principe's "Pluralism in Christian Spirituality," *The Way* 32 (1992) 54-61.

deeper fidelity and a stronger sense of discipleship? Needless to say, the followers of one model of Jesus owe respect to those who find a different emphasis in their approach to the bible.

What we ask of ourselves, of course, can also be asked of our communities: What is the spirituality of our local parish or prayer group? Is it adequate? Can it accept another way of "reading" the gospel? Do the crucifixes we display or the images we hang or the devotions we publicize reflect a particular angle of biblical awareness.

It is only when we begin to look around and listen and read that we learn where we are focused (and what we might be missing). We might well take as our plea to God a prayer once composed by one of the great Syriac fathers of the church, Ephraem of Edessa:

> Lord, who can grasp all the wealth of just one of your words?
> What we understand in the bible is much less than what we leave behind, like thirsty people who drink from a fountain.
> For your word has many shades of meaning, just as those who study it have many points of view.
> You have colored your words with many hues so that each person who studies it can see in it what he or she loves.
> You have hidden many treasures in your word so that each of us is enriched as we meditate on it.[23]

Further Reading

Lathrop, Gordon H., *Holy Things: A Liturgical Theology* (Minneapolis: Fortress, 1993). [A theology of Christian worship with careful attention to the word of God.]

Leclercq, Jean, *The Love of Learning and the Desire for God* (New York: Fordham University Press, 1961). [A classic study of the ways *lectio* developed in western monasticism.]

Schneiders, Sandra M., *The Revelatory Text: Interpreting the New Testament as Sacred Scripture* (San Francisco: Harper/Collins, 1991). [Reading the bible as the word of God by a biblical scholar who is a recognized authority on spirituality.]

---

23. From *The New Book of Christian Prayers,* edited by Tony Castle (New York: Crossroad, 1986) #1068.

Young, Frances, *Virtuoso Theology: The Bible and Its Interpretation*. (Cleveland: Pilgrim, 1993). [Scripture as a "performative" text.]

Exercises

(1) Analyze any Christian spiritual text, either classical or contemporary, with which you are familiar and note the scriptural "tone" of the text. To what images, words, etc. does the text refer and, conversely, what images or words does it seem to neglect?

(2) We have said that every person reads the bible "partially" in that a person tends to focus on a text or texts which give shape to a person's Christian life. This suggests a very simple question: What is your text? or, perhaps, What are your texts?

(3) By a meditative reading of a single part of the bible (e.g. the gospel of Mark) attempt to isolate passages that you think lend themselves well to "performance."

(4) Look at a well known piece of religious art or read a poem inspired by Christian faith. What is its text or texts?

3

The Spiritual Journey

Introduction

*I*n our introductory chapter we discussed discipleship under the image of *the way,* a term used in the primitive church to describe those who follow the Christian faith. Throughout its long history Christians who have followed the way of discipleship have attempted to describe, more precisely, the map of the way. They have responded to questions like these: How does the Christian understand the way that is to be taken? Is there a map to be followed? Are their significant signposts that point out the way to us? Are there different paths on the way?

It would be far too simple to say that as one undertakes the Christian way everything is clear and settled. The very notion of way indicates something that is not yet finished or completed. Simple reflection on one's own life would prove the point. Whether born into the faith community or a convert to it hardly qualifies one to be judged perfect at any stage of life. There are always failings to overcome and virtues to be cultivated. It is difficult to always love our neighbor (especially if that neighbor is obnoxious and living close to us!), to forgive our enemies, to turn the other cheek, to see God in the moments of disappointment, illness, or violence. Even St. Paul admitted that two contrary powers warred within him: what he wanted to do, he did not do; what he did not want to do, he often did (see Rom 7:14-19).

One of the early spiritual masters, the monk Cassian, had a wonderful metaphor in one of his conferences to describe this constant struggle: Children who learn to write first struggle with forming letters correctly. They are conscious of the effort to master penmanship. Only when they practice enough does the sheer mechanics of penmanship get internalized and become a habit. It is at that point that they forget the struggle to write and simply begin writing

Nearly a millennium after Cassian wrote, the great Dominican mystic Meister Eckhart repeated the same example as a way of understanding how one advances into a simple awareness of the knowledge of God in our lives:

> To begin with, one must memorize each letter and remember the letters' appearance. Then when one has the art one can write effortlessly and easily...it will be the same if one learns to play the fiddle or gain some other skill...so a person must be penetrated with the divine presence, and be shaped through and through with the shape of the God he loves and be present to God so that God's presence might shine out without any effort.[1]

The question, of course, is: *How* does one move from "learning the letters" to a stage where one is more fluent in the Christian life?

When one looks back on the Christian spiritual tradition it becomes clear that the great commentators on the Christian life instinctively looked to the scriptures for more precise maps and guidelines to understand the way. They found so many clues in the bible and those clues have been so variously used that it would be impossible to even catalogue them. For our purposes it will suffice to talk about three kinds of "maps" which the tradition has derived from the scriptures. They are:

(1) The spiritual life seen as a *journey*. From the New Testament period itself, the Christian tradition has read the saving acts of God in the Hebrew scriptures—God leading the children of Israel out of slavery into the desert and then on to the promised land—as a symbolic map of the Christian life. The Christian life was thus understood as a passage from slavery into the desert and beyond to the promised land.

(2) The spiritual life as an *ascent*. So many places in the bible speaking of "going up" or "ascending" (e.g. a ladder or a mountain or as a pilgrim going up to Jerusalem) that an enormous spiritual tradition of "ascent" literature developed as a way of describing the Christian life. This ascent was often used in tandem with the desert motif since the climbing of Mount Sinai is a central motif of the

---

1. "Counsel #6" in *Meister Eckhart: The Essential Sermons,* edited by Colledge and McGinn (New York: Paulist, 1981) 254. I have somewhat modified the translation. Cassian's use of the metaphor is in Conference X —chapter #8 in *John Cassian: Conferences,* ed. Colm Luibheid. (New York: Paulist, 1985) 130.

desert experience of the chosen people: Moses goes into the desert in order to ascend the mountain where God reveals the torah to Him.

(3) The spiritual life as similar to *human growth and development*. The classical model of this expression is Paul's metaphors of growth in the grace of Christ as the passage and development from being a child[2] to becoming an adult. At other places we also find the idea of leaving an old life to embrace a new life or to shed old clothes in order to assume new ones.

Each one of these great themes requires some extended comment.

The Journey

We find an example of the "journey" motif in a rather dense passage in St. Paul. Writing to the church at Corinth Paul says: "Our ancestors were all under the cloud and all passed through the sea, and all were baptized into Moses in the cloud and in the sea and all ate the supernatural food and drank the same supernatural drink. For they drank from the supernatural rock which followed them, and the rock was Christ" (1 Cor 10:1-4).

What is clear from that rather extraordinary passage is that Paul "reads" the story of the chosen people in the book of Exodus as a kind of vast code that both made sense in its own terms as the story of the exodus journey but also could be read in Christian terms. Being "under the cloud" or "crossing the sea" was a prefigurement of Christian baptism while the "supernatural food" (manna) was a sign of the eucharist. The water which flowed from the rock which Moses struck (see Ex 17) was a sign of the saving acts of Christ who is, according to Paul, symbolized by the rock.

It was New Testament readings like that which gave warrant for subsequent generations of Christians to understand the Christian life in the symbolic terms of the exodus journey from the desert and its purifications until the chosen people entered into the promised land. The passage through the desert experience, Christians

---

2. And, we might note, the words of Jesus telling us, paradoxically, that we must become like "little children" to enter the kingdom of heaven. Many Christian symbols have this "reversal" by which one journey becomes another kind; thus, for example, one "goes out" in order to "go up" or one "goes up" into order to "go down."

reasoned, was all the more pertinent because all of the gospels recorded that Jesus himself went through a desert experience of "forty days and nights" before beginning his public life.

This identification of the desert sojourn of the Jews and the Christian life goes back in the Christian tradition to Origen of Alexandria (185-254). Struck by a line which opens Numbers 33 ("These are the stages of the people of Israel when they went out of Egypt...") Origen reasoned that the deeper meaning of that passage was to explicate the "stages" of life for everyone who leaves the life of sin and vice (Egypt) in order to find God in the desert and, in turn, to enter the promised land. In a famous homily (#27 on Numbers) Origen said that it would be "wicked" to think that the sentence in Numbers 33:1 was only an historical observation with no spiritual significance. In fact, the "stages" refer to a process by which people come closer to God, for "the whole journey takes place, the whole course is run for the purpose of arriving at the river of God, so that we may be made neighbors of the flowing wisdom and may be watered by the waves of divine knowledge, and so that purified by them we all may be made worthy to enter the promised land."[3]

From those third century reflections of Origen down to the present day there has been a steady stream of literature which has meditated upon the concept(s) of the desert journey as a paradigm of the spiritual journey. Note that this literature does not deny the literal meaning of the exodus journey; what this literature assumes is that the story has a continuing and pertinent symbolic value for the believer.

From this basic journey metaphor have come a number of different emphases on the markers or "stages" along the way. Sacramental theologians, for example, have seen the sacraments as journey markers. We are born through baptism, strengthened through the Holy Spirit coming to us in confirmation, nourished by the eucharist (St. Thomas, for example, calls the eucharist, the "food for pilgrims"—esca viatorum), reconciled when we sin through reconciliation, and sustained in illness and frailty by the anointing of the sick. As the Catechism of the Catholic Church (#1210) says, "The seven sacraments touch all the stages and all the important moments of the Christian life: they give birth and increase, healing and mission to the Christian's life of faith. There is thus a certain

---

3. "Homily XXVII on Numbers" in Origen, trans. Rowan Greer. (New York: Paulist, 1979) 268.

resemblance between the stages of natural life and the stages of the spiritual life."[4]

A second way in which the Christian life can be seen as a journey was a major emphasis at the Second Vatican Council. Describing the church as a "pilgrim people," the council emphasized the *social* character of our Christian journey. What the council underscored is that as an assembled people, understood both actually and historically, we are on the way, whether we are popes or peasants, poor or rich, lay or cleric, toward a final goal which is at the end of history. All are called to a common journey because all have undertaken a common baptism.

The precise merit of the conciliar understanding of our spiritual journey as a *corporate* one is that it helps us resist the idea of the Christian life as an individual struggle and, at the same time, encourages us to be in solidarity with others who are on the same way. Finally, it insists that we are not yet at the end of the journey; that there will be failures and mistakes along the way both individually and corporately. In other words, we need to keep our eyes on the end of the journey and not become hypnotized by the shortcomings of either individuals or institutions: "The church...will attain its full perfection only in the glory of heaven. Then will come the restoration of all things" (*Lumen Gentium* VII.48).

One final reflection on the Christian life as a desert journey comes to us from the efforts of the liberation theologians to bring into close harmony our Christian life and the demands of social justice. The liberation theologians see the exodus story as the foundational event of the Jewish people, "a departure from a situation of slavery, exploitation, and destitution in Egypt, a foreign country, and a passage, via a multifaceted process of liberation, into freedom, justice, and the possession of a land of their own, the promised land...."[5]

These same theologians see that experience as a paradigm by which Christians, in the company of all who are in bondage (whether it be through poverty or oppression or enslavement of various forms), "go out" with complete faith in the providence of God to find justice, freedom, and the promises which God has given to all of us.

---

4. St. Thomas Aquinas in the *Summa* makes a similar point: there is a certain conformity between the natural and spiritual life: III. q. 65.

5. Gustavo Gutiérrez. *We Drink from Our Own Wells.* (Maryknoll: Orbis, 1983) 73.

From that perspective, Christian spirituality cannot be seen as an inner individualistic "trip" but a common journey for all who wish to take up the new way of discipleship after the manner of Jesus. These liberation theologians uniformly insist that the core of the Christian life is the following of Jesus as disciples. As Jon Sobrino has pointed out, every time there was a crisis in the life of the church, great persons—a Francis of Assisi or an Ignatius of Loyola—rose up to ask the essential question: How do I hear the voice of Jesus and how do I follow him on the way even when that way leads to the cross? The authentic response to that challenge is to join in solidarity with all those who look to Jesus as liberator and follow him to the cross and, finally, in triumph to the resurrection.[6]

The great insight that the liberation theologians give us is that whether we think of our Christian life as a journey or as an ascent or as a process of growth and maturity, it may not be thought of apart from or indifferent to the needy of the world for whom God has a special predilection and with whom we are bound in solidarity as fellow human beings saved by the great acts of Jesus the Christ.

The Ascent

Every religion has held mountains to be sacred places. They stand as a kind of link between heaven and earth; they create what the great scholar of religions Mircea Eliade has called an *axis mundi*—a symbolic link between the divine and the human.[7]

Biblical religion is no exception to this rule. It was on Mount Sinai that Moses ascended to speak with God in the clouds and receive the tablets of the law. In the New Testament Jesus takes up to the mountains his chosen disciples where he is transfigured before them. In a somewhat analogous fashion Jacob has a dream in which he sees a kind of ladder linking heaven and earth and "angels ascending and descending" (Gen 28:12). The bottom of the ladder is on earth but its top reaches to where God dwells.

Christian spiritual commentators saw in those images a kind of

---

6. Jon Sobrino, "Spirituality and the Following of Jesus," in *Mysterium Liberationis: Fundamental Concepts of Liberation Theology,* Edited by Ignacio Ellacuria and Jon Sobrino. (Maryknoll: Orbis, 1993) 677-701.

7. Mircea Eliade, *The Sacred and the Profane* (New York: Harper Torchbook, 1961) 38ff.

model for the entire Christian life. Christians, it was argued, had to ascend or climb up toward God in a manner analogous to the ascents made by the angels up the ladder or Moses up the mountain. Implicit in this understanding was, of course, the idea that as one ascends one leaves mundane realities to be closer to God. In that fashion these commentators were able to create an entire ascent literature in which they mapped out the steps which had to be taken to move up from this world to the world of God.

There is so much of this literature that it is difficult to synthesize it in an easy fashion. For example, using the image of the ladder as a starting point, one could begin with St. Benedict's *Rule* for the monastic life (chapter #7) which described the "steps" of monastic perfection as consisting of twelve steps of humility culminating in the perfect love of God which drives out all fear. The seventh century monk from Mount Sinai, John Climacus ("Climacus" means the "ladder") wrote the *Ladder of Divine Ascent* which traced out thirty steps toward perfection, a book of such authority in the Christian east that it is read in its entirety during Lent in orthodox monasteries. In the twelfth century St. Bernard of Clairvaux in his treatise *On the Love of God* uses four stages by which we pass from love of self to love of God for the sake of God,[8] while, earlier in the same century, the Carthusian monk Guigo II wrote a treatise called *The Ladder of Monks* in which he shows how one passes from the reading of scripture to meditation, prayer, and, finally contemplation. In the following century, St. Bonaventure sees the soul's journey to God as a six stage ascent (paralleling the six days of creation) until one passes over into the sabbath rest of simple union with God. Walter Hilton's *Scale of Perfection* was a fourteenth century vernacular work which drew on an earlier tradition (especially Bernard of Clairvaux) to further the "ladder" literature.

One other strain of "ascent" literature begins with Origen of Alexandria. He saw the spiritual life as passing through three stages by which we first of all purified our loves of sin in order, secondly, to be illumined by the grace of God, so that, thirdly and finally, we might find union with God. Characteristically enough, Origen roots that ascent in his understanding of how we penetrate into the mysteries of sacred scripture. Using the three wisdom books ascribed to Solomon, Origen thought that Proverbs taught us about the moral life while Ecclesiastes illuminated us through faith about how to live

---

8. Bernard also wrote "The Steps of Humility and Pride," which was an extended revisioning of Benedict's twelve steps of humility.

as true Christians. Finally, the Song of Songs teaches us about love and transformation into God under the image of the union of the bridegroom and the bride—the lover and the beloved.

A whole strand of spiritual literature used, in one fashion or another, this triple ascent of purification, illumination, and union as a background for penetrating into the mystery of God in Christ. Spiritual writers would use various metaphors to describe this gradual movement toward God: St. Bernard of Clairvaux used the image of the threefold kiss (in his sermons on the Song of Songs) while Ignatius of Loyola's *Spiritual Exercises* saw one passing through the stages as one followed the "weeks" of the *Spiritual Exercises*. St. Teresa of Avila utilized the image of entering into a castle (*The Interior Castle*), while her contemporary, St. John of the Cross, not only wrote a book entitled *Ascent of Mount Carmel* but actually drew a "map" outlining the stages of that ascent. Thomas McGonigle has noted that the "three ways" of the spiritual life is such a common theme in Catholic spirituality with a pedigree that goes back to the third century (in Origen) that a seventeenth century pope officially condemned a writer who thought the distinctions to be absurd.[9]

Spiritual Maturity

The epistle to the Hebrews uses a striking image about spiritual maturity: "...you need someone to teach you again the first principles of God's word. You need milk not solid food. Everyone who lives on milk is unskilled in the word of righteousness, for that one is a child. But solid food is for the mature, for those who have their faculties trained by practice to distinguish good from evil" (Heb 5:12-14).

This is a theme found frequently in the New Testament. St. Paul says that we are children of God but we will also be heirs (Rom 8:16), that it is only the mature who can receive wisdom (1 Cor 2:6) but that Paul had to feed first with milk before his hearers could stand solid food (1 Cor 3:1); at the end of the same epistle, Paul demands that the Corinthians be mature and not act as children

---

9. "Three Ways," in *The New Dictionary of Christian Spirituality,* edited by Michael Downey (Collegeville: Glazier/Liturgical Press, 1993) 963-64. It is worthwhile noting that Dante's *Divine Comedy* is based on a descent into hell, a climb up the mount of purgatory, and a final ascent through the heavens until the vision of God is reached.

(1 Cor 14:20). This growth will come, not suddenly, but as the end of a process of maturation; we will no longer be children but will come to maturity and "reach full stature" (Eph 4:13-14).

The notion of growth into spiritual maturity must be seen in tension with another major theme from the bible: that we are *children* of God. Jesus, after all, is depicted as the "beloved Son" or the "only-begotten Son." He is the model for all other Christians. The St. Paul who writes of spiritual maturity is the same apostle who proclaims that our dignity derives from our relationship to God as "adopted children"—that we are by the graciousness of God what Jesus is by nature: "When the fullness of time came, God sent his Son, born of a woman, born under the law, to redeem those who were under the law, so that we might receive adoption as children. And because you are children, God has sent the Spirit of his Son into our hearts crying 'Abba, Father.' So you are no longer a slave but a child, and if a child then also an heir, through God" (Gal 4:4-7; see Rom 8:14-15).

How does one account for this seeming contradiction between the notion of spiritual childhood and spiritual maturity? Two points are in order:

(a) The concept of being a son or daughter of God means, at root, that one is not a totally autonomous person but one joined to God in a real relationship by which one has a living, trustful relationship to God as one has a relationship to a human parent. That is the thrust of those spiritual writers like St. Thérèse of Lisieux who emphasize the concept of spiritual childhood. In other words, the idea of spiritual childhood reflects a sense of intimate relationship and not a statement about immaturity or arrested growth. It is an antidote to any concept of God in which God is a distant impersonal force or punishing judge. God is a loving parent.

(b) The concept of spiritual childhood carries with it the expectation of growth and maturity.[10] The gospel itself says of the youthful Jesus that he grew "in wisdom and stature, and in favor with God and man" (Lk 2:52). The point to keep in focus is that being a "child of God" says something about relationship and does not imply a need to remain fixed in immaturity or underdevelopment. After all, even when we are fully adult we are still bound to a family as a son or a daughter. Indeed, one finds any number of spiritual writers (Thomas Merton comes to mind immediately) who warn about the

---

10. Two valuable studies of growth in spiritual maturity are Joann Wolski Conn, *Spirituality and Christian Maturity* (New York: Paulist, 1989) and Walter E. Conn, *Christian Conversion* (New York: Paulist, 1986).

dangers of "infantilizing" spirituality by too much emphasis on blind obedience, fearfulness about intellectual and emotional growth, and so on. Failure to mature as responsible adults in the Christian life gives unwarranted ammunition to those who, following Sigmund Freud's *The Future of an Illusion,* argue that religion creates an unhealthy dependence on a "Father figure" who, by turns, punishes while demanding allegiance, obedience, love, and servility.

When we utilize the image of maturity and growth we must remember that the parent/child metaphor found in the bible is a metaphor. The correct understanding of that metaphor helps us resist any use of it that produces an infantilizing of the spiritual life.

Some Systematic Reflections

From this rapid sketch of some models of the Christian journey we can deduce some general statements/principles that aid us in the following of the Christian way.

(1) Both the image of the journey and the image of the ascent utilize "stages" or "steps" that mark off the path we take toward God. The crucial point is that these stages are not to be thought of in any mechanical fashion. It would be wrong, for instance, to chart one's Christian life by saying that at period X one was being purified from sin and vice and then in period Y one was illumined by the grace of the Spirit, etc. Even those great saints and mystics who lived in close union with God felt the need constantly to purify their motives, pray more for the graces of illumination, and so on. When the great saints called themselves "sinners" they were not exercising a strategy of false humility. What they understood is how different they were from the awe-ful mystery of God. Our understanding of "stages" in the Christian life, in sum, must be *dynamic* and not *static.*

All of the "maps" provided for the spiritual journey or the spiritual ascent should be understood in the context of both a person's individual and social life. Furthermore, they need to be understood as particular analyses which need not be followed in some slavish or mathematical manner. It is true that each person can see in his or her life a pattern of growth from the naive faith of childhood to a more mature understanding of what discipleship entails. Indeed, it would be unfortunate if a person were to grow physically, emotionally, and intellectually while remaining at a juvenile state of religious commitment. Not to grow religiously in tandem with the other dynamics of maturity brings with it terrible risks. Many young people who claim to "lose their faith" are, in fact, merely shedding a simple-minded concept of faith at a moment when they might well need to reach deeper understandings of what faith entails. Every person can make the prayer of the centurion his or her own prayer: "I believe, Lord. Help my unbelief."

(2) The fact that we must not understand "stages" or "steps" mechanically does not mean that such incremental moments of spiritual growth are without value or that such analyses have only an historical value. Indeed, contemporary experience teaches just the opposite. The famous "Twelve Step" program developed by the founders of Alcoholics Anonymous (and now used by many groups who have addiction or dependency problems) bears a striking family resemblance to historic analyses of the spiritual ascent/ journey. Twelve Step programs are explicitly spiritual, beginning with the need to affirm that a person must rely on a power larger than oneself and insisting throughout the steps on a need for deep personal analysis of wrongs done to oneself and others. Those steps are also incremental in that they demand that people once "spiritually awakened" (the language of step twelve) should be convinced enough of their spiritual awakening that they help others to attain sobriety. This is not to argue that Twelve Step programs and traditional ascent/journey motifs are the same; it is to argue that Twelve Step programs do bear a certain similarity to traditional Christian descriptions of the spiritual journey.[11]

In fact, many traditional devotional practices by which one assesses spiritual maturity implicitly recognize that we go through stages of Christian growth. When we keep a book of reflections or a diary or talk to a spiritual counselor or director or a "soul friend" we are, in essence, querying ourselves about where we are and, tacitly, where we would like to go. Similarly, when we reconcile ourselves in the sacrament of penance or take seriously the moment of silence at the beginning of the liturgy, we are, again, judging the present (and future) state of our Christian commitment. A healthy examination of conscience (as opposed to a morbid preoccupation with failure and sin) is a key element in Christian growth and maturity.

---

11. For an interweaving of Twelve Step spirituality and Christian sources, see Ernest Kurtz and Katherine Ketcham, *The Spirituality of Imperfection* (New York: Bantam, 1992).

For many contemporary readers, the writings of the "ascent" authors seems difficult and strange with their insistence on total "forgetfulness of the self" or their notion that God is best known through negation (e.g. in *The Cloud of Unknowing,* a fourteenth century text whose pedigree goes back to the fourth century *Life of Moses* by St. Gregory of Nyssa) or the unblinking fashion that a St. John of the Cross uses to describe the pain and sense of loss in the search for loving union with God.

What one must keep in mind is that these authors are attempting to articulate in language, rather like poets who strain for adequate words, some of the deepest *experiences* of what it means when a finite person is faced with the reality of the Infinite. They also attempt to describe some of the failures, moments of desperation, and anxiety that attend any person who tries to live the faith deeply and more maturely.

Asked by Pope Paul VI in 1967 to write an open letter to the world about the contemplative life, Thomas Merton penned some words which capture the seriousness of the spiritual ascent to God:

My brother, perhaps in my solitude I have become as it were an explorer for you, a searcher in realms which you are not able to visit….I have been summoned to explore a desert area of man's heart in which explanations no longer suffice and in which one learns that only experience counts….And in this area I have learned that one cannot truly know hope unless he has found out how like despair hope is. The language of Christianity has said this for centuries in other less naked terms. But the language of Christianity has been so used and misused that sometimes you distrust it; you do not know whether or not behind the word "cross" there stands the experience of, or only the threat of, punishment, mercy and salvation. If my word means anything to you, I can say to you that I have experienced the cross as mercy and not cruelty; truth and not deception; that the news and the truth of the love of Jesus is indeed the true good news but in our times it speaks out in strange places.And perhaps it speaks out more in you than it does in me. Perhaps Christ is nearer to you than he is to me.[12]

---

12. "A Letter on the Contemplative Life," in *Thomas Merton: Spiritual Master,* edited by Lawrence S. Cunningham (New York: Paulist, 1992) 424-25; originally published in *Contemplation in a World of Action.*

Another Model: The Widening Circle

The notion of the desert journey or the ascent of the ladder/mountain might not be one with which the contemporary Christian can easily identify. Our experience of Christian discipleship may well be too down to earth, too bound to ordinary experience, or too uncertain to attempt the desert journey (even though in our worst moments we can understand the desert!) or the ascent of the mountain. Or it might be the case that we need another alternative model of Christian growth simply as a complement to the ones we find in the classic literature.

It may be helpful, then, to think of our Christian life as an attempt to enlarge our circle of human concern in a way that helps to enter God's circle as well.

Each of us finds our young lives bound within a kind of domestic sphere. We have an immediate family, and our family is further bound, say, to the neighborhood in which we live, the parish we attend, and the school which educates us. It is within that sphere that we learn our first prayers, encounter the sacraments of the church, receive the shape of our ethical and Christian formation. This circle within which we live is not an abstraction; it is, rather, an interconnected web of relatives, friends, mentors, and colleagues.

Within that sphere we take shape. Anyone who reflects on his or her upbringing knows how formative that sphere is on who and what we are. For all of the graces and gifts that sphere brings, it is also true that the social pressures of that sphere may make us distrustful of people who do not fit within it, suspicious of those who do not share its values, and, perhaps, antagonistic to others who are very unlike us. Our sphere, familial and religious and social, is, in the worst sense of the term, parochial (remembering that the word "parochial" refers to a parish).

The first stage of religious growth often comes when we are able to shatter the narrowness, say, of our understanding of what Christianity is all about when we are confronted by others who differ from us but make claims upon our professed love and care for our neighbor. In this instance, we learn that our community of worship, within the family and within the parish, is linked to and bound up with many others who do not live in our neighborhood. In other words, we begin to see that we are really *catholic*—which is to say part of a larger reality made up of those who profess a faith in Jesus Christ but who may differ from us in race, color, nationality, and so on.

This is an extremely crucial moment of conversion. Such a moment helps us to purify one of the most toxic poisons in religion: hatred of the other in the name of a narrow understanding of our "religion." When we begin to glimpse that "our religion" cannot be professed at the expense of "their religion" we begin to shift in our thinking away from us as an ethnic or family bond to a bond which decenters us and puts God in Christ at the center of our life.

This kind of conversion is not unlike the stage of purification classically described in our spiritual literature as the dark night of St. John of the Cross. It is the time when we begin to understand under grace that what often passes for religious experience is, in reality, a kind of mask or instrument by which we articulate our prejudices, fears, and antipathies for those who are not like us.

There are many routes we can take to further this kind of purification. It may be as simple as serving the poor and the needy in the name of our faith. It may be through insight into what we really mean when we speak of *communion* as essential to our right to share in the eucharist. It may come when we reflect on whether we are hospitable persons or hospitable communities.

You will note that this widening of the circle does not appeal to a solitary ascent of the mountain or a climbing of a mystical ladder or the loneliness of the long distance runner. It makes use of our need to penetrate *into* ourselves as social beings connected to all others in this world. This moment of purification that enlarges our capacity to love and advance closer to God is strikingly described in one of the few autobiographical reflections St. Francis of Assisi left us. Late in his life, Francis wrote a testament for his companions. In a few brief lines he talks about his conversion:

> While I was in sin, it seemed very bitter to me to see lepers. And the Lord himself led me among them and I had mercy upon them. And when I left them that which seemed bitter to me was changed into sweetness of soul and body; and afterward I lingered a little and left the world.[13]

Francis, of course, had been born and raised a Catholic. He tells us, however, that it was only when he could overcome his horror at the poor segregated lepers in his native Assisi that he experienced a conversion which made him choose a new way of life.

---

13. Translation of Regis Armstrong in *Francis and Clare: The Complete Works* (New York: Paulist, 1982) 154.

Francis was, to borrow the classical formulation of it, purified of his horror of the leper and illumined about where he could find the presence of Christ—among those who were outside his social and familial community, among the most feared and despised of his world.

The widening of our circle might not be that dramatic and it may well be couched in a different kind of language. This enlargement of our way of "seeing" things grows (or should grow) by the incremental steps of testing our reactions against the imperatives of the gospel.

It should be emphasized that such a growth is not merely one of a "humanistic" character; growth in the spiritual life of a Christian is not only a way of being more tolerant or more compassionate. Christian growth holds in balance the two great commandments of love of God and love of neighbor. To the degree that we can look outside of ourselves toward another we learn our connectedness to everyone else who is created, like us, in the image of God. By the continued acts of "forgetting the self" we recognize, in those very acts, others and the Other.

Since we live in a real, tactile and gritty world we are expected to seek growth in the Christian life, not by abstracting ourselves from that world, but by finding God in creation in general and other persons in particular: "If anyone says 'I love God' and hates his neighbor, he is a liar; for he who does not love his brother whom he has seen, cannot love God whom he has not seen" (1 Jn 4:20).

One striking incident that illuminates this process of conversion may be found in the life of the late Thomas Merton (1915-68). Merton had been a monk for over fifteen years and was a well-established spiritual writer when, in the late 1950s, he had an extraordinary experience that he noted in his notebooks and later published in one of his spiritual journals:

> In Louisville, at the corner of Fourth and Walnut, in the center of the shopping district, I was suddenly overwhelmed with the realization that I loved all these people....It was...from a dream of separateness, of spurious self-isolation in a special world, the world of renunciation and supposed holiness. The whole illusion of a separate holy existence is a dream...the illusion that by making vows we become a different species of being, pseudoangels, spiritual men, men of interior life....[14]

---

14. Thomas Merton, *Conjectures of a Guilty Bystander* (Garden City: Doubleday Image, 1968) 156-57.

What Thomas Merton realized in that moment was that his Trappist life could not be one of individual contemplation, penance, and renunciation; it had to be somehow "connected" to the world outside the monastery; otherwise it ran the risk of being an exercise in egocentricity and self-absorption. It was this insight that led him to see how he might remain faithful to his monastic vocation while, at the same time, being open to and concerned with the sufferings, problems, and needs of the larger world. This led him in time to formulate more precisely how one could be in the enclosure of the monastery while still linked to the larger circle of human needs and aspirations.

Writing some years after the Louisville incident Merton said that his monastic life was not an escape from the world. It was a statement about his position in the world:

> By my monastic life and vows I am saying NO to all the concentration camps, aerial bombardments, staged political trials....If I say NO to all these secular forces I also say YES to all that is good in the world....I say YES to all the men and women who are my brothers in the world.[15]

Some Conclusions

How do we know whether we are on the right journey? How do we read the map of our own life? What do we do if we have not experienced any dramatic insight similar to that of a Thomas Merton standing at the corner of a busy intersection?

In the first place, we should not expect dramatic conversions or exquisite moments of illumination in our lives as being the normal markers on our Christian journey. Such moments may come into our lives but they are graces and should be accepted as such. If there is anything about which the great spiritual masters/mistresses assure us, it is that expectations of extraordinary graces can leave us disappointed and, even worse, upset. If God gives us such graces we should simply thank God. For the rest, we should continue on in our journey as ordinary but faith-filled wayfarers. This will mean, at times, that we may seem to be climbing a steep moun-

---

15. Preface to the Japanese translation of *The Seven Storey Mountain* in *Honorable Reader: Reflections on My Work,* edited by Robert E. Daggy (New York: Crossroad, 1989) 65-66.

tain and at other times we will travel on a level path or, to use our other image, enter into a widening circle.

Secondly, we must recognize that our journey is not a solitary one. We have *companions* (literally: "bread sharers") who have made and are making the same journey. Such companions may help us in a variety of ways and may come to us in many different circumstances. We may get help on our Christian journey from someone whom the old Irish monks called a "soul friend." This might be a confessor or a spiritual director or just a good reliable friend to whom we can go in time of need. At times, the soul friend might be a community—the people with whom we pray or the members of a St. Vincent de Paul circle or those with whom we share in the liturgy. Finally, the "soul friend" might be someone we do not know personally. Such a "soul friend" might speak to us through his or her example or writings (e.g. a Dorothy Day or a C. S. Lewis or a Thomas Merton), or this friend (perhaps a personal acquaintance) might inspire us to a more disciplined life of Christian service. Such a "soul friend" might teach us just from the example of his or her life; many people, for instance, have looked at a person like St. Francis and said that such a life is an image of the gospel and, as such, is worthy of imitation.

Whoever it is who inspires us (remembering that the "whoever," in turn, should reflect the soul friend who is Jesus Christ) we shouldn't try to become them. A recent spiritual writer makes the point well:

> However detailed the maps may appear in descriptions of the journey, they are in fact broad outlines offered by our brothers and sisters in the faith. We can learn from them and be encouraged by them. But their teachings are not rigid classifications into which we must fit our life's journeys; they must be filtered through the prism of our own uniqueness and cultures.[16]

Finally, our journey/ascent should be done in the full context of the faith, that is, in terms of the trinitarian belief that we go to the Father through the Son in the Holy Spirit. That is the way we end our prayers and that is what we affirm as Christians. We look at Christ who shows us the Father through the Holy Spirit. At that level, we are nourished by our encounter with God's word through

---

16. Richard Byrne, O.C.S.O., "Journey (Growth and Development in Spiritual Life)" in *New Dictionary of Catholic Spirituality* 576.

our common worship, by seeing Christ in others, but learning to love more deeply and more fully. We grow slowly in this journey and, at times, we may not see clearly. Affirming, however, that God's Spirit is always with us, we move forward, upward, and inward with confidence and without fear. In doing that we may pray in the words of Saint Anselm of Canterbury (died 1109):

> Lord, I am not trying to make my way to your height
> for my understanding is not equal to that.
> I do desire to understand a little of your truth
> which my heart already believes and loves.
> I do not seek to understand that I can believe
> but I believe that I may understand;
> And what is more
> I believe that unless I do believe, I shall not understand.
> Amen.

Further Reading

Gregory of Nyssa, *The Life of Moses,* trans. Malherbe/Ferguson (New York: Paulist, 1978). This classic fourth century treatise is one source for most of the "ascent" literature of later Christianity.

Gutiérrez, Gustavo, *We Drink from Our Own Wells* (Maryknoll: Orbis, 1983). A liberation spirituality focused on the "Journey." Strong on scripture and classical sources.

John of the Cross, "The Ascent of Mount Carmel," in *The Collected Works of St. John of the Cross,* trans. by Kieran Kavanaugh and Otilio Rodriguez (Washington, DC: Institute of Carmelite Studies, 1991). This is, by all estimates, *the* classic of the Christian "ascent" treatises.

Norris, Kathleen, *Dakota: A Spiritual Geography* (New York: Ticknor & Fields, 1993). A contemporary writer explores the metaphors of desert, place, and travel in terms of the Christian life.

Teresa of Avila, St., *Autobiography* (Garden City: Doubleday Image; many editions). Along with Teresa's *Interior Castle* a fine work to understand the "interior journey."

Exercises

(1) Try to describe, from your own experience, some terms that might be analogous to the three stages of Christian purification, illumination, and union. What kind of terms / stages might you find more useful to use to speak of the spiritual ascent?

(2) Choose a biography, personal reminiscence or the observation of someone you know (and admire) who exemplifies the Christian life. Can you see in that life a series of stages or insights or conversions that can be described?

(3) Think about the place of gender *in the spiritual journey. Is the spiritual path different for men and women? In what ways?*

(4) What examples from the field of literature can you think of that give us "maps" of the spiritual journey. One thinks of a classic like T. S. Eliot's Four Quartets; *can you describe others? Does your choice shed any light on question #3 with respect to gender?*

(5) Do you have a "soul friend"? If not, can you imagine the kind of "soul friend" who would best inspire you?

4

Prayer

"Let my prayer rise as incense before you..." (Ps 141).

Introduction

*O*ne cannot write a book on Christian spirituality without talking about the subject of prayer. It only takes a minute's
thought, however, to realize that prayer is an enormously complex
subject. One could devote this chapter solely to the kinds of prayer
or, from another angle, address deep philosophical questions about
the relationship of prayer to God's omniscience and self-sufficiency;
there are also issues involved in the difference between public and
private prayer, devotional practices and contemplative prayer, and
so on.

Many of these questions will be touched on in the course of this
chapter, but it may be more helpful to begin with something more
fundamental: the symbolic significance of the act of prayer itself.
By prayer, at this point, we mean something very general: those
acts which symbolize, by words and/or gestures, a person's relationship with God.

What does the act and the posture of prayer itself "say" or "signify" to one who observes a person or community in prayer?

It may say something quite superficial. When one sees a person
praying the rosary one may presume that the person is a Catholic.
Similarly, one might be able to identify Jews at prayer by their use
of a prayer shawl or Muslims who bow profoundly while on their
knees and so on. Gestures of prayer, in short, are external signifiers
of a particular religious tradition.

At a less superficial level, however—and this is the point—the
very act or gesture of prayer "says" that an individual or a community has a conviction, symbolized by the act or gesture of prayer

itself, that the person or community recognizes someone with whom they have a deep and meaningful connection who is greater than, and concerned about, those who pray. Prayer, in other words, is a fundamental gesture of belief, faith, dependence, and connectedness. In that sense, at least, what distinguishes a believer from a non-believer is the gesture of prayer. In other words, at a very fundamental level, prayer is the other side of the coin of faith.

On occasion, indeed, we note that some people who are not believers in the conventional sense feel compelled to pray (think of the proverbial saying that there are "no atheists in foxholes") simply because they are overwhelmed by circumstances of danger, despair, need, etc. and feel a deep urge to call on someone who can help them in this or that crisis moment.

In that general sense, then, prayer positively signals communication with an Other and, simultaneously, says, in effect, that a person is not totally self-sufficient and does not regard himself or herself as totally autonomous or alone. Prayer, in other words, presupposes some kind of relationship.

Those interested in the Christian way of discipleship, it is clear, may call upon God in dire circumstances just as others may do, but it is equally clear that there must be a more patterned, committed, and intense life of prayer for those persons who commit themselves to the Christian life. If one is a person of faith it follows that one must be a person of prayer. Faith and prayer have a very close bond.

It must be, then, that if one considers prayer as a constitutive part of Christian spirituality one must inquire into the life and teachings of Jesus as a resource for our understanding of prayer. We must echo, in short, the same request which the disciples once put to Jesus: "Lord, teach us to pray..." (Lk 11:1).

Jesus and Prayer

We begin with a bald statement of fact: Jesus was a profound person of prayer.[1] When the Holy Spirit descended on Christ at the

---

1. What follows here is in debt to John Wright, *A Theology of Christian Prayer,* 2nd edition (New York: Pueblo, 1988) and his article "Prayer" in *The New Dictionary of Catholic Spirituality,* edited by Michael Downey (Collegeville: Liturgical Press, 1993) 767-70 as well as #2599-2616 of the *Catechism of the Catholic Church.*

baptism which opened his public life Jesus "was praying" (Lk 3:22). The gospels tell us that immediately afterward he went into the desert to pray and fast for forty days. The gospels tell us (see Lk 5:16 and Mk 1:35) that he often rose before dawn or spent nights in prayer. He acted in a similar fashion before choosing the twelve apostles, and when the first disciples returned from their first missionary journey, Jesus uttered a prayer of thanksgiving and praise (Mt 11:25-26).

Jesus also linked his public gestures to moments of prayer. He prayed for the little children brought to him for blessings (Mt 19:13-15) just as he prayed before the tomb of Lazarus (Jn 11:41) and in the garden of Gethsemane as his passion unfolded. On the cross Jesus not only uttered the prayer of the psalms but prayed for his persecutors and uttered a prayer of resignation to the Father: "Into thy hands I commend my spirit" (Lk 23:46). Finally, we note that the early church in the New Testament writings assures us that the risen and glorified Christ intercedes for us in heaven (see Rom 8:34; Heb 7:25; 1 Jn 2:1).

Prayer, then, is woven into the life of Jesus. Not only was he a person of prayer, alone and as a faithful member of the Jewish people, but he taught people how to pray (providing his disciples and us with the Lord's Prayer), under what circumstances (e.g. not ostentatiously in order to impress people); and for whom to pray (e.g. enemies). Jesus, finally, recommends that we pray for a whole spectrum of reasons: for the things we need, for those who oppose us, to drive out the demonic, to avoid temptations, to reconcile our brothers and sisters, that workers be there for the harvest, and, finally, that we might receive the gift of the Holy Spirit.

The deepest and most fundamental characteristic of the prayer of Jesus is the radical love that Jesus has for God the Father (whom he addresses with the familiar term *Abba*). When one reads the gospels it becomes evident that everything Jesus does—and he is an incredibly active person—is done under the guidance of the Father, in union with the Father, and for the purposes of God's kingdom. When Jesus gave us the Lord's Prayer with its opening invocation addressing "Our Father" he was not expressing a sentiment but a deeply felt and real connection with the one whose will he had come to do.

For the contemporary follower of Jesus the most fundamental lesson that one learns about the prayer life of Jesus, especially as it is reflected in Luke (which can be called the gospel of prayer) or in the moving chapters in John when Jesus prays at the last supper, is that the imitation of Jesus demands a framework of prayer to the Father through the Spirit whom Jesus says the Father will send.

A careful reading of the gospels makes the following conclusion inevitable:

> The gospels generally attest that Jesus is remembered as satu-rating his life with prayer....Particularly significant is the remi-niscence that Jesus prays at especially critical moments in his ministry: before curing (Mk 9:29), when he preaches (Mt 11:25), and before his arrest in Gethsemane (Mk 14:35-36).[2]

How Does a Christian Pray?

The short answer to that question is that a Christian prays both as a member of a believing community and as an individual. Prayer has both a personal and a communal dimension.

We begin with prayer within the believing community because Jesus himself tells us that "where two or three are gathered in my name, there I am in the midst of them" (Mt 18:20). The very gath-ering "in my name" is, in itself, a gesture of prayer. When, to cite something from our contemporary experience, we gather for the liturgy we, in effect, declare that we do so in order to recall, remem-ber, re-present, and re-enact the saving acts of Jesus both by par-ticipation in the word and through the ritual action of celebrating the eucharist. In other words, we are a people who gather and our gathering is for prayer. We are most church when we gather as an assembly.

Further, for most Christians, it is within the believing commu-nity that we learn the habit and techniques of prayer. All of us have seen parents helping their children to trace the sign of the cross or instructing them with the book of the liturgy or first encouraging them to begin to commit to memory the common prayer formulas that are found in the liturgy. The gathered Christian community is not only for worship but an occasion that provides that pedagogy of worship; we *learn* from the liturgy. It is from within the liturgy that we experience Jesus Christ as Lord, savior, and risen one. Like the pilgrims on the road to Emmaus (Lk 24) we recognize him "in the

---

2. William M. Thompson, *The Jesus Debate: A Survey and Synthesis* (Mahwah: Paulist, 1985) 202-03.

breaking of the bread" and join with Christ who prays to the Father in the Spirit.

It is also obvious that from within the liturgy we see the different kinds of prayer that are common to the Christian life. Gathering for common prayer is a gesture of recognition of our relationship to God; this is the prayer of adoration by which we acknowledge our relationship to God. Eucharist means *thanksgiving,* and our prayer also expresses a sense of gratitude for everything from creation itself to the gifts and privileges we have as those who are gifted in Jesus Christ. The eucharistic liturgy begins with an acknowledgment of sinfulness and an expression of our need for forgiveness which, in turn, permits us to petition God to give us that which we require for both our material well-being and our spiritual advancement. In sum: a careful look at the liturgy reveals to us the four traditional forms of prayer which are at the heart of Christian prayer: adoration, thanksgiving, repentance, and petition.

It should also be noted, in passing, that the church provides more than the eucharistic gathering as an opportunity for prayer. There is a spectrum of institutions within the church ranging from the formal prayer of the church called the "divine office" (now largely, but not exclusively, observed in communities of vowed religious) to informal prayer groups or extra-liturgical gatherings that meet a whole variety of needs. The other sacramental celebrations (e.g. marriages, baptisms, etc.) as well as feastday observances afford communitarian opportunities for prayer. Finally, the prayer life of the church spills over into informal gatherings of families, organizations, and study groups where the prayer of the church finds extension in small and less stylized fashions. Wherever those gatherings take place they are all examples of the church at prayer.

Similarly, the Christian prays as an individual either in his or her private life as part of a regular discipline at night or in the morning or on those occasions when prayer seems peculiarly appropriate: for a sick friend or for a particular need or in the face of a personal crisis or as an act of solidarity for another person. At times, those prayers are formulaic: we use the language that comes to us from the scriptures (as in the "Our Father" or "Hail Mary" or from the psalms) or other classical sources which we obtain from manuals or books of prayers.

On other occasions, we might pray more silently and wordlessly just by being in a special place where the presence of God is felt most deeply or we find ourselves in a frame of mind that makes the presence of God well up within us out of a sense of profound need or deep gratefulness. Prayer, in that sense, may just come out of our deep sense of dependence and an equally compelling desire to connect with what lies behind our very mundane order of living. This sense was beautifully expressed by Ludwig Wittgenstein, one of the most penetrating philosophers of the contemporary period:

> What do I know about God and the purpose of life?
> I know that the world exists.
> That I am placed in it like my eye in a visual field.
> That something about it is problematic, which we call its meaning.
> That meaning does not lie in it but outside it.
> That my will penetrates the world....
> The meaning of life, i.e. the meaning of the world
> we can call God and connect with this
> the comparison of God to a Father.
> To pray is to think about the meaning of life. [3]

The deep experience of "something more" to which Wittgenstein alludes is close to that wordless state of being "in prayer" which has been described by the great spiritual masters/mistresses throughout Christian history. It has undergone many analyses and conjured up many names, each with its own history and understanding. We have words like the "prayer of simplicity" or "contemplative prayer" or "mystical prayer" or the "prayer of quiet"—all terms which point to an experience that every believer may have experienced: a moment when words are simply not enough and, by leaving aside words, one is simply in the presence of the Lord. Those experiences may come naturally or they may be consciously waited for, but they make up some of the deepest prayer experiences to which people of all ages and stripes have given witness. St. John Vianney, the patron saint of parish priests, once asked an old peasant whom he saw sitting in church each evening what he was doing. The farmer replied: "I look at the Good God [*Le Bonne Dieu*] and the Good God looks at me." That is about as good a description as one can articulate of this silent prayer, which so easily leads to contemplation.

---

3. Ludwig Wittgenstein, *Notebooks 1914-1916* (New York: Oxford University Press, 1961) 74c.

Methods of Prayer

Bernard McGinn's work on the history of Christian mysticism is still in progress but it has taken him two fat volumes to get to the twelfth century[4]—a fact which makes it clear that we cannot even begin to describe the methods of prayer used in our tradition. Another chapter will deal more precisely with issues of meditation and contemplation. In this chapter we simply paint with a broad brush.

What follows are some exemplary "paths" of prayer which have entered into our common inheritance and which still find a part in the contemporary experience of prayer. This section, then, describes some of the more common forms of Catholic prayer with an emphasis on personal appropriation.

Praying with a Bible. As a result of the biblical renewal which began early in the twentieth century more Catholics are rediscovering a tradition which is as old as the Christian tradition itself: a prayerful response to our encounter with the scriptures. That practice, of course, is embedded in the liturgy. We respond prayerfully as a community to the readings proclaimed at our common worship. The practice of responding to the bible in prayer also enjoys a privileged place in personal prayer.

Monasticism has given us the practice which goes by the simple Latin word *lectio* ("reading"). *Lectio* accepts the idea that God speaks to us through the scriptures which provides an opportunity for us to speak back. *Lectio* is, in short, a kind of dialogue with the word of God. In the middle ages a Carthusian monk, Guigo II, formulated a schema for this kind of reading. In a book called *The Ladder of Monks*[5] Guigo said that reading should trigger meditation ("thinking" about what the text means) which in turn should lead to the response of prayer (speaking in our own words in response to meditative reading), and, finally, prayer should lead us to a kind of contemplation in which we rest silently in the presence of God.

These four steps of reading, meditation, prayer and contemplation should not be thought of as four mechanical steps but ideally

---

4. *The Foundations of Mysticism* (New York: Crossroad, 1991); *The Growth of Mysticism* (New York: Crossroad, 1994).

5. *Guigo II: The Ladder of Monks,* trans. Edmund Colledge and James Walsh (Kalamazoo: Cistercian Publications, 1978).

describe a holistic approach to penetrating the word of God. Some contemporary commentators have added a further step: the process of *lectio* should spill over into resolution by which we resolve to turn our prayer into strategies for changing our lives, deepening our commitment to Christian living, and into aids for a fuller and more human life. A recent writer has developed a series of "principles" which should be part of a full exercise of *lectio;* here is an abbreviated summary of some of those principles:

- *Lectio* should be a way in which God's word breaks into our accustomed way of thinking and doing.
- It is a long term activity and not merely a source of immediate gratification.
- *Lectio* is part of our vocation so that we can hear God clearly in our present situation.
- *Lectio* should always have application to our here and now situation.
- We should try to commit to memory some of the texts which touch us most deeply.
- *Lectio* should be a physical act: begin with the sign of the cross, employ a distinct posture, perhaps read aloud, do something that is "special," etc.[6]

Making Ordinary Life a Prayer. Our tradition has proposed many different ways in which we can consciously think of our ordinary rounds of life as a form of prayer. This fits in very well with the fundamental notion that we profess as Christians that everything we are and do falls under the gaze of God. Pope John Paul II recently wrote in his best selling *Crossing the Threshold of Hope* (1994) that human beings are the "priests of creation" in that they articulate what is true of the cosmos itself, namely that the universe proclaims the glory of God. What is true of the cosmos is equally true of the life and activities of each human being.

Catholics of a certain age will remember being taught to make a "morning offering"—a prayer by which we consecrate to God the activities of that day for the praise of God.[7] That rather recent pious custom had behind it a longer history that attempted to sacralize

---

6. Michael Casey, "Seven Principles of Lectio Divina," in *The Undivided Heart* (Petersham: St. Bede's Publications, 1994) 4-9.

7. The practice of making the "morning offering" began to be popular in the first half of the nineteenth century.

our ordinary activities. The French Carmelite lay brother, Lawrence of the Resurrection (1614-1691) left notes, letters, and observations which later were published under the title *The Practice of the Presence of God.* Brother Lawrence's advice was to do everything with a consciousness that one is in the presence of God. That practice, in turn, had deep roots in the old monastic notion of *mindfulness*[8] which, in turn, had roots in the biblical teachings, both in the Old and New Testament, about God's watchfulness over us.

The actual working out of a method of prayerful mindfulness will vary from person to person. Brother Lawrence advised the use of moments of recollection together with short prayers. Here is some simple advice that he offers a soldier:

> A little lifting up of the heart is enough; a short remembrance of God; an interior act of worship, made in haste and sword in hand, are prayers which, short as they may be, are most pleasing to God....Let him [i.e. the soldier] think of God as much as he can; let him accustom himself little by little to this brief but salutary experience; nobody notices it, and nothng is easier than to make short acts of worship throughout the day.[9]

There is no reason why this form of piety cannot be melded with ordinary acts of piety commonly used today. The tradition encourages, for example, prayers to start and finish the day and thanksgiving before meals as ways to be mindful of God's presence in our lives. When those exercises are done in a family setting (e.g. grace before meals) the place of God becomes highlighted for the family which is called the "domestic church," and in that sense our meals are a mirror of the eucharist (which means, literally, "to give thanks"). Those formal gestures of recognition in our daily life can be occasions for what the great French spiritual writer Jean Pierre de Caussade (1675-1751) called the "sacrament of the present

---

8. See the essay (with abundant monastic citations) in Michael Casey's "Mindfulness of God" in *The Undivided Heart* 62-77.

9. *Brother Lawrence of the Resurrection: The Practice of the Presence of God,* trans. Donald Attwater (Springfield: Templegate, 1974) 82. There is a new translation, based on a critical edition, now available: *On the Practice of the Presence of God,* trans. S. Sciurba (Washington, DC: Institute of Carmelite Studies, 1994).

moment"—that is, a sign that we are conscious of God's guidance over us and beneficience toward us.

The benefit of such mindfulness derives not only from that fact that we are praying. It helps us realize that everything we do in our lives—work, play, study, and recreation—can be considered as prayer in the sense that what we are and do "connects" us to the reality of God. Thomas Merton expressed this concept beautifully and with simplicity:

> The requirements of a work to be done can be understood as the will of God. If I am supposed to hoe a garden or make a table, then I will be obeying God if I am true to the task to be done. To do the work carefully and well, with love and respect for the nature of my task and with due attention to its purpose, is to unite myself with God's will in my work.[10]

Meditation. We have already seen the word "meditation" as a step in the practice of *lectio*. In that context it meant thinking. The term "meditation," however, covers a wide range of spiritual practices by which we discover systematically how to "raise our minds and hearts to God" as the old catechism describes prayer. Meditation is such a complex and rich theme in the Catholic tradition that a recent writer has said, with some exaggeration, that the "history of the word in Christian spirituality sums up the history of spirituality itself."[11] The matter is all the more complex because in recent times meditation has been touted as a purely therapeutic exercise to manage stress and pain or for self-improvement or for the acquisition of better mental and physical powers.

Our brief reflections will not attempt to engage in a discussion of the various forms and methods of meditation even though such methods, ranging from the *Spiritual Exercises* of St. Ignatius to varieties of "centering prayer" are widely available to Christians today (see our chapter on meditation and contemplation). The focus of our observations will be on the ordinary ways in which we might concentrate our reflective powers on our relationship to God in a manner which adds to the ordinary practice of participating in the liturgy or "saying" prayers or even prayerfully reading the

---

10. *New Seeds of Contemplation* (New York: New Directions, 1972) 19.

11. Laurence Freeman, "Meditation," in *The New Catholic Dictionary of Spirituality*, edited by Michael Downey (Collegeville: Liturgical Press, 1993) 648.

scriptures. What we say here, in short, must be fleshed out with the materials offered elsewhere in this volume.

We might begin with the human need for some *silence* in our life. Be still, the psalmist said, and know that I am God. The meditative Christian needs both some space for external silence (by being alone or finding a quiet spot) in order to achieve some internal silence (free from distractions, worries, and day-dreaming) which allows us to be still enough to sense the presence of God in our lives. Consciously to stop in our daily routine in order to be in the presence of God, free from the noise and clutter of our passing thoughts, is the matrix out of which a meditative Christian life begins. This may be done by as simple an act as taking a walk after work or simply sitting somewhere (in a park or in a backyard) and being still with the equally simple intention of being in the presence of God both externally (where we are) and internally (through our attention). This kind of silent attention may allow us to think or meditate in the special way which we might call meditative prayer. By "thinking" we do not mean abstract acts of rumination or curiosity or "working out" problems but something far simpler and deeper— what the Oxford theologian John Macquarrie has called "passionate thinking":

> This passionate thinking, that is open to feeling the world as well as knowing it, is at least the threshold of prayer. To think of the world with longing for its perfecting is a step toward praying for the coming of the Kingdom; to think of the world with rejoicing for all that is good is inarticulately to hallow the name; to think of the world with regret for our failures is implicitly to ask forgiveness for our sins and trespasses....[12]

Thirdly, this passionate thinking, done in silence, should contain some deep sense of the self in relation to God. This may involve some personal reflection about how or how not we have lived up to the expectations of discipleship. It may well involve some attempt to understand how we are to live our lives in the near and distant future under the inspiration of the Spirit's guidance (i.e. the process of *discernment*). It may lead us further in understanding our relationships to others to whom we have obligations or from whom we

---

12. John Macquarrie, *Paths in Spirituality*, 2nd edition (Harrisburg: Morehouse, 1992) 26.

have been estranged so that our passionate thinking becomes, in Macquarrie's language, *compassionate* thinking.[13]

When we insist that prayer involves the self in relationship to God it becomes necessary to issue a word of caution. Meditative prayer should not become (and is incorrectly thought to be) merely an exercise in introspection. Much less should it be a form of self-scrutiny which dwells on failure, sinfulness, self-laceration, and so on. Meditation is not mere brooding and it certainly does not indicate a flight from the world into an interior world of timeless abstraction. For that reason alone it is well to keep our meditative practices close to the New Testament spirit of hope and faith by which, following the example of Mary, we keep all things, pondering them in our hearts (cf. Lk 2:19). The paradoxical thing about meditation is that while it invites us to ponder in our hearts it should also lead us from the self toward God in Christ and to the world and people which God gives us. In other words, the ultimate end of meditation and of all prayer should be love and wonder and gratitude.

A final note. The practice of systematic prayer and meditation is available to all. It is not an extraordinary exercise for the cloistered contemplative. It is best learned within the family and the community. Hence, it has always been advised that we accept advice, counsel, and direction from others who possess the gift of prayer. We need to learn from others; only fools, St. Bernard of Clairvaux once said, have themselves for a spiritual director. In choosing a "soul friend"[14] we need to find someone who will journey with us but not become a spiritual tyrant or a manipulator; what we need is someone who can warn us when we are acting from self-will or illusion or out of a unhealthy sense of sin or unworthiness.

That "soul friend" may be a trusted individual or it may be a supportive prayer group or it may come from a deep acquaintance with a spiritual author who provides us with the help we need at the time we need it. Martin Marty, the prominent religious historian, who does not think himself a "meditative" person, puts it rather nicely:

Meditation does not do it for me. What I do therefore—it's a kind of a crass-sounding word—is "hitchhike. I hitchhike using the

---

13. *Paths in Spirituality* 27; this leads us naturally, he says, to intercessory prayer.

14. I borrow this Celtic phrase from Kenneth Leech's *Soul Friend* (San Francisco: Harper and Row, 1977).

vehicles, the instruments of people who are better at devotion than I am. I'm not someone who could write like Mozart or who could play Mozart but I am ennobled when I listen to Mozart. I'm not a prayerful genius like the religious philosopher and scientist Pascal....But I can read him prayerfully and the thoughts he inspires will convey to me different levels of being, to new depths.[15]

Prayer as Activity. The apostle James warns us to " be doers of the word and not hearers only" (Ja 1:22). Later in that same epistle (2:14-17) he says flatly that faith without good works is dead. One could conclude from such sentiments that prayer should lead to action. That is certainly true; the great founder of the Jesuits, St. Ignatius of Loyola, wanted to form "contemplatives in action," and, earlier, the Dominicans insisted that their vocation was to hand on to others what they themselves had contemplated.

However, if it is true, as we have insisted, that prayer is a gesture that links us with God, then we would also have to say that what we do as disciples of the way of Christ is also a form of prayer. In other words, it is possible to think of our lives as Christians as a form of prayer and the moments when we formally stop to pray either individually or in common as "summing up" and "articulating" our larger, less-consciously-prayerful acts which make up the business of living.

It is at this level that some of the issues we have spoken of earlier begin to come together. If we become conscious that every moment is a possible sacramental one and that God is at the horizon of every act and Jesus walks with us in the Spirit, then every mundane thing we do is consciously connected to God as a gesture of prayer. We may not always do it, but cultivating the habit of conscious prayer in our life may prompt us, for example, to:

- offer a prayer when we see a person in need whether we see disasters on television or pass by the scene of an accident;
- express thanks for a good meal, for a helpful friend, for the love in our family;
- ask for forgivness for the ugliness of our thoughts or the inadequacies of our actions.

The more we do those kinds of things, the larger we expand our sense of attentiveness to the thickness and mystery of our human life, the interpenetration of God in our existence, and the needs of

---

15. In *How I Pray,* ed. Jim Castelli (New York: Ballantine, 1994) 92.

others who, like us, are made in the image and likeness of God. To the extent that this happens in our life, we become more human, more capable of love, and fuller in our appreciation of our life and its possibilities. Prayer, at its best, is a humanizing experience because it makes us more aware of a truth with which St. Augustine introduced his *Confessions*: that God has made us for himself and our hearts are restless until we rest in him.

Prayer and the Language of Prayer

Certain prayer words are hallowed by usage. That is certainly true of the psalms, the prayers of the liturgy, and those short prayers (like the sign of the cross) which are part of every Catholic's experience. The Lord's Prayer, for instance, has been part of the public and private life of the church from the time of the New Testament to the present. It has been called, by St. Thomas Aquinas, the "perfect prayer," but, as the whole tradition of commentary on it testifies, its fullest meaning has never been fully plumbed.[16]

Prayers, in short, have a history, and we, in using those prayers, enter into the tradition of praise, thanksgiving, penitence, and petition which has gone on before us. Nonetheless, we must be alert not to allow the language of prayer to become a rote exercise or an automatic mouthing of phrases. Jesus himself warned his disciples against "heaping up empty phrases" or thinking that God will hear one on the basis of "many phrases" (see Mt 5:7).

Even when we participate in the liturgy or "say our prayers" we need to relearn what the words actually signify when we use them. This is where word and reflection come together: what do we really *mean* when we pray "in the name of God" or "through Jesus Christ" or "in the Spirit"? Can we actually use words like shepherd, king, or lord in cultures which are not agricultural, monarchical, or aristocratic? What do we mean when we pray daily for bread in a culture where we are not hungry? Do we actually mean it when we say in the liturgy that "I have sinned"? To put the matter bluntly: Do we know what we are saying when we are praying?

One way to think about the language of prayer is to construct short phrases or words to which we attach powerful sentiments or

---

16. For a nice summary of scholarship, see Nicholas Ayo, CSC, *The Lord's Prayer* (Notre Dame: University of Notre Dame Press, 1992)

with which we find great spiritual satisfaction. The bible is stud-
ded with phrases which, when recognized, might provide us with a
powerful language for prayer. Scriptural phrases and phrases
derived from scripture have such power that they have entered
into the devotional and spiritual life of the church; some examples
would include the famous Jesus Prayer widely used in eastern
Christianity ("Lord Jesus Christ, Son of God, have mercy on me a
sinner") or the urgent petitions addressed to Jesus in the gospels:
"I believe; help my unbelief" (Mk 9:24) or "Lord, that I may see!"
(Mk 10:51) or doubting Thomas' act of faith: "My Lord and my
God!" (Jn 20:28).

Another powerful source for "relearning" the language of prayer
is to make use of anthologies of prayer which reflect the experiences
of many acknowledged spiritual masters and mistresses and not
only to learn from them but to use them as a springboard for the
composition of one's own prayers.[17] A recent compilation made by
the World Council of Churches of prayers from all over the globe
provides us with many examples of creative and moving prayers.[18]
Here is a small smattering of startling prayers:

Be Thou over me like a blanket;
Be Thou under me like a bed of furs. [Mongolia]

Lord, we know you will come through the line today.
Lord, help us treat you well; help us to treat you well.
[A foodline worker for the poor in the U.S.]

Lord, free us from the sin of believing that the slavery in Egypt is
better than the struggle here in the desert. [Nicaragua]

Lord, may I ever speak as though it were the last word that I can
speak. [Italy]

O Christ who has known fear,
Be with all who are afraid today. [Namibia]

---

17. Some anthologies and collections of such prayers can be found in the
bibliography at the end of this chapter.
18. *The World at Prayer* (Mystic: Twenty-Third Publications, 1990).

Body and Prayer

When we pray we should do so as a whole person and with those gestures and postures that seem most natural to us and are most meaningful for us. At the liturgy we should stand, sit, and kneel along with the community to provide ourselves with the sense that we are part of a larger whole. When we pray privately we should enjoy the freedom to express ourselves as we think fit.

How we pray says a good deal about the theology of our prayer. The pious Muslim kneels and bows the head to the ground as a sign of surrender (Islam literally means "surrender") to God just as the Buddha sits smilingly with eyes nearly closed as a sign that the Buddha has discovered the truth within himself (Buddha means one who is enlightened). In those gestures we learn a good deal of theology.

Catholic spirituality must insist that prayer is not only a bodiless experience done "in the head" or only "in the heart." It is an exercise of the whole person which is not incompatible with other activities such as walking or running or other forms of exercise. We may wish to pray out loud, and it is certainly helpful, when possible, to do *lectio* by reading the words audibly and slowly. Anything that integrates prayer or meditative reflection with other activities helps to integrate our ordinary pastimes with the life of prayer; Thomas Merton suggested that drawing, writing, looking at art, and staring out of the window of a train or bus are all moments when meditation and prayer are possible.[19]

The Catholic tradition also provides us with a whole series of gestures which help coordinate our prayer intentions with bodily symbols. We make the sign of the cross as a gesture of Christian belief. We may bow our heads or fold our hands or even extend the arms out in prayer (in some languages the verb "to pray" also means "to raise the arms"). These and similar gestures are all part of the "language of prayer."[20]

Just as our prayer should be the prayer of whole persons (and not only "yearning souls") so also our prayer needs to be done from

---

19. *New Seeds of Contemplation* 216.

20. We have an interesting medieval document which outlines different postures and gestures for prayer and gives us a picture of prayer at a certain historical moment in the life of the church: "The Nine Ways of Prayer of Saint Dominic," in *Early Dominicans: Selected Writings,* edited by Simon Tugwell, O.P. (New York: Paulist, 1982) 94-103.

within the midst of God's good creation. There is a side to Catholic spirituality which has linked the life of prayer with a negative and inauthentic sense of asceticism. Now it is quite true that some people are called to an austere monastic and withdrawn life, but such a life is misconstrued if it is thought of as a hatred for the body or the goodness of the created order. Our prayer ought to be affirmative and hope-filled, linked to all the good things which God has given us and filled with hope for what is yet to come.

Finally, as we noted above, along with the prayers which have come down to us as part of our tradition, we should feel free to express our prayer using our language, our usages, and our customs. Such prayers should derive from what we most deeply feel and out of what we deeply experience. In that way we will find prayer as a companion to our faith and to our daily life and ordinary experiences. In doing that we will discover the truth of what St. Augustine says in the opening page of his *Confessions:* "I shall look to you, Lord, by praying to You and in praying to You I shall believe in You."

Further Reading

Castelli, Jim, ed., *How I Pray* (New York: Ballantine, 1994). First-person accounts of people of various faiths describing their prayer life.

Catechism of the Catholic Church (various editions). Sections #2558-2864 have an excellent summary of the tradition of prayer in the Catholic Church—perhaps the best part of the catechism.

Cunningham, Lawrence S., *Catholic Prayer* (New York: Crossroad, 1989). Many of the themes in this chapter are elaborated in this book.

Egan, Keith J., *What Is Prayer?* (Denville: Dimension Books, 1974). This work connects themes from daily life with the life of prayer.

Foster, Richard J., *Prayer: Finding the Heart's True Home* (San Francisco: HarperSanFrancisco, 1992). A book on various forms of prayer by a noted Quaker author.

Wright, John, *A Theology of Christian Prayer* (New York: Pueblo, 1988). Excellent theological reflection by a noted Jesuit scholar.

Exercises

(1) Study carefully one of the collect prayers of the mass with this question in mind: What do I learn about my faith as I read and reflect on these words? Could I say them differently.

(2) Take a "classic" prayer like the "Lord's Prayer" and paraphrase it in your own words (this is an honorable exercise; we have examples of such paraphrases from both Saint Francis of Assisi and the poet Dante Alighieri).

(3) Read some selections from the gospels or the psalms and construct a prayer in response to your reading; this would be a fine way to introduce yourself to the practice of lectio.

(4) People are often asked to pray at the beginning of a public event. Assume you are asked to "bless the food" before a festive meal. What would a prayer, written by yourself, look like, assuming that not everyone at the table was of the same faith as you.

(5) Go through any anthology of prayers or prayer book or missal and pick out a prayer which is meaningful to you. Try to explain why it is meaningful.

5

Meditation and Contemplation

"Suddenly they saw two men, Moses and Elijah, talking to [Jesus]" (Lk 9:30).

*J*esus is *the* exemplar of Christian prayer. Like Jesus, Christians enter into intimacy with God through prayer. But prayer comes in many shapes as is evident in another chapter of this book. Two experiences of prayer long associated with Christian discipleship, meditation and contemplation, will be explored in this chapter. For the moment, we shall describe meditation as that reflective prayer which awakens love of God and neighbor and which may prepare one for the gift of contemplation. Contemplation we consider to be the gifted and transforming experience of the presence of God.

The Second Vatican Council insisted that all Christians, not only religious and priests, are called to holiness.[1] The unsupported myth of an exclusively clerical call to holiness had unfortunate consequences. Practices that promoted growth in love and holiness were set aside for religious and clergy. For example, meditation and contemplative prayer were considered suitable for seminarians, nuns, priests and monks, but for too long there was little promotion of meditation for the laity, and interest in contemplation was not much promoted among lay Christians.

The experiences of meditation and contemplation cannot be ignored by those who take seriously the invitation by Jesus to his disciples: "Come, follow me." Prayer is an essential response to this challenge. Prayer, especially meditation, is a search for God. Although John of the Cross wants God-seekers to know that "if

---

1. "The Call of the Whole Church to Holiness," Dogmatic Constitution on the Church, chapter 5.

anyone is seeking God, the Beloved is seeking that person much more,"[2] yet discipleship is a serious call with sobering responsibilities. With T. S. Eliot, the Christian disciple does not want to have "measured out my life with coffee spoons."[3] Serious Christians find some way to meditate. More often than we know these same Christians experience God breaking into their lives in what we call contemplation. The first five of the following lines from T. S. Eliot describe, we think, what may be called contemplation or mystical prayer, while the remaining lines are more like the peak experiences noted by writers like Abraham Maslow.

> But to apprehend
> The point of intersection of the timeless
> With time, is an occupation for the saint—
> No occupation either, but something given
> And taken, in a lifetime's death in love,
> Ardour and selflessness and self-surrender.
> For most of us, there is only the unattended
> Moment, the moment in and out of time,
> The distraction fit, lost in shaft of sunlight,
> The wild thyme unseen, or the winter lightning
> Or the waterfall, or music heard so deeply
> That it is not heard at all, but you are the music
> While the music lasts. These are only hints and guesses,
> Hints followed by guesses; and the rest
> Is prayer, observance, discipline, thought and action.
> Tho hint half guessed, the gift half understood, is Incarnation.[4]

Christians have discovered that meditation is what they can do through graced human effort and contemplation is what only God can do. To bring that search to completion is contemplative union with God.

Since Vatican II there has been a recognition that a mature spiritual formation, including meditation and a readiness for contem-

---

2. *The Living Flame of Love 3.28, The Collected Works of Saint John of the Cross,* rev. ed., trans. Kieran Kavanaugh and Otilio Rodriguez (Washington, DC: Institute of Carmelite Studies) 684.

3. T. S. Eliot, "The Love Song of J. Alfred Prufrock," *The Complete Poems and Plays,* 1909-1950 (New York: Harcourt, Brace and World, 1962).

4. T. S. Eliot, "The Dry Salvages" lines 200-215, *The Complete Poems and Plays.*

plation, belongs to all Christians. That recognition of the universal call to holiness has led to an interest in the variety of ways that Christians have meditated and experienced contemplation through the centuries.

In the years immediately after Vatican II, the Jesuits in North America worked assiduously to make available to religious, clergy and laity the *Spiritual Exercises* of Ignatius of Loyola. The Ignatian *Exercises* met the spiritual needs of countless people who wished to meditate but wanted a method that was not lost in endless details. Meditation books in the first half of the twentieth century contained extensive lists or points that often lacked biblical foundations and which seemed little connected with daily modern life. Ignatius found wisdom in the gospels and in his own experience. Retreatants resonated with the *Exercises* as they were facilitated by an experienced director. Ignatius taught, as he did in his own time, many people to meditate and to be open to contemplation.

This new openness to meditation and contemplation as important to the journey to God has led students, businesspeople, laborers, senior citizens and others to seek ways to practice meditation amid the busyness of modern culture and to be receptive to the gift of contemplation.

During this era, which has witnessed a recovery of meditation and contemplation for all followers of Jesus, the connection between meditation and contemplation must be maintained. Too often they have been separated as if meditation were for the Christian "foot soldier" and contemplation belonged only to elite Christians. A concern of this chapter is to keep meditation and contemplation in creative tension with each other as part of an ongoing journey to union with God in love. Meditation and contemplation are not the same, but they are intimately connected. This chapter explores how this connection operates in the Christian spiritual life, how meditation can prepare one for the divine gift of contemplation.

Prayer and life are two aspects of a single Christian challenge—to live as fully as possible in the presence of God. "I came that they may have life, and have it abundantly" (Jn 10:10). Meditation and contemplation are ways of praying, for, indeed, we pray as well as we live and we live as well as we pray. Christians, called to live in the presence of God, find that they can do so more fully through meditation and contemplation. With this affirmation of the creative relationship between meditation and contemplation, we must speak in these pages of one and then the other, but we shall do so aware that meditation and contemplation cannot rigidly be separated. We ask now what wisdom for modern Christians is contained in the tradition of meditation and contemplation.

An Ancient Tradition

The Jewish tradition of meditation says much about living in the presence of God. Psalm 1 says: "Happy are those...whose delight is in the law of the Lord, and on this law they meditate day and night (Ps 1:1-2).

The same call to meditate on the law of the Lord appears in the ancient book of Joshua.

> This book of the law shall not depart out of your mouth; you shall meditate on it day and night, so that you may be careful to act in accordance with all that is written in it (Jos 1:8).

The law of the Lord was the revelation of God's self to Israel, and meditation was a way of gaining access to the God revealed in that law. The word "meditation" translates the Hebrew root word *haga*. For Jews *haga* was the recitation of the word of God that made the law/word more fully present to the one who recited that word. The physical action of recitation facilitates the appropriation of the word. The bodily and the spiritual were not two disparate activities in Jewish life.

You may recall television footage of Jews at the Wailing Wall in Jerusalem where devote Jews recite or meditate (*haga*) on the word of God. This meditation on the law of the Lord is not an abstract activity but an action of the whole person, a coming under the spell of God through recitation of God's word. "Let the words of my *mouth* and the meditation of my *heart* be acceptable to you, O Lord, my rock and my redeemer" (Ps 19:14). "I commune with my heart in the night; I meditate and search my spirit" (Ps 77:6).

Jewish meditation was also a way of remembering the wonderful deeds of God on behalf of Israel and the desire to be blessed by that God: "I remember the days of old, I think about all your deeds, I meditate on the works of your hands. I stretch out my hands to you: my soul thirsts for you like a parched land" (Ps 143:5-6; see also Ps 77:11-12).

Haga is an appropriation of God's message so that this message may be remembered, reflected upon and lived. Recitation of the word of God is akin to the recitation of a mantra or a sacred word in eastern religions.[5] *Haga* also has a kinship with the Islamic practice of *dhikr* which is a constant recitation of the names of God.[6] *Dhikr* is a remembrance and reflection on God. These exercises in great world religions usher one into the divine presence. Through meditation one submits one's whole being to divine direction and love. The note of submission is especially part of the Islamic tradition of prayer and meditation.

When the Hebrew Bible was translated into Greek, the root *haga* became in Greek *melete* which emphasized meditation's movement into the depths of the human heart. Meditation as a descent into the center of one's being, into the heart, makes it possible to live more fully under the influence of the Spirit of God. "My mouth shall speak wisdom, the meditation of my heart shall be understanding" (Ps 49:3). *Melete* is a reminder that one must never let meditation be a mere formality.

The Latin bible translated *haga/melete* into *meditatio*. This Latin word described meditation as an exercise or a practice like an actor memorizing lines or a soldier undergoing military exercises. Praying or meditating with the word of God was an exercise, a practice that continued the traditions of *haga* and *melete*. Every religion requires practices that maintain the identity of the community. Religion is not an abstract theory but must be practiced and lived. Meditation is a practice that keeps the community aware of God as source and center of its life, that keeps disciples of Jesus walking the way.

Meditation became a very widely used word in the west through the Vulgate Latin bible which was *the* text of the Christian church in the west from the fourth century until the sixteenth century. Moreover, meditation became a central activity in monasticism. Monks and nuns realized that without meditation they would lose sight of the God in whose presence they sought to live.

Early Monasticism

From the late third century women and men sought God in the deserts of Egypt and Palestine. John Cassian who reported on the

---

5. Laurence Freeman, "Meditation," *The New Dictionary of Catholic Spirituality* 648-51.

6. Annemarie Schimmel, *Mystical Dimensions of Islam* (Chapel Hill: University of North Carolina Press, 1975) 167 and passim. This reference is owed to David Burrell, CSC.

life of the monks of the desert described vividly the prayer life of the monks in the desert. He wrote that this was an experience "shaped by the contemplation of God alone and by the fire of love, and the mind, melted and cast down into this love, speaks freely and respectfully to God, as though to one's own father." This "prayer of fire known to so few" occurred in a life of simplicity, growth in virtue and the practice of meditation with the hope that the monk might receive the gift of contemplation.[7]

But meditation in the desert is not an exact equivalent of the modern exercise of internal reflection and prayer. The monks of the desert gathered regularly to hear the word of God recited in public gatherings. They then recited words from the scripture in their cells. Meditation included memorization and recitation of the word of God. It was an oral exercise that kept the monk present to God's word. Abba Ammoes said, "...we went to see Abba Achilles. We *heard* him meditating on this saying, 'Do not fear, Jacob, to go down into Egypt' (Gen 46:3). For a long time he remained making this meditation."[8]

Public recitation of the word of God and meditation on the word in one's cell were crucial elements in the life of the desert dwellers. "A brother asked Abba Poemen, 'How should I live in the cell?' He said to him, 'Living in your cell clearly means manual work, eating only once a day, silence, meditation....'"[9] Meditation kept the cell a sacred place where the encounter with God might occur.

Meditation also protected the anchorite from the demons whose threatening presence in the wilderness was never far from the consciousness of the hermit and monk:

> I have seen a brother meditating in his cell and the demons standing outside the cell. While the brother was meditating they were not able to enter, but when he stopped meditating, then the demons entered the cell and strove with him.[10]

What was key and common to the whole life project of these desert dwellers and to their meditation was the bible; "the movement into

---

7. John Cassian, *Conferences,* trans. Colm Luibheid (New York: Paulist Press, 1985) 111, 117.

8. *The Sayings of the Desert Fathers,* trans. Benedicta Ward (Kalamazoo: Cistercian Publications, 1975) 29. Emphasis added.

9. Ibid. 190.

10. *The Wisdom of the Desert Fathers; The 'Apothegmata Patrum' (The Anonymous Series),* trans. Benedicta Ward (Oxford: SLG Press, 1975) 63 (n. 235).

the desert was seen above all as a response to a call from God mediated through scripture." The bible, ruminated and meditated upon, was the very fabric of monastic existence in the desert.[11]

In the west the *Rule* of Saint Benedict described a way of daily life divided into three segments: public prayer, manual labor and *lectio divina* or what may be called leisure time for God. Meditation occurred during the recitation of the divine office and during *lectio divina* when the monk turned to God through meditation on the scriptures.[12] In the words of Jean Leclercq meditation meant "to speak, to think, to remember," and this meditation was the "necessary complement, almost the equivalent, of the *lectio divina*."[13] Meditation was not a method or procedure but a personal response to the word of God heard in public prayer or leisure. This prayerful spirit is described in chapter 52 of the Benedictine *Rule*.

> After the Work of God, all should leave in complete silence and with reverence for God, so that a brother who may wish to pray alone will not be disturbed by the insensitivity of another. Moreover, if at other times someone chooses to pray privately, he may simply go in and pray, not in a loud voice, but with tears and heartfelt devotion.[14]

Jesus had warned his followers against wordy prayers: "When you are praying, do not heap up empty phrases as the Gentiles do, for they think that they will be heard because of their many words" (Mt 6:7). Benedict had similar advice for his monks.

> We must know that God regards our purity of heart and tears of compunction, not our many words. Prayer should therefore be short and pure, unless perhaps it is prolonged under the inspira-

---

11. Douglas Burton-Christie, *The Word in the Desert: Scripture and the Quest for Holiness in Early Christian Monasticism* (New York: Oxford University Press, 1993) chapters 2, 4 and passim.

12. The word "meditation" in the *Rule* of Benedict was used in the broad sense of study or rather memorization and attention to scripture. *RB 1980: The Rule of St. Benedict: In Latin and English with Notes,* ed. Timothy Fry (Collegeville: Liturgical Press, 1981) 203, 267, 446-48.

13. Jean Leclercq, *The Love of Learning and the Desire for God,* 2nd ed., trans. Catharine Misrahi (New York: Fordham University Press, 1974) 21.

14. *The Rule of St. Benedict,* chapter 52.

tion of divine grace. In community, however, prayer should always be brief....[15]

Meditative prayer is an opportunity to be before the Lord in simple, quiet attention to the Lord's presence especially through attention to God's word. Yet, meditation tends toward wordless attention which, in turn, can become a gifted contemplation of God. The early church and much of the middle ages constantly reminded those who meditate that Christian meditation belongs within the rhythm of the liturgy and that contemplation is a flowering of the baptismal event. Meditation and contemplation are, therefore, sacramental events, that is, they are graced moments in which God's presence is manifested.

The *Epistle of Barnabas,* written around the end of the first century, captured in a few lines many elements that became distinctive of Christian meditation especially as it became a regular feature of monastic life. Commenting on a text from Leviticus (11:3) and Deuteronomy (14:6), the *Epistle* says that these words meant this:

> Seek the company of men who fear the Lord; who muse in their hearts on the purport of every word they have received; who take the statutes of the Lord on their lips, and observe them; who know that meditation is a delight—who do, in fact, *chew the cud* of the Lord's word.[16]

Meditation is thus a seeking, a musing in the heart, a recitation, a rumination, even a mastication of the word, a delightful partaking of the word of the Lord. A quote from a twelfth century Benedictine, John of Fecamp, sums up a conviction about meditation that monasticism forged from its very inception: "It is altogether impossible to come to purity of heart save through constant meditation in praise of God."[17]

Medieval Monasticism

Bernard, the twelfth century abbot of Clairvaux, was the key leader in the Cistercian retrieval of the spirit of the *Rule* of

---

15. Ibid., chapter 20.

16. *The Epistle of Barnabas* 10, *Early Christian Writings: The Apostolic Fathers,* trans. Maxwell Staniforth (Baltimore: Penguin, 1968) 208.

17. Quoted by Bernard McGinn, *The Growth of Mysticism* (New York: Crossroad, 1994) 135

Benedict and especially in the recovery of *lectio divina*. Bernard realized that monasticism suffers when *lectio divina* is neglected. Monastic life loses its soul whenever meditation and contemplation are not honored. For Bernard this meditation or *lectio divina* was the wine cellar of the Holy Spirit where one is anointed by the Spirit. Bernard urged all his monks to enter this wine cellar. There lambs can paddle and elephants can swim. Meditation in this monastic climate was biblical, simple, affective and oriented to contemplation.

The medieval monks knew well the tradition of *lectio* and *meditatio* but meditation had not yet become a set or precise exercise with definite periods of time set aside for its practice as would become the norm in religious life after the Reformation. Yet, twelfth century monasticism did not escape the same trends that brought about the scholastic revolution that led to so many new ways of thinking.

Meditation and Method

During the late eleventh century and the twelfth century meditation, like the rest of culture, was affected by the incipient scholasticism with its interest in logic, order and especially method. This development is evident in the life and writings of Anselm of Canterbury (d. 1109) who composed prayers and meditations for the inspiration and instruction of others and as models for their prayer. Anselm's meditations contain a spirit of theological inquiry not discernible in previous prayers.[18] This famous archbishop of Canterbury began his meditation, the *Prosologion,* in this way: "At the pressing entreaties of my brethren I published a short work as an example of meditation on the meaning of faith...."[19] But, as with all monastic meditation, Anselm's meditations were intended to lead one "to the contemplation of God."[20] Anselm concluded the *Prosologion* with a prayer typical of his spirituality:

---

18. Bernard McGinn points to John of Fecamp as another monastic author whose meditations had taken a turn toward method: *Growth of Mysticism* 136.

19. *The Prayers and Meditations of St. Anselm,* trans. Benedicta Ward (Baltimore: Penguin, 1973) 238.

20. Ibid. 239.

God of truth,
I ask that I may receive,
so that my joy may be full.
Meanwhile, let my mind meditate on it,
let my tongue speak of it,
let my heart love it,
let my mouth preach it,
let my soul hunger for it,
and my whole being desire it,
until I enter into the joy of my Lord,
who is God one and triune, blessed forever. Amen.

Anselm, through his prayers and meditations, taught the rest of the middle ages how to pray and to meditate, always with the presumption that meditation could lead to seeing the face of God in contemplation.

The development of methods of meditation became more pronounced in the hands of the influential scholastic author Hugh and his followers at the Abbey of Saint-Victor in Paris. Hugh of Saint-Victor set out stages of thinking and praying. He wrote that "there are three visions of the rational soul: thinking, meditation, contemplation."[21] Note that, like the whole monastic tradition, Hugh pointed those who studied, prayed and meditated toward the contemplation of God. Ever since Gregory the Great, monks of the west claimed that the goal of their way of life was to see God, a metaphor for contemplation. Teresa of Avila with her usual exuberance captured the power of this tradition when she wrote in the sixteenth century: "I was dying to see God."[22]

Monastic letters abounded in the twelfth century. One of them, written by the Carthusian Guigo II to his friend Gervase and known as *The Ladder of Monks*, was one of the most popular texts during the middle ages. This little treatise outlined the steps or rungs on the ladder to God: reading, meditation, prayer and contemplation. Reading is an encounter with the word of God, meditation seeks the hidden meaning of this word, prayer is the turning of the heart to God, and contemplation occurs "when the mind is in

---

21. *Commentary on Ecclesiastes,* quoted in McGinn, *The Growth of Mysticism* 375.

22. *The Book of Her Life* 29.8, *The Collected Works of St. Teresa of Avila,* trans. Kieran Kavanaugh and Otilio Rodriguez (Washington DC: Institute of Carmelite Studies, 1976) 191.

some sort lifted up to God and held above itself, so that it tastes the joys of everlasting sweetness."

This brief letter was circulated widely and gave the subsequent tradition a handy, simple and well-organized view of the journey to God in prayer. Typical of the personalism of twelfth century monks, Guigo concluded his letter on this note:

> So, my brother Gervase, if it is ever granted to you from above to climb to the topmost rung of this ladder, when this happiness is yours, remember me and pray for me. So, when the veil between you and God is drawn aside, may I too see Him....[23]

Four centuries later the Spanish mystic, John of the Cross, was still passing on the wisdom of Guigo's ladder of prayer to his directees: "Seek in reading and you will find in meditation; knock in prayer and it will be opened to you in contemplation."[24] Guigo's letter to this day has valuable wisdom for any who commit themselves to prayer as a way of following Jesus.

Thomas Aquinas, the Late Middle Ages and the Reformation

After the twelfth century the literature on meditation became ever more methodical, especially in the fourteenth and the fifteenth centuries. But, before that era, Thomas Aquinas knew meditation and contemplation to be terms with a variety of meanings both intellectual and religious. For some time during the middle ages the phrase "contemplative life" had described the monastic life, that is, a way of living that was oriented to religious contemplation.

Thomas Aquinas as a Dominican friar was part of an important revolution in monasticism. He and other friars explicitly joined evangelization to traditional monasticism. Pastoral ministry had always been incidental to the monastic call to live in stability. Critics saw this innovation of the friars as a betrayal of the ideal of contemplative life which was a way of describing monasticism before St. Francis and St. Dominic joined ministry to monasticism.

---

23. Guigo II, *The Ladder of Monks: A Letter on the Contemplative Life and Twelve Meditations*, trans. Edmund Colledge and James Walsh (Garden City: Doubleday, 1978) 82, 99.

24. *The Sayings of Light and Love* 158, *The Collected Works of St. John of the Cross* 97.

Thomas Aquinas justified the ministry of the friars by citing the ministry of Jesus as their exemplar. Thomas also took a saying in the Dominican constitutions as a warrant for the participation by the friars in evangelization. The Dominican constitutions and Thomas saw that their call was "to share with others the fruits of their contemplation."[25] Thomas Aquinas developed a spirituality that was oriented to contemplation, a contemplative spirituality.[26]

The late middle ages witnessed further systematization of meditation. More steps are added to the meditative process. Emphasis in this era was on meditation that led to the imitation of Jesus. The classic text from this era was Thomas à Kempis' *The Imitation of Christ* (1,1) which makes this point: "Let it, then, be our chief study to meditate on the life of Christ." In particular there was an emphasis on the passion of Jesus Christ as the content of meditation. During the late middle ages guidebooks for meditation and books with sample meditations multiplied especially after the advent of printing.

The Protestant Reformation reacted against the seeming complicated character of late medieval meditation. The Protestants and many Catholic reformers turned to a more simple reading of and praying with the scriptures. This reaction against meditation accounts also in part for the lack of interest in contemplation over the centuries by Protestant denominations since faithfulness to meditation often enough leads to contemplation. Protestant spirituality developed a different vocabulary for their attentiveness to the word of God.

The Spanish Mystics

Ignatius of Loyola, founder of the Jesuits, took his own spiritual and mystical experiences as the basis for his highly influential *Spiritual Exercises,* published first in 1548. The *Spiritual Exercises* involve the exercitant in a series of meditations and contemplations, terms used without great differentiation by Ignatius. These exercises enable the retreatant to come to terms with sin, to identify with Christ, and to make choices or confirm choices that are in conformity with God's will. Jerome Nadal spoke of his friend

---

25. *Summa theologiae* II, II, 188.6.

26. Walter Principe, *Thomas Aquinas' Spirituality* (Toronto: Pontifical Institute of Mediaeval Studies, 1984) 27.

Ignatius as a "contemplative in action." This happy aphorism describes Ignatius as a model who overcame the false dichotomy between action and contemplation. The human capacity to know and to love God comes to fruition in contemplation; however contemplation is not an end itself but a description of the human person in love with God. One who is in love with God has the capacity and the mandate to love one's neighbor through whatever actions are called for by the circumstances of one's life. Action and contemplation are like T. S. Eliot's fire and rose that have distinctive histories but, in the end, are joined in a single reality.[27]

The meditations and contemplations of the *Exercises* of Ignatius have enabled Christians to become more conscious of the implications of belief in Jesus Christ. The impact of the *Exercises* has been far-reaching. By the end of the sixteenth century the steps of meditation fostered by the followers of Ignatius not only influenced countless Christians who made the *Exercises* but had an impact on metaphysical poets like John Donne. Professor Louis Martz drew attention to this integration of meditation and poetry some four decades ago.[28]

Martz' insights remind one to pay attention to the meditative character of all authentic poetry and to realize the power of poetry to teach one to be more attentive to one's inner self, to be more focused in prayer, to engage in the reading of scripture and to be a more centered person. The reading of poetry, silently or aloud, is an excellent preparation for meditation and often enough is, in fact, prayer.

For Teresa of Avila and John of the Cross meditation was oriented to mystical contemplation. Teresa taught her nuns to meditate which she called the prayer of (active) recollection. She described this prayer in chapters 28-29 of *The Way of Perfection*, which has as its premise the faith that God is within, a truth Teresa says she learned from St. Augustine.[29] This prayer or meditation consists in turning often in faith during the day to a mystery from Christ's life. Teresa felt that this regular turning to Christ, along with self-

---

27. "Little Gidding," *Four Quartets*: "And the fire and the rose are one."

28. Louis L. Martz, *The Poetry of Meditation* (Garden City: Doubleday, 1954) and *The Meditative Poem* (Garden City: Doubleday, 1963).

29. *The Way of Perfection* chapters 28-29, *The Collected Works of St. Teresa of Avila,* Vol. 2, trans. Kieran Kavanaugh and Otilio Rodriguez (Washington, DC: Institute of Carmelite Studies, 1980).

knowledge and detachment, makes one available for contemplation or God's mystical presence.[30]

Teresa colorfully described the happiness derived from meditation with the Spanish word *contentos* (consolations), but mystical prayer and gifted contemplation Teresa described as *gustos* (spiritual delights). Teresa accented the giftedness of contemplation, mystical prayer or what she called spiritual delights over meditation which she saw as achieved by human effort and ordinary grace.

> The spiritual delights begin in God, but human nature feels and enjoys them....O Jesus, how I long to know how to explain this! For I discern, I think, a very recognizable difference, but I don't have the knowledge to be able to explain myself. May the Lord do so.[31]

What Teresa had no hesitations about was her insistence on the central and necessary place of the humanity of Jesus in Christian prayer. In her day there was a tendency among some spiritual writers to advocate prayer that seemed to bypass Christ's humanity. Teresa would have no truck with this tendency to neglect the humanity of Christ in prayer.[32]

Teresa's collaborator, John of the Cross, was also more interested in describing contemplation than meditation. For John "the purpose of discursive meditation on divine subjects is the acquisition of some knowledge and love of God." John sees a "spirit of meditation" as a precursor to contemplation.[33] John's eye is always on union with God in love.

> God desires to withdraw them [beginners] from this base manner of loving and lead them on to a higher degree of divine love. And he desires to liberate them from the lowly exercise of the senses and of discursive meditation, by which they go in search of him so

---

30. Teresa of Avila, *The Interior Castle,* Dwelling Place 1-3, *The Collected Works of St. Teresa of Avila;* see Keith J. Egan, "The Foundations of Mystical Prayer: Teresa of Jesus," *Peaceweavers,* Vol. 2 of *Medieval Religious Women,* ed. L. T Shank and J. A. Nichols (Kalamazoo: Cistercian Publications, 1987) 330-44.

31. *The Interior Castle* 4.1.4, *The Collected Works of St. Teresa of Avila* 318.

32. *The Book of Her Life,* chapter 22, *The Collected Works of St. Teresa of Avila.*

33. *Ascent of Mount Carmel* 2.14.2, *The Collected Works of St. John of the Cross* 191.

inadequately and with so many difficulties, and lead them into the exercise of spirit, in which they become capable of a communion with God that is more abundant and more free of imperfections.[34]

For both Teresa of Avila and John of the Cross, meditation is what we can do and contemplation is what God does within us. John, with a poet's insight, described the inauguration of God's work of contemplation as the dark night, a night that liberates one for union with God in love.

Souls begin to enter this dark night when God, gradually drawing them out of the state of beginners (those who practice meditation on the spiritual road), begins to place them in the state of proficients (those who are already contemplatives), so that passing through this state they might reach that of the perfect, which is divine union of the soul with God.[35]

John has become well known for his articulation of the signs that mark the transition from active meditation to contemplation: one can no longer meditate, one finds little satisfaction in the spiritual life, yet one desires "to remain alone in loving awareness of God."[36]

John of the Cross' poetry is not only an example of focused attention on the presence of God, but his three major poems[37] are, in fact, reports of his mystical experience. In the past, exclusive attention has been given to John's commentaries to the neglect of his poems as spiritual resources.[38] John's poetry is a resource for meditation which prepares one to be more contemplative.

---

34. *The Dark Night* 8.3, *The Collected Works of St. John of the Cross* 376.

35. *The Dark Night* 1.1.1, *The Collected Works of St. John of the Cross* 361.

36. *The Ascent of Mount Carmel* 2.13 and *The Dark Night* 1.9, *The Collected Works of St. John of the Cross.*

37. "The Dark Night," "The Spiritual Canticle" and "The Living Flame of Love."

38. Keith J. Egan, "A Mystic's Poetry: John of the Cross," forthcoming in collection of lectures delivered by various persons at Trinity College, Dublin, October–November 1994.

Post–Vatican II Era

Directions for meditation from the seventeenth century until the first half of the twentieth century tended to be overly detailed. Often there was insufficient biblical content and meditation was not much connected to the liturgy. However, religious renewal since Vatican II has brought a new appreciation for meditation and contemplation. Elsewhere in this book the change in attitudes to mysticism after Vatican II have been mentioned. What is said there applies to contemplation as a mystical experience, that is, contemplation as an experience that is a special gift of God but which is rooted in one's baptismal, confirmational and eucharistic identity and is nourished by the word of God.

Meditation and contemplation can no longer be seen as esoteric and elitist experiences. No one has done more to liberate meditation and especially contemplation from this elitism than the Trappist monk Thomas Merton. Merton did much to retrieve the contemplative tradition without falling into the trap of trivializing contemplation. Merton asked: "What does the contemplative life or the life of prayer, solitude, silence, meditation, mean to man in the atomic age?"[39] Merton, read by more people than any monk from any age, alerted Christians to their heritage of meditation and contemplation, and he showed by his life that meditation and contemplation lead inevitably to a ministry of justice and peace.

During the time since Vatican II, there has also been a widespread interest in meditative techniques like transcendental meditation. While such techniques may have therapeutic benefits and may aid the Christian who seeks to be still and to be prayerful, Christian meditation is more than a technique. It is an act of faith, a religious exercise carried out as part of one's following of Christ. Its foundation is the word of God, and it is always open to the gift of contemplation.

Developing a Contemplative Disposition

The practice of meditation requires that one live with an attentive mind and heart. One cannot hope to pray meditatively if one's life and mind are cluttered and unfocused. The culture in which we

---

39. "Contemplation in a World of Action," *Thomas Merton: Spiritual Master,* ed. Lawrence S. Cunningham (New York: Paulist Press, 1992) 369.

live is loud, even boisterous and overly frazzled. It can drown out the inner voice of the Christian conscience which calls one to stand with one's sisters and brothers in the presence of God.

Yet, everyone has a capacity for developing what Solomon sought from God in a dream—a listening heart (1 Kgs 3:9). Everyone, indeed, has a capacity for God. Fr. William McNamara, some years ago, spoke of contemplation as "taking a long loving look at the real." McNamara's contemplation is a listening stance, a contemplative life that bids one to attend to God and to be open to the loving presence of God. There are obstacles in our society that make it difficult to pray, to meditate or to be open to contemplation. There is much clutter, busyness and distraction in our lives. Prayer requires simplicity, time for quiet and a heart willing to search for God in hard-won moments of silence and solitude. These moments are not easy to find by a mother with small children, by students juggling class assignments, jobs and a social life, or by the homeless oppressed by undignified poverty. What is more, as Teresa of Avila said, some of us have minds like "wild horses"[40] that make it difficult to be still.

Yet, choices must be made that insure that there are regular times when one can turn to the God who is always and everywhere trying to break into the human heart. The indwelling of the Holy Spirit in the human heart beckons one to attend to that saving presence. Meditation, according to one's spiritual personality, is a way of listening attentively to the guidance of the Spirit of God.

Lest we be enslaved to a culture that has little appreciation of the human capacity for God, we must become free for God to the extent that our responsibilities allow. One may choose a time each day to be still for even a brief time, select a scene from the life of Christ as one's focus, and listen quietly for a God who speaks in something like "the sound of sheer silence" (1 Kgs 19:12).[41]

Centering Prayer

Taking inspiration from Thomas Merton, spiritual writers like Thomas Keating, Basil Pennington and John Main have advocated

---

40. Teresa of Avila, *The Way of Perfection* 19.2.

41. See Walter Burghardt, "Contemplation: A Long Loving Look at the Real," *Church* (Winter 1989) 14-18. Note that Burghardt's contemplation is more like the meditation described in this chapter.

a practice known as centering prayer. With eyes closed, one becomes still, repeats a sacred word like Jesus, and allows oneself to be drawn into the presence of God. When distractions come, one repeats the sacred word, and finally one takes a few moments of quiet before returning to one's daily routine.[42] Centering prayer is not a technique for its own sake but a way of habitually turning to God so that God's love can become more manifest in one's life.

Many people from many walks of life have discovered that this centering on the presence of God in their lives transforms the way they perceive themselves, their relationships and even their work. God is then known more directly as their center, source and destiny. This centering on God as present within one also makes one more vulnerable to the sacramental presence of God in creation. Medieval hermits were known for the affection they developed for creation and the animal kingdom—sacramental environmentalists, one might say.

The same criterion advocated by Teresa of Avila as the test of mystical experience is the test for all meditation and contemplation: growth in love of neighbor which is the sign that one loves God.[43] This love of neighbor Teresa saw as a result of meditation: "Let truth dwell in your hearts, as it should through meditation, and you will see clearly the kind of love we are to have for our neighbor."[44] Teresa was merely restating the wisdom of the early church: "If we love one another, God lives in us, and his love is perfected in us" (1 Jn 4:12).

Meditation clearly is not only for clergy and religious but is a practice for every disciple of Jesus. Holiness, as Vatican II has said, is a universal call; the means to holiness are, therefore, needed by all. Meditation is the birthright of every Christian, and every human person has the capacity for contemplation which is our destiny, if not in this life, then in the next. Meditation prepares one for the contemplation which is ultimately indescribable. John of the Cross described contemplation as "nothing else than a secret and peaceful and loving inflow of God...."[45]

---

42. Thomas Keating, "Centering Prayer," *The New Dictionary of Catholic Spirituality* 138-39.

43. *The Interior Castle* 5.3.8-9,12, *The Collected Works of St. Teresa of Avila* 351, 353.

44. *The Way of Perfection* 20.4, *The Collected Works of St. Teresa of Avila* 115.

45. *The Dark Night* 1.10.6, *The Collected Works of St. John of the Cross* 382.

Whatever method best helps one to live more habitually in the presence of God is the way to meditate. Method must suit the person and his or her personality, but method is never the goal of meditation—loving attention to God is.

A long cherished way of preparing for meditation and contemplation is praying the psalms alone or with others. These ancient songs that rose from the hearts of Jews seeking God run the whole gamut of human emotions—from anger and fear to joy and love. It is no accident that monks and nuns from the earliest times recited the psalms. The psalms prepared the hearts of monastic women and men to recognize God as active in every facet of their lives. Not a few laity find that the daily recitation of the morning prayer and evening prayer called the liturgical hours is a way of allowing the psalms and other prayers to shape their spiritual lives and keep them in touch with the church at prayer.

Christian meditation has always tried to arouse the emotions, the deepest of human feelings and the desires of the human heart so that the whole person, not just the mind, may participate in the search for God. Unfortunately meditation has often been called mental prayer as if the intellect were the only capacity involved in the search for God. When one prays, the whole person is involved in the search for God.

Regular meditation also fosters self-knowledge which is absolutely necessary for Christian maturity. Self-knowledge is not only a recognition of sin and weakness, it is also—what is harder for most of us—an acceptance of our gifts and of the fact that God has loved us first (1 Jn 4:19).

Meditation, practiced regularly by members of the Christian community, leads to a more contemplative church where God's presence is honored and even experienced in a special way when God enters more deeply into human persons with the gift of God's presence called contemplation.

A contemplative church will also be a more fully human church since contemplatives are those who embrace as fully as possible the human condition which, for its fulfillment, requires the manifestation of God's love in the human heart. This process of becoming more human is for the Christian a process of being *in Christ*. "So if anyone is in Christ, there is a new creation: everything old has passed away; see, everything has become new" (2 Cor 5:17). Meditation and, above all, the gift of contemplation are the means by which disciples heed the challenge of Paul: "Let the same mind be in you that was in Christ Jesus" (Phil 2:5). Contemplation is God taking delight in the human person and the human community.

Further Reading

Finley, James, *The Awakening Call* (Notre Dame: Ave Maria, 1984). This book is an invitation to heed the God's call to enter divine presence.

Keating, Thomas, *Intimacy with God* (New York: Crossroad, 1994). The Cistercian Keating has been a key leader in spreading the good news of centering prayer.

Main, John, *The Word into Silence* (New York: Paulist Press, 1980). The Benedictine Main captured the imagination of numerous people with his call to practice meditation.

Merton, Thomas, *New Seeds of Contemplation* (New York: New Directions, 1962). The publication of the first edition of this modern classic may have been the moment when Christians discovered that meditation and contemplation did not belong to the elite.

Pennington, Basil, *Centering Prayer* (New York: Doubleday, 1980). Pennington has been another leader in the dissemination of the practice of centering prayer.

Shannon, William, *Seeking the Face of God* and *Silence on Fire: The Prayer of Awareness* (New York: Crossroad, 1990 and 1994). This author continues the work of his spiritual mentor, Thomas Merton, by introducing modern readers to the tradition of meditative prayer.

Exercises

(1) Practice centering prayer for two or three days, about ten or fifteen minutes each day. How did you feel? Did you notice any difference in the way you spent the rest of the day? What do you think might be the effect of practicing centering prayer regularly?

(2) Tease from this chapter and elsewhere a definition or a description of meditation, one that you think is down-to-earth and useful in your life and in the lives of your friends.

(3) Write a description of contemplation. Do you detect a desire for contemplation in yourself or in others? Do you think Christians can become more contemplative in the twenty-first century?

(4) List those factors in our culture which seem to make meditation and contemplation difficult for modern Christians.

(5) List advice that you would give to a friend who says that he or she would like to practice meditation despite the cluttered culture in which he or she lives.

6

Asceticism

"To come to possess all/desire the possession of nothing."
St. John of the Cross

Introduction

One thing that is common to all of the great religious traditions of the world is an appreciation for ascetic practice. The forms this ascetic practice may take differ according to the specific religious tradition but, in general, asceticism is known in all religious traditions and in many philosophical "schools."

What, in general, do we mean by religious asceticism? Perhaps the best generic description is. "...a voluntary, sustained, and, at least partially, systematic program of self-discipline and self-denial in which immediate, sensual, or profane gratifications are renounced in order to attain a higher spiritual state or a more thorough absorption into the Sacred."[1]

How does that definition or description work when we consider *Christian* asceticism? We might begin with an intriguing passage in the New Testament.

Saint Paul, quite evidently, knew the world of athletic competition; more than once he makes reference to sporting events. In one famous passage he actually mixes metaphors from competitive running and boxing:

Do you not know that in a race all the runners compete, but only one receives the prize? So run that you may obtain it. Every athlete exercises self-control in all things. He does it to win a

---

1. Walter O. Klaeber, "Asceticism," in *The Encyclopedia of Religion*, edited by Mircea Eliade (New York: Macmillan, 1987) I:441.

perishable wreath, but we an imperishable. Well, I do not box as one beating the air; but I pummel my body and subdue it, lest after preaching to others I myself should be disqualified [1 Cor 9:24-27].

Paul, of course, recommends, through analogy, that the followers of Jesus Christ should be like athletes: they compete for an imperishable wreath (unlike the wreath of ivy which was the crown for winners of races) and they do that by the exercise of self-control and pummeling and subduing the body. Paul's example, of course, must have been drawn from his own experience watching athletic games in the Roman cities around the Mediterranean as competitors "worked out" to get their bodies in shape for competition.

The Greek word for "training" (e.g. of athletes) was *askesis* from which we derive the English word *asceticism*. Long before the time of Christ Greek philosophers used the term to mean the disciplined kind of life (of withdrawal from the world, of the life of virtue) required of anyone who wished to take up a life devoted to the pursuit and love of wisdom: i.e. *philosophia*. The word *askesis* came into the Christian vocabulary to describe the disciplined life of the Christian. For our purposes we can describe asceticism as the systematic use of the various exercises found in the Christian tradition which train us to be more committed disciples of the way of Jesus Christ.

What are those "various exercises"? Taking its clue from the New Testament, the Christian tradition has highlighted practices of self-denial in the form of fasting and abstinence, voluntary celibacy for the sake of the kingdom of God, following the example of the poverty of Christ by the sharing of goods, a life of charity and service to others, a regular life of prayerful withdrawal, resistance to the world as a witness of peace, cultivation of the virtues and the avoidance of vice, a conscious willingness to adopt a simplicity of life so as not to be trapped by the acquisition of goods or their possession, and so on.

In the popular imagination the term "asceticism" has conjured up a gloomy picture of self-punishing monks and body-hating hermits, and a generally negative picture of the Christian life as suspicious of the good things of the earth, a repugnance toward human relations and sexuality, a fear (as someone once said of the Puritans) that somewhere and sometime people were having a good time. It is quite true that such practices did and do happen in the Christian world. What is not true is that such attitudes and practices say everything about asceticism or its legitimate place in the Christian life.

To counter those kinds of stereotypes it would be helpful to grasp what theory stands behind asceticism, how it relates to the Christian life, what dangers may be in asceticism, and what a healthy Christian asceticism should look like. We will take up those topics in turn.

Why Asceticism?

We need to begin with the plain fact that the New Testament has an ascetical doctrine which is proposed for the Christian. Jesus fasted and recommended fasting; he held out the ideal of voluntary poverty and celibacy for the kingdom; he insisted that people "stay the course" even when it meant following him in his own journey toward Calvary. To his disciples, as they are called, Jesus demands that they give up everything for the purpose of following him as disciples.

These demands, however, were interpreted and lived out in various ways with different emphases. People did not fast all the time; not everyone was expected to remain single for the sake of God; not all Christians gave up everything for the sake of the kingdom. Indeed, there is evidence in the New Testament that the followers of Jesus were seen as not being sufficiently ascetical in their lives. Critics of Jesus and his followers contrasted the ascetical life of John the Baptist and his disciples with those of Jesus (see Lk 5.33-39).

The very first thing that needs recognition is that the ascetic life in general and ascetical practices in particular are only *means* to greater ends. Jesus always commends ascetical practices not for their own worth but as they relate to some greater good. Prayer and fasting, for example, are ways of exorcising evil; one remains celibate for the "kingdom of God"; one gives up all things for the sake of perfectly following in the way of discipleship. To say it another way: one does not become an ascetic because that is seen as an absolute but a relative good; it should always be seen as a strategy or a path for someone who seeks a greater and more praiseworthy goal.

Asceticism in athletics helps us to see this point. Training is a means to gain a specified goal (faster time, higher score, etc.). When training becomes done for its own sake it is no longer training; it is addiction.

Perhaps we can clarify the point further if we consider, for a moment, asceticism as something which impinges on every stage of our developing life as members of the human community.

There is, for example, a kind of "training" (asceticism) that is imposed on every child as he or she grows out of infancy. Parents, family members, and teachers begin this training with "rules": do not strike your sister, do not throw food at the table, do not get in a stranger's automobile, say good night to mommy and daddy, be sure to brush your teeth, etc. Now the point of issuing these rules is not for the purpose of getting the child to memorize them or even repeat them back. The purpose of this training is to get the child to internalize the rules so that one can, in a sense, "forget" them as rules once they have become the way the child is and acts. They are part of the child's identity.

At each stage in life there are other rules of "training" which function in the same way: one learns the rules, internalizes them, "forgets" them once they have become a pattern for living. In this sense, there is an asceticism of married life or student life or working life. One learns the rules not to obey them but in order to be a loving spouse or a serious student or a satisfied professional. This training has been fully absorbed when a person can get to the stage of not saying "That is against the rules." One is a natural ascetic when one says something like "This is not the way I am or the person I wish to be."

The great lesson for the Christian—and it is so often forgotten—is this: Being a Christian is not about obeying the "rules" of asceticism; it is rather about living according to Christian asceticism in such a way as to be able to say, always tentatively and always seeking, that "I am a follower of the way of Jesus; I am a disciple."

This point is made over and over again by those who led the most ascetical lives in the church. The early monastic writer Cassian, for example, cites a desert monk as saying: "...fasting, vigils, scriptural meditation, nakedness, and total deprivation do not constitute perfection but are the means to perfection. They are not the end point of our discipline."[2] What is the end point to which Cassian refers? Quite simply, he says, it is the "kingdom of God."[3] Cassian's point, of

---

2. *The Conferences of John Cassian,* trans. Colm Luibheid (New York: Paulist, 1985) 42.

3. Ibid. 39.

course, is merely a gloss on those famous chapters (five through seven) in Matthew's gospel where Jesus demands that what we do and say, how we act and what we profess, be in conformity to God and not immediate gain or for the sake of fidelity to law. Indeed, the ascetical practices recommended in Matthew 5–7 will be the subject of some closer scrutiny further in this chapter.

The Asceticism of Discipleship

We go back then to what we said in the beginning: Christian spirituality is the working out of the call to follow the way who is Jesus. What training (*askesis*) does that entail? What must we assimilate into our lives in order to be responsive to the grace which calls us to discipleship? Everyone will have a personal response to that question; let ours be summarized in some simple words or concepts.

(1) The asceticism of *risk*. One must learn, when confronted with Jesus saying "Come and see" (Jn 1:39) or, more pointedly, "Follow me" (Jn 1:43), how one will answer. The asceticism of risk is the preparation (which is to say, the grace-filled "training") to be open enough to accept the invitation even when one does not know where that invitation will lead. What is the direction embedded in the imperative verbs "Come" and "Follow"?

The ascetic risk has its sharp edge because we know that to come and follow demands that we encounter the first great denial of the self. When we yield to the invitation of another to come and see, in that very act we give up our own plans, our own direction, and our own aspirations. Note that such a "giving up" is a fundamental form of asceticism.

Christian ascetic literature is full of sayings about "denial of the self," and not a little of that literature is quite unsatisfactory. Nonetheless, there is a fundamental insight in the concept of "denial of the self" when it is understood to mean that the self (with the self's plans, desires, aspirations) only thinks of its self. The fundamental basis of biblical faith is that the self is inextricably bound to the Other. Therefore, denial of the self is only half of the equation. The other half is love of God and love of neighbor.

To take that risk of coming to see and following is to make oneself open relative to a larger demand. Indeed, that demand can be extremely costly; Jesus puts it quite starkly in a passage where he treats our subject explicitly: "If any would come after me, let them deny themselves, take up their cross, and follow me" (Lk 9:23).

(2) The asceticism of *love*. The great Catholic spiritual figure Dorothy Day loved to quote a line of the saintly monk Zossima from Fydor Dostoevsky's *The Brothers Karamazov:* "Love is a harsh and dreadful thing." That phrase seems odd to our ears. Our music, popular culture, and literature hymns love in terms of endearment, gifts of roses, soulful glances across a crowded room or the touching gestures of two lovers or parent and infant. And, of course, all those things are signs of love and, further, they are all good and a sign of God's love for us.

There comes a time, however, when the Christian is called upon to love when there is little taste for loving and no natural appetite for loving another. This kind of loving is intimately connected with the denial of the self which we have described above. It is the love by which we forgive enemies, turn the other cheek, accept the unlovable, and reach out to others regardless of cost. It is that love which is called *agape*: the "pure gift, sheer grace which ennobles, empowers, elicits Christians to love God and neighbor in the self-sacrificial manner God first loved us in Jesus Christ."[4]

It is that kind of love which is described in the gospel parables of the good Samaritan and the prodigal son; it is the same love which Jesus showed as he forgave those who had sent him to the cross (Lk 23:34).

(3) The asceticism of *denial*. This, of course, comes closer to what we ordinarily understand by the term asceticism. For a person to be a follower of Jesus it becomes necessary to say *no* to certain ways of thinking, acting, and being. St. Paul puts this graphically by insisting that the Christian life involves a kind of symbolic "death" in order to possess a new kind of "life." Paul, using the model of the life of Jesus, sets out this death/life motif in a classical passage: "But if we have died with Christ we believe that we shall live with him...so you must consider yourself dead to sin and alive to God in Christ Jesus" (Rom 6:9 and 11).

Now the crucial point to see in this text is that one does not "get rid" of sin and then become a Christian; it is, rather, the reverse: one becomes identified with Christ (through faith, baptism, etc.), and in that identification one loses the appetite for sin. To say it in other words: being a Christian does not mean embracing an ethical

---

4. David Tracy, "The Catholic Model of *Caritas*," in *On Naming the Present* (Maryknoll: Orbis, 1994) 94.

philosophy. It does mean being a believer so that certain forms of behavior become antagonistic to the pledge of faith. That is what St. Augustine meant in his famous aphorism "Love God and do what you will!"

The asceticism of denial, at this level, then, means seeking to find out what it is that might make us less likely to be a follower of Christ.

How do we discover what it is that we must deny?

Obviously, we must begin with both the sources that are available to us (preeminently the word of God as it is proclaimed in the Christian community) that tell us what a "Christlike" life is, and, secondly, we must see what those sources tell us in the light of our own experience and life story.

At one level, certain things are obvious. One does not have to meditate on the gospels for a long time to see what Jesus demands of us, e.g. love of God and love of neighbor. The working out of the particular applications of that most universal biblical law creates a Christian moral tradition as we ask how, in particular, we manifest a love for God or how we are to love a neighbor. The working out of that Christian moral tradition moves from the more obvious forms of denial (a Christian does not blaspheme God, does not do a neighbor harm) to a deeper sense of the radical imperatives embedded in the gospel (we should give up everything for the love of God and turn the cheek after being struck).

At times, this asceticism of denial requires a precise "giving up" of specific desires, wants, and aspirations. To choose the Christian life may well require a personal election not to pursue a certain kind of career, to avoid certain kinds of people, to stand against very powerful cultural trends, to make choices in the face of social opposition, etc. This asceticism works itself out in a certain capacity for simplicity of life, one that is free from the addiction to possessions and grasping in order not to fall into that greediness or avarice which traps us into mindless consumerism and consumption.

There is also a positive side to "giving up" when our very choices, by the very fact that they are chosen, require self-denial. A parent might give up a certain level of personal comfort in order to nurture a family just as one called to the consecrated life might give up a family altogether for the "sake of the kingdom." Persons might give up personal possessions for the sake of the poor; others, impelled by grace, might choose to live under severe conditions out of love for neighbor. "Giving up" in these or similar instances creates a curious but wonderful paradox: it allows us a priceless freedom that flows naturally from our choices. In that sense, asceticism creates freedom.

In all of the instances we have given above, the asceticism of denial does not mean pure negativity or some sort of loathing for the world and its beauties. What an asceticism of denial does imply is a certain kind of "no" in order to express a "yes" to the call of God's grace. This expression of no and yes was once beautifullly explained by the late Thomas Merton. Writing a preface to one of his books which had been translated into Japanese, Merton tried to explain to his largely non-Christian readers the motive for living a life of a Trappist monk with all of its severity and withdrawal from the active world:

> To adopt a life that is essentially non-assertive, non-violent, a life of humility and peace, is in itself a statement of one's position.... By my monastic life and vows I am saying NO to all the concentration camps, aerial bombardments, the staged political trials, the judicial murders, the racial injustice.... If I say NO to all these secular forces I also say YES to all that is good in the world and in man. I say YES to all that is beautiful in nature, and in order that this may be a "yes" of a freedom and not of subjection, I must refuse to possess anything in the world as purely my own....[5]

The surest way of knowing whether our asceticism is a healthy one (i.e. not merely self-punishment or guilt-ridden hatred of the self or others) is to ask this question: Is every "no" we make with regard to ourselves combined with a "yes" to some value which we find in the following of Christ? Otherwise, even if "I have prophetic powers and understand all mysteries and all knowledge and have faith to move mountains but have no love, I am nothing" (1 Cor 13:2).

Some Ascetic Practices

Once we have put asceticism into the broader context of discipleship it is worthwhile to reflect on some of the traditional ascetic practices of the Catholic tradition. We have left these practices to

---

5. Preface to the Japanese translation of *The Seven Storey Mountain* found in Thomas Merton's *Honorable Reader: Reflections on My Work,* edited by Robert Daggy (New York: Crossroad, 1981) 65-66.

this part of the chapter in order to make again our very important and fundamental point: ascetic practices (whatever they may be) are not ends in themselves; they are simply strategies to aid us in the development of the Christian life. The early monastic writers are very precise on this point. They warn against a kind of pride that develops in those who think that because they are rigorous ascetics that they are "perfect" people. The fourth century writer Cassian tells the story of a desert monk named Hero who was so completely wrapped up in his life of fasting and withdrawal into the desert that he refused to join the other desert ascetics for the Easter liturgy or the common meal which they enjoyed after the liturgy was completed. Cassian tells us that Hero was blinded by Satan and threw himself into a well, convinced that he was too perfect to be harmed. He died of his injuries, and only the intervention of some of the monks kept him from being considered a suicide.[6] According to Cassian, Hero's fault was that he lacked "discernment"—that kind of discretion which distinguishes means and ends.

It will be in the light of the cautions written above that we will consider the ascetic practices discussed below.

Fasting. One of the most frequently mentioned ascetic practices in the bible is the voluntary abstinence from food and drink that we call fasting. A glance at any standard biblical encyclopedia[7] reveals not only numerous references to fasting but different reasons for the practice. The ancient Hebrews observed a special period of fasting as a sign of repentance on the Day of Atonement (*Yom Kippur*) just as Jews do today. Fasting was a sign of mourning or an act of reparation for sins or a practice done before some momentous undertaking. Jesus, as all four of the gospels report, spent forty days in fasting and prayer on the eve of his public ministry. Jesus, again, provides rules for fasting and other acts of piety which are to be done without public display (Mt 6:1-18). The members of the early church quite naturally linked fasting with prayer (see, for example, Acts 13:2-3).

In the history of the Christian church fasting was both encouraged and later mandated as a duty. Despite the fact that fasting today in the Catholic Church is an obligation only in restricted periods of

---

6. The story is found in Cassian's Conference II in *John Cassian: The Conferences,* edited by Colm Luibheid (New York: Paulist, 1985) 64-65.

7. For example, "Fasting," in *The Anchor Bible Dictionary,* Vol. II (New York: Doubleday, 1992) 773-76; see also J. Wimmer, *Fasting in the New Testament: A Study in Biblical Theology* (Mahwah: Paulist, 1982).

Lent, the discipline of fasting is still regarded as a recommended Christian ascetical practice.

What we will say below will be in the context of the reflections of Jesus himself as they are found in Matthew 6 since it is there that Jesus talks about practices of piety.

Why fast? Beneath all of the stated aims (such as fasting as a signing of repentance or mourning) is the more fundamental idea of putting one's person in focus. When one wants to express sorrow for sin, for example, the prayer of forgiveness is linked to an actual *bodily* practice which is out of the ordinary, i.e. stopping the normal intake of food and drink. Fasting, in short, is a "making physical" of a spiritual sentiment or desire. In that sense, fasting, like all ascetical practices, has a "sacramental" value: it is an outward sign of an inward disposition.

Once we have understood that, there are many creative ways in which fasting may be undertaken to "make physical" sentiments of discipleship. Some people, for example, designate days in which they eat only the amount of calories available to the poorest of the world as a sign of human solidarity and as a way of saving some money for the poor. Others fast on days when they are on retreat or having a quiet day as a method to sharpen their sense of attention and as a way to remember to be thankful for what they normally receive at table.

Fasting has certain subheadings like abstinence (restricting certain kinds of food or drink, e.g. flesh meat or wine) or other acts of self-denial (restricting television watching or getting up earlier), but for all these activities, the same principle applies: they are means and not ends. Such acts conform to Christian discipleship only when they are linked to the larger desire to do or not do something as part of following the way of Christ.

Almsgiving. In Matthew 6 Jesus speaks about three ways of "right conduct" (*dikaiosyne*) before God, three acts of traditional piety: almsgiving, fasting, and prayer. This conduct is a gift to be sought from God (see Mt 6:33) and is a sign of discipleship.

Almsgiving can be understood as a shorthand way of speaking of self-denial in favor of another. It implies giving away what is one's own in favor of another in need. The gospel tells us that it can be a simple gesture like offering a cup of water or, as in the case of the widow who gives her penny for the poor, a giving of something from one's own substance. The ultimate act of almsgiving, in this sense, is the giving away of one's own life for the sake of another: "No one has greater love than this, to lay down one's life for one's friends" (Jn 15:13).

The asceticism of discipleship that values giving to another (of time or goods or friendship or whatever) is a concrete way of expressing solidarity with all other humans who, after all, are "made in the image and likeness of God" and in imitation of Christ who gave himself up for others "even unto death on a cross."

Again, the self-giving implied in almsgiving is only an asceticism of discipleship when its motives are shaped by a desire to be a follower of Jesus. To give charity for tax purposes (or to fast in order to be more fashionable) is morally neutral but does not fit into the gospel understanding of almsgiving.

A final point: a fully *Catholic* account of almsgiving must not rest only on the act of one individual toward another. Nor can such acts be seen simply as "charity." All Christians, socially bonded as they are, must ask the hard questions: Can my parish be a lavish one when so many are poor? Can I be satisfied to be among the "rich" families or "powerful" states when so many families or states teeter on the edge of extinction through want of basics? The church-wide concerns with the right use of resources, aid to refugees, international cooperation, etc. are not exercises in pious social work. They are attempts to plumb the full meaning of giving to the other in the name of Jesus Christ. The whole complex of ideas and motivations which we call "social justice" is nothing more than a working out of the asceticism of almsgiving "writ large."

Prayer. A separate chapter will devote itself to prayer, but there is one point in Matthew 6 that is especially pertinent for our discussion of asceticism. Besides fasting and almsgiving, Jesus adds prayer as one of the three acts of traditional piety. Jesus emphasizes two things in that section: the necessity to pray to God for the right motive (not for the praise of people—6:5) but "in secret" as communion with God (6:6). Secondly, one should pray not with a babble of phrases but with that purity of heart which speaks directly to God. Jesus then gives the example of the Lord's Prayer (6:7-15).

The point to be emphasized is that prayer must be part of the Christian's life, that it should be done from the right motive, and that it should come from the heart and be aimed directly to God. The ascetic lesson to be learned from all of this is simple: part of one's "training" in discipleship involves a regular regime of turning to God in prayer.

We can systematize the three main points of Matthew 6 in this fashion: all three traditional activities involve a kind of "turning" (i.e. a kind of "conversion") that allows us to gain a greater sense of our way of discipleship. Each has its own end:

- Fasting leads us to forget the ordinary and the routine so that we can focus more intensely in a bodily fashion as followers of the Lord.
- Almsgiving allows us to forget the self by a focus on the individual or social other by acts of self-giving.
- Prayer permits us to let loose of the self as we turn from the self to the supreme Other who is God.

Asceticism as a Way of Life

It becomes apparent, when one looks back over the long history of the Catholic tradition, that certain forms of "training" (asceticism) have become institutionalized into quite diverse ways of discipleship. These institutionalized forms (often called *schools of spirituality*) evolve along a rather regular road of development. Someone discovers a way of being faithful to the gospel and lives it such a way as to attract others to it. The core person or group produces texts which reflect on the experience, and, finally, this way of life is offered to the Catholic community as one way of living out the gospel and becomes part of the tradition.[8] For example, St. Francis of Assisi lived a life of gospel poverty and attracted disciples who, like Francis, lived out and wrote about these experiences. From this came a kind of "Franciscan" way of life in the world.

These schools of spirituality (whether they be inspired by monasticism or by great mystics like John of the Cross and Teresa of Avila or the founders of the Catholic Worker Movement) have certain characteristics in common. The most conspicuous characteristics would include:

a) A given number of emphases or constants regarding one or another aspect of the Christian faith or life in the Spirit.

b) A certain way of praying and a specific understanding of mission.

c) A specific pedagogical method to form people, whether it be a rule of life (like a monastic rule) or a shaping document to form

---

8. We borrow this notion from Gustavo Gutiérrez's *We Drink from Our Own Wells* (Maryknoll: Orbis, 1984).

people (like the *Spiritual Exercises* of St. Ignatius of Loyola) or a text which teaches a way of union with God (like the writings of the mystics) or a doctrine of formation to help people serve a particular evangelical purpose.

d) Every school of spirituality has its preferred biblical texts that receive special emphasis and attention.

e) Every school of spirituality is rooted in an intense spiritual experience(s) which seeks to shape those who follow it into being more authentic disciples of Christ.[9]

It is easy to see how these characteristics work out in real practice. The monastic tradition, for instance, emphasizes withdrawal from the world in order to live in prayerful community as a "school of the Lord's service" (*Rule* of Benedict). They have a formation document (the Rule), they have a predilection for certain biblical texts (e.g. those places in the Acts of the Apostles which talk about the common sharing of goods and the life of fraternity and prayer), and they intend to provide monastic followers with a plan for continuous conversion of life.

There are many such schools in the tradition. What is not often recognized, however, is that these "schools" need not be restricted to those who live under religious vows in convents or monasteries (although, obviously, these are easy cases to discern). Indeed, reflection on schools of spirituality can lead us to ask creative questions about how one might think of other ways of discipleship that would be pertinent to the age in which we live or the future which we envision.

One example as a thought experiment: What kind of training and spirituality is characteristic (or: should be characteristic) of a married couple? It is obvious that such a spirituality could not simply duplicate an asceticism more geared to a contemplative monastic order (even though, obviously, there may be resources in such a tradition that would be helpful). The actual living out of the Christian life must be geared to who one is and where one finds oneself. St. Francis de Sales made this clear in a classic work he wrote to help a married woman enter more deeply into her Christian life:

Devotion must be exercised in different ways by the gentleman, the worker, the servant, the prince, the widow, the young girl, and

---

9. These characteristics are taken from Raymond Deville's *The French School of Spirituality* (Pittsburgh: Duquesne University Press, 1994) 153-54.

the married woman. Not only is this true, but the practice of devotion must be adapted to the strength, activities, and duties of a particular person. I ask you, is it fitting for a married man to want to own no more property than a Capuchin friar or for a skilled workman to spend all day in church?...Would not such devotion be laughable, confused, impossible to carry out?[10]

Obviously, a married spirituality demands a certain asceticism; there is a learning and training in the married life by which people learn to be sensitive to the other, to be faithful, to enter into a partnership (and, more importantly, a friendship) that is mutually enriching, to sacrifice for the sake of the family, and so on. For Catholics, then, one seeks out the resources of the tradition which allows such constants to be present and to grow in order to be with each other "in sickness and health until death they do part."

Such a spirituality demands a maturity through which people learn about deepness of love, expressed in their sexual, social, and family life. It also presupposes that married people would deepen their understanding of the married state as having a sacramental ("sign") value involving an authentic reflection of the creative work of God and and the love between God and humanity.

Here is what the *Catechism of the Catholic Church,* quoting Pope John Paul II's *Familiaris Consortio* and Vatican II's *Gaudium et Spes,* holds out as the ideal of marriage:

The Christian family constitutes a specific revelation and realization of ecclesial communion, and for this reason it can and should be called a "domestic church." It is a community of faith, hope, and charity; it assumes singular importance in the church, as is evident in the New Testament.... The family is a privileged community called to achieve a "sharing of thought and common deliberation by the spouses as well as their eager cooperation as parents in the children's upbringing." [11]

Obviously, this is an ideal and it may be one far removed from the gritty reality of making a living, worrying over children, keeping peace in the household, etc. The point, however, is that there is an ideal to be reached through being open to grace and those

---

10. In *Introduction to the Devout Life*, trans. John K. Ryan (New York: Harper Torchbooks, 1966) 37.

11. #2204 and #2206, slightly amended.

resources available in the tradition to develop a sense of the spiritual shape of the married person and family member.

Unfortunately, a good deal of writing about Christian marriage and the family is done either by church professionals who "think" professionally or by religious who, unmarried, have a rather idealized and romantic view of marriage somewhat distanced from its reality in real life. Such a state of affairs presents a great opportunity for people who are committed to the faith to begin to think of what a spirituality and an asceticism should look like in this present time. Such thinking, obviously, would be pertinent not only for married persons but for those who are single, divorced, workers or students, and other "life forms" which make up the fabric of our society.

How do such spiritualities develop?

First of all, they must derive from experience and not from the mechanical imitation of some past tradition. One cannot simply translate the ascetical practices of the past into the present without "testing" them against what we deeply experience as human beings and believers. Ascetical practices, for example, which turn people into neurotics or self-punishers in the name of spirituality, would seem, on the face of it, unhelpful. Attitudes and orientations which engender a distrust of God's creation or a judgmental attitude toward others are not authentically Christian.

At the same time, the Christian cannot expect spiritual experience to be an easy "feel good" form of therapy. Disciples must expect both the cross and the resurrection. As we have earlier argued, one of the purposes of ascetical practice is to help us say "no" to the self, not for the sake of saying "no" but for the sake of saying "yes" to another and to God.

One area of asceticism which deserves special mention concerns sexuality. Historically, the Catholic tradition has honored those who choose sexual continence as a way of discipleship. From antiquity we have honored those who embrace the path of virginity either individually or in the social context of the monastic or religious life. For well over a millennium the western priesthood has been a celibate one. The strong value that the church places on sexual continence has had, at times, the negative effect of undervaluing the positive and sacramental worth of sexual love, especially when continence was praised partially as a result of suspicions about bodiliness and pleasure.

The great task of contemporary spirituality is to achieve a positive asceticism of sexuality in a culture which overvalues the erotic and the sexual. To be sexually chaste according to one's state of life; to be faithful in a monogamous relationship; to have a healthy respect for and celebration of physical love—all of these challenges presuppose a kind of discipline which values the bodily without ignoring the religious dimension of human sexual relationships.

Sexuality, of course, means more than genital acts; sexuality encompasses holistically the bodily in relationship to another. In that sense, it implies a whole range of experiences appropriate to one's condition and one's sense of self. It is for that reason that Elizabeth Dreyer can write:

> There is something amiss if one's sexuality is not a primary locus of the revelation of God. As relational, sexuality is replete with potential elements for the spiritual life—self-knowledge; self-gift; love; kindness; intimacy; touch; kiss; embrace; nakedness; trust; vulnerability; pleasure; union; ecstasy; self-transcendence; play; self-denial; creativity; companionship; forgiveness....[12]

A Final Note

If Christian asceticism is to be fully understood it is crucial not to divide body and soul into two separate compartments. Disciples of Jesus are persons, not bodiless angels or brute animals. Authentic asceticism, like spirituality itself, must account for whole persons who are made in the image and likeness of God. Asceticism should always be linked to human integration, i.e. for the sake of the whole person.

Nor can asceticism be concerned only with the needs and desires of the solitary self. One may diet for one's own self-image but one undertakes a Christian fast for the sake of others and for the sake of God. Furthermore, if we are authentically *Catholic* our asceti-

---

12. Elizabeth A. Dreyer, *Earth Crammed with Heaven: A Spirituality of Everyday Life* (Mahwah: Paulist, 1994) 116. The same point has been made recently by the British spiritual writer and theologian, Philip Sheldrake: "Every human person is unavoidably a sexual person. This emphatically includes those in various forms of the singleness, including the option of celibacy. We can try to ignore sexuality and to repress it, or we can seek to live positively and healthily within it. What is not open to us is to bypass it or to escape completely from it." In *Befriending Our Desires* (Notre Dame: Ave Maria Press, 1994) 67.

cism will involve our neighbor. One of the more persistent themes of contemporary spirituality is the critique of those who would understand the spiritual life only as a vertical relationship of a solitary person with God. Spirituality, like asceticism, demands a social context that embraces self, friends, neighbors, strangers, the earth itself refracted in, and bound by, the goodness of God.

Finally, asceticism must be seen as something integrated into the whole of life. Asceticism is intertwined not only by that training by which we pray, fast, and do acts of charity with regularity but also with our ordinary lives as healthy Christians. It must also intertwine with the way we have certain obligations, with the ways we are related to family, friends, companions, and the larger world, with what we desire to do with our lives in terms of occupation, and so on.

There is a constant tension in asceticism between desire and the denial of desire. A true ascetic must experience joy (in eating, loving, reading, living, etc.) just as an ascetic knows how to integrate sorrow and self-denial into life. An ascetic must always keep an eye on the self just as the ascetic keeps an eye on others in God. The final test of asceticism is whether it brings a greater capacity to love, grow humanly, yearn for what is not yet, sense the presence of God in ordinary moments as well as extraordinary ones, dwell in friendship, celebrate the eucharist with joy, and embrace others.

Further Reading

Brown, Peter, *The Body and Society: Men, Women, and Sexual Renunciation in Early Christianity* (New York: Columbia University Press, 1988). A scholarly study which attempts to describe the many motives underlying the Christian practice of sexual continence.

Bynum, Caroline W., *Holy Feast and Holy Fast: The Religious Significance of Food to Medieval Women* (Berkeley: University of California, 1987). A fascinating but demanding study of the symbolic relationship of food, the eucharist, and medieval women's spirituality.

Elgin, Duane, *Voluntary Simplicity* (New York: Bantam, 1982). One of several fine books which argues for an ordinary asceticism based on ecological awareness.

Miles, Margaret, *Fullness of Life: Historical Foundations for a New*

Asceticism (Philadelphia: Westminster, 1981). An attempt, not always successful, to argue for a new asceticism in Christian life.

Sheldrake, Philip, *Befriending Our Desires* (Notre Dame: Ave Maria Press, 1994). A very balanced work with a positive and nourishing view of the Christian life.

Wimbush, Vincent and Richard Valantasis, eds. *Asceticism* (New York: Oxford University Press, 1995). A collection of scholarly essays on asceticism in the world's religions. Excellent studies on Christian asceticism. Good bibliography.

Exercises

(1) There are many ascetic "rules of life" in the history of the Christian tradition. What would be the basic "rules" which you would think appropriate for your own state of life (e.g. as a student or worker) as basic for Christian living?

(2) How might one relate traditional Christian ascetic practices as instruments to become more consciously compassionate toward those who are victims of injustice, poverty, and violence in the world? What does a "social justice" asceticism look like?

(3) What are the major issues that one must confront when attempting to integrate a balanced sexuality and a desire for discipleship?

(4) Can you relate the Christian emphasis on simplicity of life with your own style of life as a person who lives in a consumer society?

(5) Can you think of persons who have manifested clear ascetic values in their pursuit of a certain kind of life, e.g. as an athlete or artist or scholar or professional person? How do those ascetic tendencies reflect certain religious values?

(6) What ascetic values do you see as being most conspicuous in the life of Jesus as that life is depicted in the gospels?

7

Living in the Presence of God: The Way of the Mystics

"Go out and stand on the mountain before the Lord, for the Lord is about to pass by" (1 Kgs 19:11).

*T*he prophet Elijah heard the above words on the same mountain where Moses stood in the presence of the burning bush (Ex 3). The disciples of Jesus, moreover, witnessed these two prophets conversing with Jesus at the transfiguration (Mk 9:2-8). The Christian mystical tradition looks back to these prophets, Moses and Elijah, as archetypes, primitive models, of the Christian mystical experience.

This chapter explores the Christian mystical tradition as a resource in the modern search for God. As Karl Rahner wrote: "...the devout Christian of the future will either be a 'mystic,' one who has 'experienced' something, or he will cease to be anything at all."[1] The future of Christianity requires a descent into the depths of the human spirit, for, as Eliot has said, "prayer is more/Than an order of words...or the sound of the voice praying."[2]

The mystics have reported their encounters with God in various ways. They have called their experiences union with God, seeing God, contemplation, etc. In this book we follow a suggestion made by Bernard McGinn whose monumental study of mysticism has adopted presence as the basic category for speaking about the mystical experience of God.[3] Listen to Teresa of Avila, the first

---

1. Karl Rahner, *Theological Investigations* 7, trans. David Bourke (New York: Herder and Herder, 1971) 15.

2. T. S. Eliot, "Little Gidding," *Four Quartets, The Complete Poems and Plays, 1909-1950* (New York: Harcourt Brace and World, 1962).

3. Bernard McGinn, *The Foundations of Mysticism: Origins to the Fifth Century* (New York: Crossroad, 1991) xvii.

woman doctor of the church, tell about her experience of divine presence:

> This presence is a great favor from God and should be highly esteemed by the one He gives it to, for it is a very sublime prayer, but it is not a vision; in this prayer of union or quiet one understands that God is present by the effects that, as I say, He grants to the soul—that is the way His Majesty wants to give the experience of Himself.[4]

Teresa and other mystics write so intensely and passionately about the mystical encounter with God that their texts constitute a compelling exploration of the inner journey to God. We shall look at some moments, texts and figures in this mystical tradition so that we may better understand the meaning of the mystical life. The mystical life is an embrace of one's humanity, a humanity that finds its fulfillment in living more consciously in the presence of God.

Since Vatican II, interest in mysticism has revived dramatically. On balance Christian life had been more ascetical (human effort) than mystical (God's work) since the end of the seventeenth century when mysticism became suspect. However, during the 1960s many young people turned to eastern non-Christian mysticism because they had not found the mystical tradition of the west. But, as Thomas Merton discovered from personal experience, the turn to the east was not as productive as it could have been if the searchers had known better their own mystical tradition.

This chapter can sample this multi-faceted Christian mystical tradition only briefly. The hope is that this sampling will send readers to texts of the many fascinating mystics of Christianity to become conversation partners with mystics who have left records of their encounters with the divine. There is much to be learned from dialogue with the mysticism of non-Christian traditions. One may better dialogue with other mystical traditions once one has become conversant with one's own tradition.

----

4. *The Book of Her Life* 27.4; Vol. 1: *The Collected Works of St. Teresa of Avila,* trans. Kieran Kavanaugh and Otilio Rodriguez (Washington, DC: Institute of Carmelite Studies, 1976) 175; Vol. 2: *The Way of Perfection / The Interior Castle* (1980); Vol. 3: *The Book of Her Foundations* (1985).

Vocabulary

The study of mysticism requires mastery of some basic terminology. The word "mystic," much abused in our day, is used so loosely that it refers to anything esoteric. Early Christians took the word "mystic" from the Greeks whose *myo*, to close the eyes, described the action of one reacting to religious experience. The same root is the basis for the Greek word *mysterion*, mystery, which is what mysticism concerns—an encounter with divine mystery.

Christians began early on, with Clement of Alexandria, to speak of the hidden or deeper meaning of scripture as mystical. *Mystikos* also described the encounter with Christ in the sacraments of baptism and eucharist. Mystical body referred to the eucharist until the twelfth century when Christians began to refer to the church as the mystical body of Christ. Previously the Pauline phrase, the body of Christ, described the church. The patristic and medieval use of mystical presupposes an ecclesial, corporate context rather than some individualized mystical experience.

About A.D. 500 a Christian, perhaps in Syria, composed a text, *Mystical Theology,*[5] which has had an incalculable impact on Christian mysticism. The unknown author passed himself off as the convert of St. Paul (Acts 17:34). Thus he is often called Pseudo-Dionysius. The title of his little treatise, *Mystical Theology,* refers not to the study of mysticism, a modern notion, but to intimate experience of God. But it was not until the late middle ages, perhaps even later, that union with God was perceived in an individualized fashion. This conception gave rise to the modern idea that mysticism is the transformation of individual consciousness. A ninth century Irishman John Scotus Erigena translated into Latin the Greek texts of Pseudo-Dionysius. This translation made Pseudo-Dionysius' dynamic mystical thought available to many in the middle ages including Thomas Aquinas.

The term *mysticism* did not come into use until the early seventeenth century in France[6] when mysticism was a much discussed topic in the salons of Paris. In this chapter we hope that various contexts will provide a background for the use of the words mystic,

---

5. *Pseudo-Dionysius: The Complete Works,* trans. Colm Luibheid (New York: Paulist Press, 1987) 133-41; Andrew Louth, *Denys the Areopagite* (Wilton: Morehouse-Barlow, 1989).

6. Bernard McGinn, *The Growth of Mysticism: Gregory the Great Through the Twelfth Century* (New York: Crossroad, 1994) 266.

mystical and mysticism. Mystic here describes both those who lay claim to the experience of the divine and to those who have written about the mystical life, not a distinction to make too finely.

Reading the Mystics

To read the bible intelligently one has to develop skills that avoid rigid literalism or fanciful interpretations not supported by the text. Biblical hermeneutics is the science that articulates principles for reading the bible responsibly. The mystics present like hurdles for the unwary reader. Principles from biblical hermeneutics can prepare one to read the mystics intelligently.[7] Christian mysticism formally began with the biblical interpretations of Origen who searched the scriptures for the mystical (hidden) presence of Christ. Mysticism must never be divorced from the bible which is the foundation for all Christian mystical experience.

Reading the mystics also requires that one bring to the text one's own religious search and experience in order to connect with the spiritual journey of the author of the text. One can then recognize in these texts themes common to every search for God and some that differ radically from one's own search. As with all texts, one must be open to what the mystic says on her or his own terms. John S. Dunne speaks of the process of "crossing over" to the experience of the other so that one may be with, feel with and understand the experience of the other. Then one can return to one's own experience enlarged by the other's experience.[8] To pass over to Elijah's experience of the "sound of sheer silence" (1 Kgs 19:12) is to gain an appreciation of the Spirit speaking through silence. Elijah's experience enlarges one's own capacity for God.

Texts of the mystics cannot be lumped together as if they were all alike. Each mystic is unique. Indeed, the mystics come from different eras, different locations and cultures, with all that these differences mean for understanding this or that mystic. One cannot read Origen, the early church exegete, in the same way one reads the sermons of Bernard of Clairvaux, the passionate Cistercian abbot, or the twelfth century theologian Hildegard of Bingen or the

---

7. See *The New Jerome Biblical Commentary,* eds., R.E. Brown, J.A. Fitzmeyer, R.E. Murphy (Englewood Cliffs: Prentice-Hall, 1990) 1146-65.

8. John S. Dunne, *The Way of All the Earth: Experiments in Truth and Religion* (New York: Macmillan, 1972) ix-xiii, *passim.*

Showings of Julian of Norwich, the fourteenth century English visionary. As with biblical texts, one must identify the genre at hand. Is the text a biblical commentary by Origen, a sermon by Augustine, a theological treatise by Richard of Saint-Victor or an essay on contemplation by Thomas Merton?

Each mystic, moreover, must be studied in historical context. The twelfth and the seventeenth centuries are very different eras with consequences for how one reads mystics from these two times. Mystical texts of the early church are different than the visionary accounts of Catherine of Siena or the mystical treatises of the Franciscan theologian St. Bonaventure. A reader must honor the distinctiveness of each mystic, each genre, each era.

Common, however, to all the mystical writers is the need to stretch their imaginations beyond the ordinary limits of language. Mystics agree that what they have to say is ineffable, unsayable. They write about the indescribable encounter with the mystery who is God, a God revealed in the scriptures but also a God hidden in the depths of unspeakable mystery. About this encounter one can only say with the prophet Jeremiah, "Ah, Lord God! Truly I do not know how to speak..." (Jer 1:6). Mystical writers resort to numerous symbols like water and fire, mountains and mansions, in an effort to pierce, if ever so slightly, the veil of mystery. Some mystics turn to poetry to offer "hints and guesses" (T. S. Eliot) of the experience of God. The Spanish Carmelite John of the Cross said this about his mystical poetry: "It would be foolish to think that expressions of love arising from mystical understanding, like these stanzas, are fully explainable."[9] Nevertheless, like the poets they sometimes are, the mystics keep trying to share the beauty and love which they have experienced in their encounters with the divine.

Christian mystics seeking to describe the human-divine encounter have often turned to the Song of Songs. The erotic language and symbols of these songs allow mystics to express the intensity, power and beauty of the loving relationship between God and the Christian community or between God and the mystic. This inspired text, filled with passionate symbolism, offers mystical writers a rich mine in which they plumb the depths of the experience of the divine present in the human.

Origen's mystical interpretation of these biblical love songs

---

9. Prologue to *The Spiritual Canticle, The Collected Works of St. John of the Cross,* trans. Kieran Kavanaugh and Otilio Rodriguez, rev. ed. (Washington, DC: Institute of Carmelite Studies, 1991) 469.

initiated a long Christian tradition wherein the Song of Songs has served as the source of metaphors and symbols for the mystical journey to God.[10] Readers of the mystics do well to become acquainted with this unique book of the bible and with Origen's writings on the Song of Songs.[11] Bernard of Clairvaux and John of the Cross are only two of many Christian mystics for whom the Song of Songs has supplied language and symbols for reports about the journey to union with God in love.[12]

Mysticism in the Early Church

Jesus challenged his followers to avoid the formalism that infected religion in his time as it does in other eras. The call of Jesus was to love the Lord God with all one's heart, mind and soul and to love the neighbor as one's self. Jesus died for his commitment to his Father and for what he taught his followers about God. The integrity and commitment which led to Jesus' death was an example for martyrs who with their lives witnessed to their faith in Christ. During the era of martyrdom there arose an element in Christianity that called for a radical, transforming love of God which would much later be called mysticism. The mystic is one whose single-minded love of God and love of neighbor leads to an awareness of the presence of God.

This mystical tradition began with the desire to know and to love God as deeply as possible through contact with Christ hidden in the scriptures. As mentioned above, this encounter was called mystical, an encounter with Christ hidden in the scriptures and a mystical encounter with Christ hidden in the sacraments of baptism and eucharist. In the era before Vatican II the study of mysticism too

---

10. See list of Christian commentators in Marvin Pope, *Song of Songs: A New Translation with Introduction and Commentary,* "Anchor Bible" (Garden City: 1977) 114ff.

11. Origen, *An Exhortation to Martyrdom, Prayer, First Principles: Book IV, Prologue to the Commentary on the Song of Songs, Homily XXVII on Numbers,* trans. R.A. Greer (New York: Paulist, 1979); Origen, *The Song of Songs, Commentary and Homilies,* trans. R.P. Lawson, "Ancient Christian Writers" (New York: Newman/Paulist, 1957).

12. Bernard of Clairvaux, *On the Song of Songs,* 4 vols., trans. Kilian Walsh and Irene Edmonds (Kalamazoo: Cistercian Publications, 1971-1980). *The Spiritual Canticle* of John of the Cross is a reworking of the Song of Songs.

often lacked biblical and sacramental foundations. In addition, a rationalistic and individualistic approach robbed Christian mysticism of its ecclesial dynamism and its ability to inspire a sense of mystery.[13]

The early Christian experience of mysticism contained these elements neglected in modern times. The mystical writings from that era act as a resource for keeping the word of God and the sacraments as the authentic basis for the Christian mystical life. This emphasis also keeps mysticism from becoming privatized as happens too easily. Mysticism in the Christian tradition has an ecclesial (corporate) context and sacramental roots, and is always incarnational, that is, related to God as become flesh in Christ. Mysticism must never be body-hating.

This ecclesial mysticism is a remedy for the extreme individualism of modern North American life. Scripture and the sacraments keep the mystical life under the influence of the Holy Spirit who is the architect of the mystical life. McGinn has written that "mysticism is *primarily* (not *solely*) an ecclesial tradition of prayer and practice nourished by scripture and liturgy in order to foster awareness of whatever direct forms of divine presence may be available in this life...."[14] This return to the biblical and sacramental foundations of mysticism is what makes possible the "everyday" or "ordinary" mysticism articulated by Karl Rahner. A watered-down mysticism this is not but rather a connecting of mystical graces with the sacramental realities of the Christian life.

The encounter with Christ, begun at baptism, sealed with the Holy Spirit at confirmation and nourished at the eucharist lays the foundation for all Christian mysticism. The mystic is one who says with St. Paul: "I have been crucified with Christ; and it is no longer I who live, but it is Christ who lives in me" (Gal 2:19-20). This quotation captured the imagination of Teresa of Avila who referred to this Pauline sentiment when she described the consequences of her conversion to a mystical life at the age of thirty-nine.[15] Mysticism is commitment to the demanding discipleship of the gospels.

There is space here to mention only a few of the mystical authors

---

13. Keith J. Egan, "The Prospects of the Contemporary Mystical Movement: A Critique of Mystical Theology," *Review for Religious* 34 (1975) 901-10.

14. McGinn, *The Growth of Mysticism* 81.

15. *The Book of Her Life* 23.1, *The Collected Works of St. Teresa of Avila* I, 152.

from the early church. We have already noted Origen whose importance is impossible to exaggerate. Every renewal of Christian mysticism has included a return to Origen's writings. Origen influenced
another key figure, Gregory of Nyssa, a married man who became
the bishop of Nyssa. Gregory had an immense impact on eastern
Christian mysticism, but westerners heard little of his wisdom
until this century. Gregory has intrigued many readers, including
Thomas Merton, with his notion of *epektasis*.[16] This term means
that the core dynamism of the Christian life is the never-ending
growth in love of God here and in eternity. Eternally becoming new,
one grows forever in an ever greater participation in God's life and
glory.[17] *Epektasis* is an earthly mysticism become eternal.

Origen developed a mysticism of light while Gregory of Nyssa
saw the mystical experience of God as an encounter with darkness.
Gregory wrote the following about the experience of his brother, St.
Basil, the great monastic legislator of the eastern church.

> Often we saw him enter into the darkness where God was. By the
> mystical guidance of the Spirit he understood what was invisible
> to others, so that he seemed to be enveloped in the darkness in
> which the Word of God is concealed.[18]

This experience of darkness or incomprehensibility is known as
apophatic or imageless mysticism. Gregory stressed the absolute
transcendence of God. This apophatic experience of the absolute
mystery of God eludes all description. God is beyond anything that
one can say about the divine. Apophatic mysticism is a hallmark of
eastern Christianity, but every mystic comes face to face with the
otherness of God. Eastern theologians, like Vladimir Lossky, insist
that the apophatic experience is neither impersonal nor abstract but
a personal encounter with the triune God in darkness. In fact,
Lossky even speaks of the apophatic encounter with the incarnation,
the hiddenness of God in Christ,[19] a notion that deserves further

---

16. For example, *The Hidden Ground of Love* (Letters), ed. by William
H. Shannon (New York: Farrar, Straus, Giroux, 1985) 348.

17. *From Glory to Glory: Texts from Gregory of Nyssa's Mystical
Writings,* Introduction by Jean Daniélou, trans. H. Musurillo (New York:
Charles Scribner's Sons, 1961) 56-71.

18. Ibid. 28.

19. Vladimir Lossky, *The Mystical Theology of the Eastern Church*
(London: James Clarke, 1957, 1968) 44, 43.

exploration. Mystics in the west less often emphasize the apophatic, but there are those like the author of *The Cloud of Unknowing* who in the fourteenth century composed a handbook for prayer where knowing is a kind of unknowing.[20]

The counterpart to the apophatic experience is known as kataphatic mysticism. Kataphaticism focuses on the experience of what can be known, said or symbolized about God. The kataphatic is what has been revealed or manifested about God in creation, the scriptures, the sacraments, and the personal experience of God in prayer. Did not mystical experience make it possible for the nearly blind Francis to see God's beauty in creation?

> All praise be yours, my Lord, through all that you have made/And first my lord Brother Sun,/Who brings the day; and light you give to us through him./How beautiful is he, how radiant in all his splendour!/Of you, Most High, he bears the likeness./All praise be yours, my Lord, through Sister Moon and Stars; In the heavens you have made them, bright/And precious and fair.[21]

There is a modern tendency to distinguish mystics as apophatic or kataphatic. Eastern mysticism sees *the* culmination of mystical experience as apophatic. Western writers are becoming comfortable with the idea that, while a mystic like Meister Eckhart may be called apophatic, he is at the same time kataphatic. In other words, western mystics may lean one way more than another, but the totality of their experience of God contains both the apophatic and the kataphatic. Mystics never tire of the paradoxes that express their experiences. The apophatic/kataphatic paradox is a mark of western mysticism that needs to be kept in creative tension

Monastic Mysticism

Christian monasticism got underway at the end of the third century in Egypt. The solitude of the hermits and the anchorites as well as the solitude provided for the monks and nuns in the

---

20. *The Cloud of Unknowing and the Book of Privy Counselling,* ed. William Johnston (Garden City: Doubleday, 1973).

21. Selection from Francis' "The Canticle of Brother Sun," *English Omnibus of the Sources for the Life of St. Francis,* ed. Marion Habig, 3rd rev. ed. (Chicago: Franciscan Herald Press, 1973) 130-31.

communal monasteries of the desert gave birth to the mysticism that found a special home in monasticism for centuries. The mysticism of the first eleven Christian centuries "was inseparable from the history of monasticism," and this monasticism had a "decisive role in the history of the earliest layer of Western mysticism," says Bernard McGinn.[22]

The writings of Evagrius of Pontus and his disciple John Cassian, both influenced by Origen's mysticism, communicated a monastic mysticism that left a special mark on Christian mysticism. Cassian's description of the "prayer of fire" inspired for centuries those who turned often to his *Conferences*. The Lord's Prayer, Cassian wrote,

> lifts them up to that prayer of fire known to so few. It lifts them up, rather, to that ineffable prayer which rises above all human consciousness, with no voice sounding, no tongue moving, no words uttered.[23]

In the western church two figures, Augustine of Hippo and Gregory the Great, exerted an enormous influence on subsequent mysticism. Augustine's *Confessions* left an indelible mark on everyone who has felt as he has that one's "heart is restless until it rests in you."[24] For many centuries the ecstatic experience of Augustine and his mother Monica which occurred as they were "leaning out of a window overlooking a garden" at a tavern in Ostia has been etched in the imagination of Christians.[25] But Augustine's mystical teaching is scattered throughout his voluminous writings, and Professor McGinn has summarized its scope in this way:

> ...first, his account of the soul's ascension to contemplative and ecstatic experience of the divine presence; second, the ground for the possibility of this experience in the nature of the human person as the image of the triune God; and third, the necessary role of Christ and the church in attaining this experience.[26]

---

22. McGinn, *The Foundations of Mysticism* 131-32.

23. John Cassian, *Conferences,* trans. Colm Luibheid (New York: Paulist, 1985), Conference 9, 25.

24. Augustine, *Confessions,* trans. Henry Chadwick (New York: Oxford University Press, 1992) 1.1.1.

25. *Confessions* 9.10.23-26.

26. McGinn, *The Foundations of Mysticism* 231.

Along with Augustine, Gregory the Great, monk and pope, thoroughly shaped the religious language and symbolism of western Christianity. Here we cite only Gregory's pervasive impact on subsequent mystical language, symbols and theory. In particular Gregory insisted "that it is only in and through the study of the bible that contemplation is possible."[27] The imprint of Augustine and Gregory the Great appears on every subsequent page of western mysticism.

From the middle of the sixth century, when the Benedictine *Rule* was composed, until 1153, when Bernard of Clairvaux died, nuns and monks gave to Christian mysticism a distinctively monastic profile. But it was Bernard, abbot of the Cistercian monastery of Clairvaux, who left the most personal imprint on monastic mysticism. Medieval authors, from Thomas Aquinas to Martin Luther, quoted and cited Bernard extensively. Bernard's most pervasive influence on mysticism came from his eighty-six sermons on the Song of Songs. These passionate sermons use imaginatively the text, language and symbols of the Song of Songs, and they celebrate exuberantly the experience of the mystical encounter with Christ.

Bernard's sermons on the songs are a key text in the transmission of the bridal mysticism that mystics of the middle ages and the Counter-Reformation found so congenial. Bernard's skillful and creative use of Latin is a prime example of the way mystics can take a malleable langauge and push it to its limits in the exploration and expression of mystical experience. Julian of Norwich did this with Middle English in the fourteenth century and John of the Cross with Castilian Spanish in the sixteenth. A mystic with a poetic imagination is able to take a flexible language and to shape words and symbols in a way that expresses deep interior experience. Bernard of Clairvaux made Latin sing with melodic phrases that invited others to participate in his spiritual and mystical experiences. Bernard's prose is as poetic as prose can be.[28] Meister Eckhart's fiery German sermons electrified his audiences with the power of his language and symbolism.

---

27. McGinn, *The Growth of Mysticism* 39.

28. See Bernard McGinn's remarks on vernacular theology in "Meister Eckhart and the Beguines in the Context of Vernacular Theology," *Meister Eckhart and the Beguine Mystics: Hadewijch of Brabant, Mechtild of Magdeburg, and Marguerite Porete,* ed. Bernard McGinn (New York: Continuum, 1994) 1-14.

Bernard's fellow Cistercians, like William of Saint-Thierry, explored avidly mystical themes and bequeathed to posterity theoretical foundations of the mystical life. The Carthusians, who stressed solitude within community, produced a steady stream of mystical writings. The Victorine canons of Paris, e.g. Hugh of Saint-Victor and Richard of Saint-Victor, as practitioners of the new scholastic theology, wrote treatises that systematically explored the mystical life and provided guidance for the development of mystical theology during the rest of the middle ages.[29]

Later Medieval Mysticism

The half-century after the death of Bernard in 1253 was an explosive era that saw a rising population, new towns and flourishing commercial ventures throughout Europe. A popular religious revival among the laity took a keen interest in poverty and in evangelization. Dissent against church and monastic practices emerged. This turbulent era gave birth to one of the most significant movements in the history of Christianity: the friar movement. The Italian Francis of Assisi and the Spaniard Dominic Guzman inaugurated this movement that sent friars to every corner of Europe and well beyond to renew the faith of Christians in the light of the challenges of the Fourth Council of the Lateran (1215).

Francis of Assisi, founder of the Franciscans, wrote little but lived a mysticism that so identified him with the naked and crucified Christ that he bore on his body the stigmata. Dominic, founder of the Dominicans, laid the foundations for a renewal of Christian preaching and spiritual direction based on a study of the scriptures.[30] This preaching and teaching by the four mendicant orders, the Dominicans, Franciscans, Carmelites and Augustinian Friars, spread among clergy, religious and laity numerous ideas from the mystical tradition.

This mendicant preaching, in particular, affected the Beguines, women who espoused an evangelical life outside of the established ways of being a religious woman. The fervor of the Beguines made them apt listeners to the preaching of the friars. Freedom from the usual constraints of female monastic life at the time left the

---

29. See Richard of St. Victor, *The Twelve Patriarchs, The Mystical Ark, Book Three of the Trinity*, trans. Grover Zinn (New York: Paulist, 1979).

30. Benedict Ashley, *Spiritual Direction in the Dominican Tradition* (New York: Paulist, 1995).

Beguines open to the mysticism percolating in medieval Europe. The Dominican Meister Eckhart both influenced and was influenced by these women[31] whose role in the life of medieval Europe is only now receiving the attention it deserves.

The two most outstanding friar theologians of the middle ages were Thomas Aquinas and Bonaventure. The former articulated a theology of contemplation. However, after the middle ages theologians often put the study of mysticism within a version of Thomas' theology that robbed Thomas of the dynamism of his original thought. Post-Reformation theologians read Thomas too exclusively through his commentators.

Bonaventure became the minister general of the Franciscans and developed a theology of the mysticism that Francis lyrically lived. This Franciscan mysticism, profoundly Christological and intensely affective, touched profoundly and extensively all subsequent Christian mysticism. Bonaventure produced one of Christian mysticism's key masterpieces, *The Journey of the Soul into God,* in which Bonaventure reflected symbolically and theologically "on various ways by which the soul ascends into God."[32]

In the last quarter of the twentieth century the women's movement has sparked a widespread interest in the long neglected women mystics of the middle ages. No longer foreign to us are names of women like Elizabeth of Schonau, Hadewijch of Antwerp, Mechtild of Magdeberg, Mechtild of Hackeborn, Gertrude of Helfta, Angela of Foligno, Marguerite d'Oingt, Bridget of Sweden, Julian of Norwich, Catherine of Siena, Catherine of Genoa and many others. The modern literature on these female mystics and visionaries of the middle ages has grown at a rapid pace and is yielding valuable new insights into the spiritual life of the middle ages.[33] This chapter passes on reluctantly from these women but also from the mystical authors who followed in the footsteps of Meister Eckhart: Johann Tauler, Henry Suso and Jan van Ruysbroeck who made a decisive impact on Christian mysticism.

---

31. McGinn, *Meister Eckhart* 1-14.

32. Bonaventure, *The Soul's Journey into God, The Tree of Life, The Life of St. Francis,* trans. Ewert Cousins (New York: Paulist Press, 1978).

33. The literature on medieval women mystics is vast. Perhaps one can begin with Elizabeth Petroff, ed., *Medieval Women's Visionary Literature* (New York: Oxford University Press, 1986) and idem, *Body and Soul: Essays on Medieval Women and Mysticism* (New York: Oxford University Press, 1994).

The Reformation and Catholic Reform

Martin Luther's rejection of the mystical tradition was unfortunate for Protestantism and for Protestant-Catholic relations. Indeed, there was something of the mystic about Luther who effectively mined much wisdom from this tradition. Luther reacted not so much against the mystical tradition as against late medieval piety that seemed to him devoid of biblical warrants. However, Luther's opposition left Protestantism without much access to the mystical tradition and deprived this tradition of creative input from Protestant mystics.[34]

Among Catholic reformers in the sixteenth century, the names of three Spanish mystics come to the fore immediately: Ignatius of Loyola, founder of the Jesuits, Teresa of Avila, reformer of the Carmelites, and John of the Cross, poet and spiritual director. These three mystics have had a remarkable influence on Catholic spirituality despite the fact that, before Vatican II, theologians interpreted Teresa and John rather mechanically and neglected the mysticism of Ignatius.

Ignatius of Loyola, hell-bent on a life of soldiery adventure, was stopped in his tracks when he was wounded at the battle of Pamplona. A *Life of Christ* and a collection of saints' lives turned Ignatius from a swaggering soldier to a courageous saint. Till the end of his life Ignatius was the recipient of mystical graces. His *Spiritual Exercises,* intended to dispose retreatants to conversion, were the result of Ignatius' mystical experiences.

Some followers of Ignatius failed to appreciate the mystical character of his spirituality. They reduced his mysticism to asceticism. However, his associate, Jerome Nadal, knew the depth of Ignatius' experiences. Nadal described Ignatius as a "contemplative in action." Ignatian mysticism has been rediscovered in the twentieth century and spiritual pilgrims have found the *Exercises* to be an immense help in discerning the will of God. Ignatius of Loyola developed a "spirituality of service" and ministry[35] rooted in contemplative prayer. Moreover, the primitive texts of Ignatian spirituality

---

34. See *The Study of Spirituality,* eds. C. Jones, G. Wainwright, E. Yarnold (New York: Oxford University Press, 1986) 342-56, 431-80.

35. John O'Malley, "Early Jesuit Spirituality: Spain and Italy," *Christian Spirituality: Post-Reformation and Modern,* Vol. 18 of *World Spirituality,* ed. Louis Dupré and Don E. Saliers (New York: Crossroad, 1989) 3-27.

are crucial to contemporary attempts to develop a spirituality of ministry with mystical roots.[36]

Ignatius was still pursuing his military exploits when, at a village near Avila, a daughter named Teresa was born to a family who had to hide its Jewish ancestry. Teresa was a warm, friendly and talented young woman who became at twenty a member of a large Carmelite monastery outside the walls of Avila. At the age of thirty-nine Teresa experienced a conversion that initiated a mystical life that resulted in the reform of the Carmelite order and in the composition of mystical classics.

Urged by her advisors, Teresa described her spiritual journey in *The Book of Her Life*. Chapters 11-22 of this book tell the story of mystical prayer using the symbolism of water. Teresa's mystical masterpiece is *The Interior Castle* which she wrote in five months on-the-run. She showed herself a masterful story-teller in *The Book of Her Foundations*. For the young women in her reformed monasteries Teresa composed *The Way of Perfection* as a description of their way of life.

Teresa of Jesus became the first woman doctor of the church in 1970, one week before the church accorded the same title to the Dominican third order member Catherine of Siena. Teresa's gift was the ability to describe with warmth and wit, accuracy and appreciation, the action of God that led her through the "mansions" of her journey to spiritual marriage with God. Teresa perceived that her journey could be a pattern for others. Teresa thought that anyone who was detached from the silly things that keep one from God, who knows one's self well and who prays regularly with a listening heart can expect God's special presence.[37] Teresa of Jesus was a mystic with her feet firmly on the ground. For her the test of mystical experience is always growth in love of neighbor. She, who called herself a "daughter of the church" as she lay dying, wrote: "If we fail in love of neighbor we are lost."[38]

In the fall of 1567 Teresa of Jesus met for the first time the newly

---

36. For a selection of Ignatius' texts in English with an appreciation of their mystical character, see Ignatius of Loyola, *The Spiritual Exercises and Selected Works*, ed. George E. Ganss (New York: Paulist Press, 1991).

37. *The Interior Castle*, Dwelling Places 1-3, *The Collected Works of St. Teresa of Avila;* see Keith J. Egan, "The Foundations of Mystical Prayer: Teresa of Jesus," *Medieval Religious Women,* eds. L. Shank and J. Nichols (Kalamazoo: Cistercian Publications, 1987) 331-44.

38. *The Interior Castle* 5.3.8,12.

ordained John of the Cross. Teresa recognized immediately John's gifts. She convinced him not to transfer to the Carthusians but to help her reform the Carmelite order. The rest is Carmelite history. John, raised by his mother in poverty, worked as a teenager in a venereal disease hospital. These experiences left John compassionate and sensitive especially to the ill and the elderly.

However, John's single-minded commitment to reform left some fellow friars angry and vengeful. They imprisoned him at Toledo for nine months. Yet in that small prison cell John composed some of mysticism's most celebrated lyrics. Besides other poems, John wrote in prison the first thirty-one stanzas of the "The Spiritual Canticle," a powerful rewriting of The Song of Songs. John of the Cross' poetry is an expression of his mystical experience and should be read first before one turns to his commentaries: *The Ascent of Mount Carmel, The Dark Night, The Spiritual Canticle* and *The Living Flame of Love*.[39] John of the Cross' writings received little attention for three centuries after his death in 1591. In the twentieth century Spanish poets discovered the beauty of his poems several of which are considered to be among Spain's finest poetry. In 1926 John was named a doctor of the church.

Students of mysticism should keep in mind John of the Cross' advice for those interested in the psychological phenomena sometimes associated with mysticism, e.g. locutions and visions. Ignore them, says John; God has already done what God intended long before you noticed the phenonmena. Besides, these phenomena are the result of human weakness. Growth in love of God and neighbor is what counts. Rather than seek visions and revelations, John has God say this: "Fasten your eyes on him [Christ] alone because in him I have spoken and revealed all and in him you will discover even more than you ask and desire."[40]

Early Modern Mysticism

The focus on mysticism shifted in the seventeenth century from Spain to France. The spiritual energy in France at this time was

---

39. After John's poetry, one would do well to sample letters. *The Ascent of Mount Carmel* is best read after *The Living Flame of Love* and *The Spiritual Canticle*.

40. *The Ascent of Mount Carmel* 2.22.5; see also chapters 18-21, *The Collected Works of St. John of the Cross*.

extraordinary. One influence was the arrival in France of the writings of Teresa of Jesus along with several of her collaborators. If not too hackneyed to say, a who's who of French mysticism was involved in this mystical revival, e.g. Francis de Sales, Cardinal Berulle, Benedict Canfield, Barbe Acarie, Anne of Saint Batholomew, Anne of Jesus, Blaise Pascal, Madame Guyon and Felix Fenelon, to name only the better known.[41]

This mystical era was also a time of endless religious controversies especially over the relationship between grace and free will, predestination and Christ's will for universal salvation. Movements that began with fervor and good intentions ended in negativity, e.g. Jansenism and Quietism. Both of these movements adversely affected mysticism. A suspicion of mysticism that took root in the late seventeenth century intensified during the enlightenment of the eighteenth century and during the rationalism of the nineteenth century. In these centuries the mystics were interpreted individualistically, rationalistically and with little reference to mysticism's biblical, patristic and sacramental roots. Christianity for too long prized its mystical tradition too little.

The Future of Mysticism

Will the mystical tradition thrive in Christianity's third millennium? The interest is currently present, but much will depend on a willingness by Christians to become thoroughly acquainted with the mystical tradition in its biblical and liturgical contexts and on a willingness to read the signs of the times.

This chapter has quickly explored some moments in the Christian mystical tradition. There are many gaps in this coverage. Clearly few can digest the voluminous literature of the mystical tradition in all its fullness. But each one can find a few mystics who speak to one's heart and mind, whose experiences and instruction can make these mystics friends for the journey to God.

Where might these mystics be leading us at this stage of salvation history? David Tracy of the University of Chicago believes that important voices of the last hundred years are pointing us to a spirituality that is "mystico-prophetic." Tracy cites the voices of John

---

41. See Michael J. Buckley, "Seventeenth Century French Spirituality: Three Figures," 28-68, and Louis Dupré, "Jansenism and Quietism," 121-42 in *Christian Spirituality,* III.

Henry Newman, Thérèse of Lisieux, Baron Friedrich von Hügel, Maurice Blondel, Teilhard de Chardin, Joseph Maréchal, Jacques Maritain, Karl Rahner, Hans Urs von Balthasar, Edith Stein, etc. Tracy also mentions the liberation theologians who see the mystics as resources in the liberation of the human family.[42]

Finally, Tracy discovers in the lives and writings of Thomas Merton and Dorothy Day a reminder that the mystical tradition is a powerful resource for prophetic action. In these modern spiritual writers Tracy sees a church regaining its identity as the "presence of Christ's indwelling Spirit."[43] Mystics remind us that Christian growth in love of God and neighbor is the work of the Holy Spirit. The mystics are those who pray and live under the influence of this Spirit. As friends from the tradition the mystics can prepare us to welcome the Holy Spirit as the architect and "principal guide" of the spiritual life.[44]

The characteristics of mystical experience begin to characterize the communities where living in the presence of God is honored. Mystical experience is ineffable. It is also simple, unifying and integrating—all characteristics that raise the human spirit to a higher quality of life and dispose it to live more fully under the direction of the Holy Spirit. Moreover, the mystical encounter with the divine is experience, not theory. For the mystic the divine presence is felt. Yet mystical experience transcends the emotions because this experience occurs in the depths of the human spirit. Mystical experience is a transforming experience that makes one truly what one was intended to be—free and loving. Finally, the mystical experience is all gift, not the result of human effort. These are qualities that one finds in the reports by the mystics of their experience. They are also characteristics that make for a more fully human life lived in faith.

We began this chapter with a quotation from Karl Rahner about the mystical future of Christianity. This modern prophet of the mystical character of Christianity felt deeply the need to live under God's abiding influence. In 1980 Rahner imagined Ignatius of Loyola saying to modern Jesuits:

---

42. See Segundo Galilea, *The Future of Our Past: The Spanish Mystics Speak to Contemporary Spirituality* (Notre Dame: Ave Maria Press, 1985).

43. David Tracy, "Recent Catholic Spirituality: Unity amid Diversity," *Christian Spirituality* III, 143-73.

44. John of the Cross, *The Living Flame of Love* 3.46, *The Collected Works of St. John of the Cross* 691.

I have experienced God, the nameless and incomprehensible, the silent but near God, who turns to me in eternal Trinity....Whether one calls such experience mysticism or not is here unimportant....But I have met God, I have experienced God's own self.[45]

The category of mysticism is, as Rahner says, unimportant; it comes late in the tradition anyway. What counts in the mystical tradition is growth in love of God and love of neighbor by living out of the deepest of human capacities—the capacity for God. The mystics have much wisdom to offer those who struggle to become in their search for God free and loving. What Augustine heard in the garden we may take as an invitation to learn from the mystics: "Pick up and read, pick up and read."[46] Finally, John of the Cross has consoling words for those who desire to see the face of God: "If anyone is seeking God, the Beloved is seeking that person much more."[47]

Further Reading

Cunningham, Lawrence S., "Mystics," *The Catholic Heritage* (New York: Crossroad, 1983). This chapter introduces the mystics to those with only a vague notion of mysticism.

Dupré, Louis and James Wiseman, *Light from Light: An Anthology of Christian Mysticism* (New York: Paulist, 1988). See excellent General Introduction.

Egan, Harvey D., *Christian Mysticism: The Future of a Tradition* (New York: Pueblo, 1984). A useful anthology.

Egan, Keith J., "Mysticism," *The HarperCollins Dictionary of Religion*, ed. Jonathan Z. Smith (San Francisco: HarperCollins, 1995), pp. 186-89. A brief overview of Christian mysticism.

Katz, Steven T., ed., *Mysticism and Religious Traditions* (New York: Oxford University Press, 1983). Contains perceptive essays.

---

45. Leo J. O'Donovan, "To Lead Us into Mystery," *America* (16 June 1984) 456.

46. *Confessions* 8.12.29.

47. *The Living Flame of Love* 3.28, *The Collected Works of St. John of the Cross* 684.

Louth, Andrew, *The Origins of the Christian Mystical Tradition: From Plato to Denys* (Oxford: Clarendon, 1981). This is an important study of its subject.

Principe, Walter, "Mysticism: Its Meaning and Varieties," *Mystics and Scholars: The Calgary Conference on Mysticism 1976,* ed. H. Coward and T. Penelhum, *Sciences Religieuses,* Supplement, 13 (1977). A very helpful essay.

Underhill, Evelyn, *Mysticism* (New York: World Publishing, 1955). A modern classic.

Williams, Rowan, "Mysticism and Incarnation," *Teresa of Avila* (Harrisburg: Morehouse, 1991), pp. 143-73. A very perceptive essay.

Wiseman, James, "Mysticism," *The New Dictionary of Catholic Spirituality,* ed. Michael Downey (Collegeville: Liturgical Press, 1993). An insightful, brief account of Christian mysticism.

Exercises

(1) Read the Song of Songs. Make a list of passages that express the dynamism of human love as well as suggest the beauty of the encounter with God. Note especially some favorite passages of the mystics, e.g. 1:2; 2:16-17; 4:1,7; 6:1; 8:6. What do these passages tell you about the connection between human love and divine love?

(2) Read Paradiso, *Canto 33 of Dante's* Divine Comedy *where Saint Bernard asks the Virgin Mary to grant to Dante the grace of "seeing" God. List from this canto themes which characterize mystical experience. How well has Dante represented in this canto the mystical tradition?*

(3) Read aloud John of the Cross' poem "Dark Night." What is the story here of human love and how well does it help to understand loving union with God? Reflect on this paradox: this poem about love and about a "night more lovely than the dawn" is for John a story of the night experience of loss and pain.

(4) Make some suggestions about ways in which the Christian mystical tradition might be more fully retrieved by the church of the twenty-first century.

(5) Who is your favorite mystic? Why does she or he appeal to you?

8

Solitude in Community

What can we gain by sailing to the moon if we are not able to cross the abyss that separates us from ourselves?[1]

*M*any voices accuse modern culture of prizing solitude too little; yet one of those voices, Thomas Merton's, has aroused an intense and widespread interest in the recovery of solitude. To his dying day, Merton never ceased seeking solitude about which he thought and wrote constantly.[2] Solitude is central to the life and writings of this Trappist monk who knew so well the spiritual pulse of this age.

Solitude is key to becoming fully human and to becoming a spiritual person. Some perceive solitude as the antithesis of community. Solitude is, indeed, a paradoxical dimension of community but not its opposite. Every Christian is called to the community of New Testament discipleship. This community finds its ultimate model in the loving relationships of the triune God. The real paradox is this: solitude is a necessary component of community, a key ingredient in the relationships that constitutes community. So, this chapter is entitled: Solitude in Community.

Without solitude one runs the risk of conformism, unhealthy dependencies, a failure to discover and to respond to one's gifts, group illusions, mechanical relationships, an absence of mystery and much more. Yet solitude is not only a preparation for genuine community, it is an ongoing essential ingredient of any healthy community.

As mentioned above, modern philosophies, at least implicitly,

---

1. *The Wisdom of the Desert: Sayings of the Desert Fathers of the Fourth Century*, trans. Thomas Merton (New York: New Directions, 1960) 11.

2. Cf. R. A. Cashen, *Solitude in the Thought of Thomas Merton* (Kalamazoo: Cistercian Publications, 1981).

have treated solitude and community as opposites. Marxism sacrifices the person to community while radical existentialism affirms the person at the expense of community. However, the Christian tradition sees community as its core experience with solitude as crucial to the achievement of community. Solitude is a unique encounter with mystery, the mystery who is God and the mystery of one's self and others. The Jewish-Christian tradition has discovered that there is a special entree into these mysteries through solitude.

This chapter explores some key figures and events in the long tradition of solitude and consults the wisdom of this tradition by sampling some of the significant moments in the Jewish-Christian tradition. It is an exploration not of loneliness but of what has been called blessed solitude. No one escapes the anguish of loneliness, not even the dedicated hermit. However, while it knows loneliness, solitude transcends the pain of human isolation.

Solitude in the Hebrew Scriptures

In Genesis 2:18 one reads: "The Lord God said, 'It is not good that the man should be alone; I will make him a helper as his partner.'" Here is an affirmation of the social nature of women and men. But elsewhere one hears about a dimension of human society where solitude is the context for the encounter with the divine. Recall Jacob who dreamed of a ladder that reached from earth to heaven with God's angels ascending and descending (Gen 28:10-17). On another occasion the Lord stood beside this Jacob who "was left alone" and who wrestled with God. Jacob, in his solitude, is the one who contends with God—encounters the divine (Gen 32:24-32).

A memorable moment of solitude in the Hebrew scriptures is the experience of Moses on "Mount Horeb, the mountain of God" where "the angel of the Lord appeared to him in a flame of fire out of a bush...[and] Moses hid his face, for he was afraid to look at God." From this solitude God sent Moses to lead the Israelites out of Egyptian slavery. But first God instructed Moses: "Remove the sandals from your feet, for the place on which you are standing is holy ground" (Ex 3). Solitude discovers sacred places that nourish the human spirit, where, like Moses, one comes to know God and God's will. The wilderness is a place where divine revelation occurs.

The exodus event, Israel's escape from Egypt and the forty year sojourn in the wilderness, is a model for liberation. The Lord told

Moses and Aaron how to celebrate this deliverance: "This day shall be a day of remembrance for you. You shall celebrate it as a festival to the Lord..."(Ex 12:14). Solitude, like the vast Sinai wilderness, strips one of pretenses, petty attachments and dependence on human contrivances. In the desert Israel learned to depend on God alone. Solitude, in whatever shape it comes, is a place for liberation from illusions of all sorts.

Like Moses, Elijah the prophet was a pilgrim to Horeb/Sinai. There Elijah encountered the Lord on the same mountain where Moses had stood before the burning bush. Elijah grievously offended Queen Jezebel when he slaughtered the prophets of Baal. In one of the finest crafted narratives of the Old Testament, Elijah's journey through the wilderness, from Mount Carmel in the north to Horeb in the south, culminates in Elijah's meeting with God on this mountain (1 Kgs 19:1-16). That encounter was not in the expected and usual ways—in a great wind or in an earthquake or in fire, the ways Israel knew God to appear. Rather Elijah experienced God in "a sound of sheer silence," from which God sent Elijah to anoint Hazael, Jehu and Elisha. Once again the wilderness was the setting in which a great prophet of Israel was missioned by God.

Elijah's journey to Horeb reveals parallels with the common journey of faith. When the going gets tough, we, like Elijah, seek escape: "Then he lay down under the broom tree and fell asleep" (v. 5). "Get up and eat, otherwise the journey will be too much for you," says the angel of the Lord (v. 7). This arduous journey to Horeb of about 480 kilometers took forty days and forty nights and was a matter of life and death for Elijah. Not human but divine sustenance was needed. But Elijah persevered to the mountain, already made sacred by the Lord's encounter with Moses.

As early as Athanasius' *Life of Antony* (356), Elijah became a model for lovers of solitude,[3] and John Cassian considered the anchorites of the desert to be imitators of Elijah and of his follower Elisha as well as John the Baptist.[4]

---

3. Athanasius, *The Life of Antony and the Letter to Marcellinus,* trans. Robert C. Gregg (New York: Paulist Press, 1980) 37.

4. John Cassian, *Conferences,* trans. Colm Luibheid (New York: Paulist Press, 1985) 187.

Solitude in the Christian Scriptures

Moses and Elijah reached their fullest expression as archetypes of the experience of God at the transfiguration when Peter, James and John saw Moses and Elijah talking with Jesus (Lk 9:28-36). On the mountain of the transfiguration, Moses and Elijah experienced intimacy with Jesus as they had with God on Mount Horeb. Retreat from usual concerns makes space for intimacy with God, an intimacy that requires a leaving behind of life's pre-occupations by ascending the mountain, even if only metaphorically.

Discipleship, as the basic model of Christian living, calls for the imitation of Christ which, in the context of this chapter, is an imitation of the Jesus who regularly went off alone to pray: "In the morning, while it was still very dark, he got up and went out to a deserted place, and there he prayed" (Mk 1:35).[5] Jesus recommends that one find a hidden place to pray: "...whenever you pray, go into your room and shut the door and pray to your Father who is in secret..." (Mt 6:6).

Jesus is also a model of the desert or wilderness experience: "Jesus, full of the Holy Spirit, returned from the Jordan and was led by the Spirit in the wilderness, where for forty days he was tempted by the devil." Like Jesus, Christian hermits discovered that the wilderness is a place where demons confront the desert dweller. The presence of the Holy Spirit enables one to overcome these demons who become more stark and fearsome in the wilderness which lacks the usual supports of normal, communal life. Note that the foray into the wilderness by Jesus culminates in mission: "Then Jesus, filled with the power of the Spirit, returned to Galilee, and...he began to teach in their synagogues..." (Lk 4:14-15). In the wilderness one faces one's demons so as to be receptive to the Holy Spirit.

Many disciples since Jesus have relived his experience of the wilderness, e.g. Ignatius of Loyola (d. 1556) whose solitary experiences taught him God's will and who composed his *Spiritual Exercises* so that others may go aside for a period of silence and solitude to discern the will of God.

Solitude, though it can greatly benefit one physically and psychologically, is always for the sake of spiritual solitude and spiritual growth. Profoundly significant experiences of solitude in the life of Jesus were Gethsemane and his dying and rising. At Gethsemane

---

5. See also Lk 5:16, 6:12, 9:18 and 28, 11:1.

Jesus encountered the dark night experience, the exhaustion of human power. At Gethsemane Jesus foresaw the collapse of his ministry. His followers, having fallen asleep during his agony, betrayed him, denied him or ran away.[6] Jesus accepted this collapse of his ministry because to do so was his Father's will: "Not what I want but what you want" (Mk 14:36).

Jesus moved on to the depths of the terrible solitude of the cross where he felt abandoned by his Father: "My God, my God, why have you forsaken me?" (Mk 15:34).

Like Jesus, every human person faces death alone. Life's moments of solitude are a foretaste and preparation for the solitude of death. Martin Luther recognized that death occurs for each person one at a time: "The challenge of death comes to us all, and no one can die for another. Everyone must fight his own battle with death by himself, alone....I will not be with you then, nor you with me."[7] In an earlier time, Abba Theophilus, about to die, said: "You are blessed, Abba Arsenius, because you have always had this hour in mind."[8]

From the cross Jesus went into the deepest realms of solitude from which he was raised up by the Father, raised to live in eternal community with the Father and the Spirit. In his living, dying and rising Jesus is the archetype of Christian solitude. He fully embraced his humanity in and through the solitudes of his life, death and resurrection. Solitude offers the followers of Jesus the opportunity to accept one's redeemed humanity and to plunge more deeply into the baptismal identity of dying and rising with Jesus.

The desert or wilderness is a place where God feeds his people. A crowd looking for Jesus told him: "Our ancestors ate the manna in the wilderness; as it is written, 'He gave them bread from heaven.' ...Jesus said to them, 'I am the bread of life'" (Jn 6:31-35). The gospel writers described this event, the multiplication of loaves, as taking place in a deserted spot (Mk 6:32-35; 8:4; Mt 14:13; Lk 9:12) like the place where God provided manna for the Jews in the

---

6. David Stanley, *Jesus in Gethsemane* (New York: Paulist Press, 1980) 119-54.

7. Quoted in Dietrich Bonhoeffer, *Life Together* (London: SCM Press, 1954) 67.

8. *The Sayings of the Desert Fathers: The Alphabetical Collection,* trans. Benedicta Ward (Kalamazoo: Cistercian Publications, 1975) 70. Henceforth *Sayings.*

wilderness (Ex 16:1-36; Num 11:4-9). In solitude one receives the nourishment that God alone can give.

The habitual withdrawal of Jesus to places where he prayed alone sets an example for all who seek the face of God. If one wishes to pray with a pure and undivided heart, then one must also withdraw, at least occasionally, and, if not in the wilderness, at least from the noise and turbulence which keep one enmeshed in lesser concerns and deprived of the wisdom to be gained in solitude.

Although Jesus is the central archetype of Christian solitude, his precursor, John the Baptist, is an important symbol of solitude. John was a man of the wilderness where he "wore clothing of camel's hair with a leather belt around his waist, and his food was locusts and wild honey." John, in the words of Isaiah, was "the voice of one crying out in the wilderness" (Mt 3:3-4).

John's identification with the wilderness made him a natural patron of monasticism, but for all Christians John is a man of solitude who reveals how to prepare the way of the Lord. John's asceticism—he came "eating no bread and drinking no wine" (Lk 7:33)—created a space in Israel where the incarnate God could minister. The silence, the fasting and other practices that intensify solitude are for the sake of the emptiness to be filled by the overshadowing by the Holy Spirit who brings about the fullness of Christ within the human person. However, ascetical practices must never be blasphemous attacks on the sacredness of the human body but rather acts of liberation that free the human heart from enslavement to the trinkets of frivolous desire.

One may also recall from the New Testament the desert experience of the apostle Paul.

> But when God, who had set me apart before I was born and called me through his grace, was pleased to reveal his Son to me, so that I might proclaim him among the Gentiles, I did not confer with any human being nor did I go up to Jerusalem to those who were already apostles before me, but I went away at once into Arabia... (Gal 1:15-17).

The call of prophets to minister God's word is once again associated with the experience of solitude. Every Christian is called to prophetic action. The call to this action is often heard in the experience of solitude.

Solitude in the Early Christian Tradition

The first heroines and heroes of the early Christian church were the martyrs who forfeited their lives for their faith in Jesus and all those who remained unmarried for the sake of the kingdom. Martyrdom like all death is an experience endured alone even if the martyr is surrounded by a crowd. Virginity or celibacy is a choice to live apart from the sexual expression of marriage. Martyrdom and celibacy are chosen solitudes not possible on one's own. The French speak of *cas limit* situations that can only be embraced through help beyond one's own power. Grace, God's loving presence, makes the solitude of martyrdom and celibacy possible and fruitful for those called to witness to the value of this solitude embraced for the kingdom of God. Martyrdom and celibacy are counter-cultural moves discerned, embraced and empowered within graced solitude.

Once Christians were able to practice their faith freely and publicly in the early fourth century, monasticism became a popular way to follow Jesus. Men and women went to Egypt and Palestine to become disciples in the wilderness. This wilderness had captured the imagination of Jews and Christians ever since Israel's exodus. In the monastic experience of the wilderness the archetypal figure of solitude is Antony (d. 356) who gave up a prosperous inheritance to live in the wilderness. *The Life of Antony* by Athanasius (d. 373) became a powerful Christian conversion story and a wondrous advertisement for the monastic vocation.

Antony's story thrilled Augustine who mentioned a man in Trier whom this story "set on fire." Antony's response to a passage from the gospel of Matthew (19:21) inspired Augustine to seek the Lord's will in the scriptures.[9] Tradition refers to Antony as the father of monks and especially as the father of hermits. Jean Leclercq has called *The Life of Antony* "a living text, a means of formation of monastic life."[10] Augustine's enthusiasm for this archetypal hermit ensured that Antony's story would be read widely in the middle ages and into our own time. Anyone interested in solitude should "pick up and read"[11] this powerful portrait of Antony.

The monasticism of the deserts of Syria, Egypt and Palestine

---

9. Augustine, *Confessions*, trans. Henry Chadwick (New York: Oxford University Press, 1992) 8.6.15; 8.12.29.

10. Jean Leclercq, *The Love of Learning and the Desire for God,* 2nd ed. (New York: Fordham University Press, 1974) 125.

11. *Confessions* 8.12.29.

acts as a paradigm for Christian religious life, and in fact for any Christian experience of solitude. Leclercq writes that "during each monastic revival, they hark back to ancient Egypt; they want, they say, to revive Egypt, to inaugurate a new Egypt and they call upon St. Antony, his example and his writings."[12] From the late third century desert monasticism has cast a spell upon Christians. The desire for intimacy with God drew Christians into the wilderness with echoes of Hosea's words (2:14): "I will now allure her, and bring her into the wilderness, and speak tenderly to her."

The wisdom of the desert era is captured in the pithy sayings of the desert. These koan-like sayings were responses by fathers and mothers of the desert who passed on their wisdom to those disciples who found themselves puzzled by ways of the wilderness. Here is an interaction between two abbas:

> Abba Isaiah questioned Abba Macarius saying, "Give me a word." The old man said to him, "Flee from men." Abba Isaiah said to him, "What does it mean to flee from men?" The old man said, "It means to sit in your cell and weep for your sins."[13]

Long involved explanations and wordiness are out of place in the vastness of the desert. The desert is for the silence that allows one to know oneself better and permits one to listen to God. Wordiness pollutes the heart. "It is said of Abba Agathon that for three years he lived with a stone in his mouth, until he had learnt to keep silence."[14]

There is inexhaustible wisdom in these sayings, garnered from struggles with the harshness of the desert where one lives always at the edge of human existence. The desert sayings are classic formulations of the wisdom of the wilderness. Like all classics, they wait to be heard by each generation that is willing to let their wisdom penetrate to the ear of the spirit. These sayings foster self-knowledge, a key experience of the desert. They explore deftly the frailties and illusions that afflict human beings on the spiritual journey where pride and other deceptions assert themselves in numerous subtle ways.

Douglas Burton-Christie's study of the sayings of the desert has demonstrated the centrality of scripture in these sayings and in the

---

12. Leclercq 125.
13. *Sayings* 112, n. 27.
14. *Sayings* 19, n. 15.

lives of the monks of the desert. He writes that the texts of scripture "...were proclaimed, recited (in solitude and in community), memorized, ruminated upon, and discussed. They served as a basic frame of reference and primary source of sustenance to the early monastics."[15] Christian solitude without the word of God is doomed to futility. The desert, without this word, becomes a place of madness, lacking in the divine wisdom that makes sanity and holiness possible. The desert is for dialogue with the Holy Spirit who makes the desert blossom: "The wilderness and the dry land shall be glad, and the desert shall rejoice and blossom; like the crocus it shall blossom abundantly...."[16]

Desert dwellers knew that the wilderness was a special place for listening to the Holy Spirit: "One of the Fathers asked Abba Poemen, 'Who is he who says, "I am a companion of all who fear Thee" (Ps 119:63)?' And the old man said, 'It is the Holy Spirit who says that.'"[17] The monk or nun in the wilderness knows from experience that he or she cannot do without the companionship of the Holy Spirit who speaks through the scriptures. Moreover, the psalms held a unique role in the life of the desert. These Hebrew songs which cover the whole range of religious sentiment were never long off the lips of the hermits and made up much of communal prayer that hermits prayed when they joined communities on weekends.

Moreover, the psalms were easily committed to memory in this highly oral culture. Memorized psalms did their work when the hermit was engaged in daily activities and even at times of hospitality. In the middle ages one story goes like this: Ask a hermit what his prayer book is, and he will tell you that it is the psalter. If you ask him where he keeps his psalter, he points to his head. The psalms, a unique resource for the solitary, develop a language of prayer and keep one in touch with the strong feelings that often erupt when one seeks God in solitude. Like the solitaries of old, one ought to bring the psalms as friends when one ventures into the wilderness.

While there was a great variety of desert dwellers, e.g. monks, nuns, hermits, anchorites, ascetics, for simplicity's sake we shall

---

15. Douglas Burton-Christie, *The Word in the Desert: Scripture and the Holiness in Early Christian Monasticism* (New York: Oxford University Press, 1993) 298.

16. Is 35:1-2.

17. *Sayings* 156, n. 136.

refer to both the women and men of the desert as monks, from the word *monachos* meaning a solitary person, rather than get lost in interminable distinctions. Neat categories do not do justice to the identities of hermits and others whose lifestyles were much more fluid than now imagined.

In the desert, monks encountered demons who acted as a revelation of the evil that stirs in the hearts of even seasoned monks. It is easy to see the evil done by others when one mixes with other people in a crowd, but in solitude one's own evil becomes graphically apparent. That is why tears often occur when one takes time aside to search one's heart. It was said of Arsenius that "...he had a hollow in his chest channelled out by the tears which fell from his eyes all his life...."[18] The desert was and is a place to mourn for one's sins and the sins of others. *Penthos* or compunction for sin was a key experience among the desert dwellers.

But the desert and solitude are every bit as much opportunities for discovering one's gifts and for learning to live with those gifts honestly and humbly. The discovery of one's gifts may also elicit tears—tears of gratitude. In the desert people knew first-hand the gift of tears. In solitude the gift of tears cleanses the heart of its illusions as one grieves over sins and weeps in joy for God's gifts.

Because the women and the men of the desert lived without the usual protection of family and urban life, they endured very primal experiences: the discovery of sinfulness and gifts, the constant struggle to become virtuous, temptations to anger and to sexual fantasies, and the demands of becoming a loving person. Therefore, they realized the need for guidance. Spiritual direction as practiced today was not known in the desert, but the seeds of spiritual direction were sown when desert dwellers sought help from their elders in the wilderness. Scripture and a word from an elder were the companions that one needed in the desert. Solitude arouses awareness that one needs the guidance and companionship of someone experienced in the ways of the wilderness.

A classical source of information about the desert experience of the early monks is contained in the writings of John Cassian who lived the monastic life at Bethlehem and who with his friend Germanus visited the monks and hermits of Egypt. His *Institutes* offer principles and particulars of monastic life, while his *Conferences* are reports of dialogues that he and Germanus conducted with the elders of Egyptian monasticism. The conferences

---

18. *Sayings* 16, n. 41.

are a must for anyone who seeks a first-hand account of the spirit of the monastic desert. The Benedictine *Rule* recommends the *Institutes* and the *Conferences*.[19] Saint Dominic kept Cassian's *Conferences* at his bedside,[20] and Thomas Aquinas read Cassian every day. Aquinas' early biographer, William Tocco, quotes Thomas as saying: "From this reading I reap devotion, and that makes it easier for me to lift myself up into speculation. So, the *affectus,* attachment to God, widens into devotion, and thanks to it, the intellect ascends toward the highest summits."[21] The *Conferences* of Cassian are a vivid portrayal of the early monastic wisdom. Purity of heart, self-knowledge, asceticism, sorrow for sins, the desert prayer of fire, discernment and a host of other themes appear in these *Conferences.*

Theoretically John Cassian considered the life of the hermit who lived alone in the wilderness to be the highest expression of the monastic calling. However, he realized the dangers that befell the hermit who was not prepared for the rigors of the eremitic life. Few were ready for its demands according to Cassian. One of his *Conferences* is an interview with Abba John who spent thirty years in a cenobium, twenty years as a hermit, and then returned to the cenobium "to aim at a lower target and hit it more easily, and to avoid the risk of failing at the effort after a loftier way."[22]

Recognition that the cenobium, the community, was a safer way than eremitism soon became a constant of monastic wisdom. A strong proponent of community over the eremitic life, though not exclusively so, was Basil of Caesarea, the monastic lawgiver of eastern Christianity.[23] The Benedictine *Rule* emphasizes community and speaks of the "cenobites...who belong to a monastery, where they serve under a rule and an abbot." For Benedict, anchorites or hermits have come through the test of living in a monastery for a long time, and have passed beyond the first fervor of monastic life.

---

19. *RB1980: The Rule of St. Benedict,* ed. Timothy Fry et al. (Collegeville: Liturgical Press, 1981) chapter 73.

20. M.-H. Vicaire, *Saint Dominic and His Times* (New York: McGraw-Hill, 1964) 43.

21. Jean Leclercq, François Vandenbroucke, Louis Bouyer, *The Spirituality of the Middle Ages* (New York: Desclee, 1968) 331.

22. "The Conferences of Cassian," *Western Asceticism,* trans. Owen Chadwick (Philadelphia: Westminster Press, 1958) 281.

23. Basil, *Long Rules,* cited in Tomas Spidlik, *The Spirituality of the Christian East,* trans. A. P. Gythiel (Kalamazoo: Cistercian Publications, 1986) 160.

Thanks to the help and guidance of many, they are now trained to fight against the devil. They have built up their strength and go from the battle in the ranks of their brothers to the single combat of the desert. Self-reliant now, without the support of another, they are ready with God's help to grapple single-handed with the vices of body and mind.[24]

What Cassian, Basil, Benedict and others were grappling with was the social nature of the human person, the need for companions on the spiritual journey, the corporate character of Christianity and the dangers of extended aloneness that can become isolation rather than solitude. Isolation from human companionship can make one odd and can expose one to temptations that go beyond one's endurance. Monastic writers appreciated the grace of being alone with God, but they also knew that community is a grace that protects one against the demons and the illusions of the wilderness. Facing long periods of solitude requires spiritual maturity.

Already in fourth century monasticism there was a semi-eremitic life that recognized that hermits needed at least a modicum of community. In the middle ages the Camaldolese, the Carthusians, and the first Carmelites were semi-eremitic orders who recognized the need for the guidance of a community.

But, on the other hand, is it not the struggle of every human person, whether religious, clergy, married, or single, to create within community enough solitude to attend to the need for quiet and seclusion? The Holy Spirit, if listened to attentively, will lead one further into solitude if that is God's call. Teresa of Avila recognized that her nuns could be contemplatives in community only if that community were small enough to make solitude possible.

From the stoics, Christian monks as they lived in the wilderness borrowed the term *apatheia*—without emotion—to describe a condition in which the emotions no longer enslaved the monk. But the term can be misunderstood as a crushing of the human spirit. John Cassian avoided this term. In its place he used the phrase "purity of heart"—a unified and undivided heart, capable of love and contemplation. Solitude purifies the heart and prepares it for this purity by liberating the God-given desires of the heart. *Apatheia,* purity of heart, is freedom to love which is the purpose of the Christian life whether in the wilderness or in the city.

In the desert the Jesus Prayer was born and developed. This

---

24. *Rule of St. Benedict* chapter 1, 168-69.

remembrance of Jesus by the repetition of his name or later by the use of the phrase "Lord Jesus, Son of God, have mercy on me" stamped eastern Christianity with a unique approach to prayer. With the Jesus Prayer is associated *hesychia,* stillness and image-less prayer. Further development of the Jesus Prayer and *hesychia* occurred on Mount Athos, the Greek monastic peninsula where monasteries of men seeking solitude were founded from the end of the tenth century. A contemporary revival of the Jesus Prayer or other mantra-like prayers prepares one to come into solitude focused on God. Solitude is not an aimless roaming of the mind, but a time for attention to God and God's affairs.

Early monasticism recognized that liturgy provided contact for anchorites with a worshiping community. Monks in the desert who lived at a distance from their churches returned on weekends for communal worship, the divine offices and eucharist. More research needs to be done on the intense devotion of the early monks and nuns to the celebration of the eucharist and to the consecrated bread which they often carried to the ill and to those at a distance, and which they sometimes kept reserved in their cells.

While cenobitic monasticism recognized the danger of the solitary life for someone not prepared for being alone, it also made sure that, within community, there were opportunities for solitude. Thus *lectio divina,* mentioned in the Benedictine *Rule,* was an insurance that the monk and the nun had access to solitude. Whenever monasticism has neglected *lectio divina,* what St. Bernard called the "wine cellar of the Holy Spirit," the monastery became not a community but a pious federation of individuals. *Lectio divina,* leisure for God, transforms isolation into solitude. Rules of silence are another attempt to provide solitude as are the provisions in some communities for separated cells.[25] Retreats and days of recollection are attempts to secure solitude for religious and laity who otherwise may have little opportunity for it.

The monastic life is a source of wisdom for the Christian life. Hermits may appear to live on the fringes of society, but if the hermit is truly living in the presence of God, he or she is not on the margin but at the center of Christian existence. Hermits are witnesses to the universal call to live in the presence of God so that the rest of us may know where our center is. Hermits, like the early

---

25. Rule of St. Albert (Rule of the Carmelites), *Albert's Way,* ed. Michael Mulhall (Barrington: Province of Most Pure Heart of Mary, 1989) 4-5.

martyrs, are witnesses to the reality of the living God in whose presence Elijah stood (1 Kgs 18).

Solitude in the Middle Ages

The great experiment in the Egyptian desert inspired a renewed interest in solitude during the eleventh and twelfth centuries in western Europe. One of the new orders, the Carthusians, was said to renew the "ancient fervor of Egypt."[26] This medieval love affair with solitude arose among religious and laity, with women taking a prominent role in this movement. While there were individual hermits and anchorites in this era, new orders practiced what Jean Leclercq called "collective eremitism." These orders emphasized solitude but within a cenobitic context: the Camaldolese and the Carthusians are perhaps the best remembered of these new orders. An early Carthusian wrote: "Our chief anxiety and the object of our life is to care for silence and the solitude of the cell."[27] Since the days in Egypt, monks had heard this advice: "Go, sit in your cell, and your cell will teach you everything."[28] The cell was where conversation with God took place.

Important to the medieval hermit was the theological realization that solitude for the Christian is not isolation, not a negative attitude about one's neighbors. On the contrary, a hermit referred to himself or herself as *ecclesiola,* a little church. This was a recognition of the interdependence of all Christians. The Christian has been baptized into the body of Christ, one body with many members. Christian solitude, being with the Christ within, is a sacramental activity, initiated at baptism and celebrated at eucharist where individual Christians come together to partake in a common meal at the table of the Lord. Separation from others so that one may be alone with God is not isolation but an act of solidarity, a manifestation of love for one's sisters and brothers as well as a witness to them of the primacy of God in their lives. The Christian solitary is an ecclesial and sacramental person.

The medieval hermit had a sense of the sacramentality of creation as a manifestation of the presence of God. Thus creation supplied symbols that connected the hermit with the divine presence. Stories tell of the affinity of the medieval hermit with wild animals

---

26. *The Spirituality of the Middle Ages* 157.
27. Ibid. 154 (Guigo I).
28. *Sayings* 118.

who symbolize a restoration of paradise, and early monasticism saw itself as an anticipation of heaven and as an angelic existence.

When Francis of Assisi and Dominic Guzman initiated the mendicant movement in the early thirteenth century, they brought monasticism into the marketplace. Would not hermits be out of place among these friars who were busy ministering to the growing number of town dwellers in Europe? Not so. Francis himself often sought solitude and made provisions for Franciscan hermitages where several friars acted as "mothers" to their "sons" who lived in solitude.[29] About the same time some lay hermits gathered in cells around a chapel on Mount Carmel. Within less than half a century these Carmelite hermits became friars, but their early eremitic existence eventually gave birth to Carmelite mysticism.[30] The friars of the middle ages affirmed the intimate connection of solitude with ministry. As spiritual directors to anchorites and others, the friars fostered solitude in the later middle ages.

Looking back to early eremitism and to the resurgence of the solitary life in the middle ages, Jean Leclercq detected certain characteristics of a hermit's life: more prayer, greater austerity and an intensification of devotion to the humanity of Jesus. The hermit found congenial the identification with Jesus contained in this aphorism: naked to follow the naked Christ. Solitude was conducive to the discovery of this identity.

A picturesque movement in England during the middle ages consisted of anchorites who lived in anchorholds attached to parish churches. The anchorite, supported by parishioners, participated in liturgies and acted as spiritual guides to those who sought spiritual guidance. Julian of Norwich is now the best known of these anchorites who sought solitude in the midst of busy parish life and whose wisdom, gained in solitude, was much prized by laity, religious and clergy.[31] The Reformation brought the anchoritic movement to an near end in England and elsewhere in Europe.

Neither Protestantism nor Catholicism emphasized solitude very much in the post-reformation centuries. Though too simplistic to

---

29. *St. Francis of Assisi: Writings and Early Biographies,* ed. Marion Habig (Chicago: Franciscan Herald Press, 1973) 38, 72-73.

30. Keith J. Egan, "Carmelite Spirituality," *The New Dictionary of Catholic Spirituality,* ed. Michael Downey (Collegeville: 1993) 117-25.

31. Ann K. Warren, *Anchorites and Their Patrons in Medieval England* (Berkeley: University of California Press, 1985); Julian of Norwich, *Showings* (New York: Paulist Press, 1978).

say, Protestants fostered scripture and fellowship while Catholics concentrated on the sacraments and on parish life. Solitude was not a high priority with either group, especially as mysticism fell from favor in the late seventeenth century. Solitude has often been the birthplace of mysticism. The hermit knew that contemplation could be the gift that capped solitude.

John of the Cross, a Spanish mystic of the sixteenth century, who had wanted to be a Carthusian monk and who did not, as a Carmelite, neglect opportunities for physical solitude, emphasized in his writings spiritual solitude, an inner solitude, where the heart is free to be alone with God. In one of his poems, John wrote this of the soul's solitude:

> She lived in solitude,
> and now in solitude has built her nest;
> and in solitude he guides her,
> he alone, who bears
> in solitude the wound of love.[32]

Solitude in the Twentieth Century

In the search for God solitude always has a role. Space does not allow for the exploration of moments where solitude emerged as a value even in the post-Reformation era. So we jump ahead to the twentieth century when a rugged Frenchman lived alone in the depths of the Sahara Desert. The life of the hermit Charles de Foucauld has stirred the Christian imagination with a renewed appreciation for solitude. De Foucauld's followers, the Little Brothers of Jesus and the Little Sisters of Jesus, have moved into the wilderness of modern cities. Their hour of silent prayer before the Blessed Sacrament after a day at a secular job is a reminder of the deep devotion to the eucharistic presence that goes back to the early deserts of Palestine and Egypt. Once better understood, this tradition of prayer before Jesus in the eucharist awaits an integration with the contemporary emphasis on the eucharist as meal.

The twentieth century's prophet of solitude is, without a doubt, Thomas Merton whose life and writings turn over and over again to

---

32. "The Spiritual Canticle," Stanza 35, *The Collected Works of St. John of the Cross,* trans. Kieran Kavanaugh and Otilio Rodriguez, rev. ed. (Washington, DC: Institute of Carmelite Studies, 1991) 607.

the theme of solitude.[33] In fact, Merton's writings are a school for solitude. Merton felt that his cenobitic Trappist monastery did not provide the solitude for which he yearned. As a culmination to these yearnings, Merton moved permanently to a hermitage in the woods at Gethsemani Abbey three years before his death. This lover of solitude has reminded countless readers of the human need for authentic solitude. There one can discard the false self, discover the true self and be more fully present to God. Merton, who "always felt a great attraction to the life of perfect solitude," saw it as the source of compassion and gentleness. In a journal entry from January 1950 he wrote:

> It is in deep solitude that I find the gentleness with which I can truly love my brothers. The more solitary I am, the more affection I have for them. It is pure affection, and filled with reverence for the solitude of others. Solitude and silence teach me to love my brothers for what they are....[34]

Paradoxes fill the days of the hermit, and Merton discovered that solitude is a place where these paradoxes become manifest. Emptiness for the sake of fullness, language that imposes silence, solitude that is neither practical nor useful, and solitude that is, in fact, a sharing in the life of God and of one's neighbors are some of the paradoxes noted by Merton.[35] For anyone who seeks solitude for a day, a weekend or a lifetime, Thomas Merton's advice is apropos: "Do not flee to solitude from community. Find God first in the community, then he will lead you to solitude."

Like hermits of old, Merton suggests that one turn in solitude to the psalms: "The Psalms are the true garden of the solitary and the scriptures are his paradise." Is not solitude also a place where one learns what everyone on the spiritual journey must learn: all of life and love are gift? That was Merton's conviction: "The great work of the solitary life is gratitude."[36] Merton expressed his most cherished convictions in poetry. Here he sang of solitude:

---

33. See note 2 above.

34. Thomas Merton, *The Sign of Jonas* (New York: Harcourt, Brace, 1953) 10, 268.

35. Thomas Merton, "The Solitary Life," *The Monastic Journey,* ed. Patrick Hart (Garden City: Doubleday Image, 1978) 200, 210.

36. Thomas Merton, *Thoughts in Solitude* (Garden City: Doubleday Image, 1958) 114, 121, 119.

If you seek a heavenly light
I, solitude, am your professor.

· ·

For I, Solitude, am thine own self:
I, Nothingness, am thy All.
I, Silence, thy Amen![37]

A modern theologian, Dietrich Bonhoeffer, writing about community, devoted a chapter to "The Day Alone," where he shared this conviction about solitude: "One who wants fellowship without solitude plunges into the void of words and feelings, and one who seeks solitude without fellowship perishes in the abyss of vanity, self-infatuation, and despair." Bonhoeffer adds: "Let him who cannot be alone beware of community."[38]

Conclusion

There is much more to be said about solitude, but we are sure that the elders of the desert would caution against wordiness. So after this sampling of the Jewish-Christian tradition of solitude, what does one conclude?

First of all, this review does not intend to send anyone headlong into the Sahara. Yet this tradition of solitude invites one to reflect on wisdom unearthed by hermits. Quiet times, some silence, some time alone is necessary for everyone who seeks sanity and holiness. Moreover, the search for God and the discernment of important decisions in life require reflection and prayer that only solitude makes possible.

Yet even brief periods of solitude are not easy to come by in our often chaotic culture. But we must not be victims of a noisy culture that deprives us of the time and space to embrace our humanity. To be fully human and to be wise, one must have a "listening heart,"[39] which is the fruit of solitude. The example of hermits from the desert or of anchorites like Julian may not send one to deserts, forests or anchorholds, but the wisdom these solitaries have dis-

---

37. "Song: If You Seek..." *The Collected Poems of Thomas Merton* (New York: New Directions, 1977) 340-41.

38. Bonhoeffer, 68.

39. Solomon sought and received from God a *leb somea,* a listening heart (1 Kgs 3:9).

covered in the crucible of solitude should send us, at least now and then, for a day alone at the beach or by a lake, a walk in the woods, a day of recollection, to a directed retreat, or to wherever there is enough silence and solitude to become whole, wise, happy and holy. God gave the Jews manna in the desert: Jesus gave those who followed him bread in a deserted place. The Holy Spirit feeds with the bread of wisdom those who seek God in solitude. Modern culture may remain selfish, violent and compulsive unless enough of us seek our true selves in whatever solitude we can manage.

Further Reading

Egan, Keith J., *Solitude and Community: The Paradox of Life and Prayer,* (seven audio-cassette tapes) (Kansas City: Credence Cassettes, 1981). These tapes survey the tradition of solitude and its connection with community.

Gould, Graham, *The Desert Fathers on Monastic Community* (Oxford. Clarendon Press, 1993). This book deftly explores the meaning of community among the desert dwellers.

Kelty, Matthew, *My Song Is of Mercy: Flute Solo and Sermons and Talks*, ed. Michael Downey (Kansas City: Sheed and Ward, 1994). With lovely imagery, especially in *Flute Solo,* a Trappist monk shares his experience of solitude.

Louth, Andrew, *The Wilderness of God* (London, 1992), Louth explores creatively various themes in the tradition of solitude.

Merton, Thomas, "Notes for a Philosophy of Solitude," *Disputed Questions* (New York: Farrar, Strauss and Cudahy, 1960) 177-207. This essay contains some of Merton's fundamental attitudes to solitude.

Thomas Merton: Spiritual Master, ed. Lawrence S. Cunningham (New York: Paulist Press, 1992). Contains selections from Merton's *Thoughts in Solitude* and *The Wisdom of the Desert.*

Exercises

(1) Read 1 Kings 17–19 and record how Elijah was both a busy prophet and a solitary pilgrim and why monks looked to Elijah for inspiration.

(2) Using the section above on solitude in the Christian scriptures, record and comment on the importance of solitude in the life of Jesus. What does Jesus' habit of solitude mean for the modern Christian?

(3) Taking a hint from the philosopher Hans Georg Gadamer, play with some of the sayings of the desert. What wisdom do they contain for modern living? For the sayings, see above, notes 1 and 8.

(4) Design for yourself, amid your present responsibilities, several opportunities for solitude where you can be alone with God.

(5) Write for a friend reasons why some regular moments of silence and solitude might bring greater peace to his or her life.

9

Friendship

"No one has greater love than this, to lay down one's life for one's friends" (Jn 15:13).

Few joys compare to the joy of friendship. A walk, a meal, even a letter from a friend are memorable gifts. Friends, however, too often are taken for granted, and today friendship is considered by many as a mere secular asset. This chapter, on the other hand, explores the religious and spiritual dimensions of friendship.

Not even Aristotle need be invoked to show the necessity of friends for a satisfying and fulfilling life.[1] Stories of friendship among the great and among the small abound. These stories reveal how gracious and good life is when it is shared with friends, and stories of friendship instill hope when dark moments threaten to becloud one's days.

Stories of Friendship

One of the most poignant stories in the Jewish-Christian tradition concerns the unlikely friendship of Jonathan and David: "The soul of Jonathan was bound to the soul of David, and Jonathan loved him as his own soul." Jonathan "took great delight in David" and made a covenant with his friend David to which the son of King Saul was eminently faithful. When Saul and Jonathan were killed in battle, David sang a lamentation for the king and his son in which the future King David mourned Jonathan's death with these words:

I am distressed for you, my brother Jonathan; greatly beloved were you to me; your love to me was wonderful, passing the love of women (1 Sam 18:1-3; 19:1, 14-17; 2 Sam 17:26).

---

1. *Nicomachean Ethics* VIII, 1155a.

The bible uses the words "friend" and "friendship" far less often than Greco-Roman literature. That may be so because scripture so emphasizes the notion of covenant.[2] But the covenantal relationship has much in common with friendship. Think of the tender covenant of faithfulness between the daughter-in-law, Ruth, and her mother-in-law, Naomi, who became Ruth's friend:

> Where you go, I will go;
> where you lodge, I will lodge;
> your people shall be my people,
> and your God my God.
> Where you die, I will die—
> there will I be buried.
> May the Lord do thus and so to me,
> and more as well,
> if even death parts me from you (Ruth 1:16-17).

Indeed, the Hebrew scriptures have a clear sense of friendship with God. Job talked of the time when "the friendship of God was upon my tent" (29:4), and Psalm 25:14 says that "the friendship of the Lord is for those who fear him." Those who have wisdom "obtain friendship with God" (Wis 7:14). Human friendship is also a notable biblical value: "Wine and music gladden the heart, but the love of friends is better than either" (Sir 40:20).

We now return to stories of friendship. One doesn't think of popes as weary and depressed, but Pope Gregory the Great (d. 604) wrote that he was "feeling quite depressed" and "sick at heart." Gregory missed the peace and quiet of the monastery, and he minded the "noisy wrangling" among those who approached him as bishop of Rome. Gregory sought peace and consolation in conversation with the deacon Peter "who had been a very dear friend to me from his early youth and was my companion in the study of sacred scripture." This story of friendship appears in Gregory's *Dialogues,* a text that was read widely throughout the middle ages and that remains fresh and fascinating to this day.[3]

Two friendships between a woman and a man deserve a word here. The first is the mutually enriching relationship between

---

2. S.K. Williams, "Friendship," *Harper's Bible Dictionary,* ed. Paul Achtenmeier (San Francisco: Harper & Row) 322.

3. Gregory the Great, *Dialogues,* trans. Odo J. Zimmerman (New York: Fathers of the Church, 1959) 3.

Francis of Assisi and Clare. This first woman Franciscan, during the twenty-seven years after the death of Francis, lived gospel discipleship so faithfully that her life is a witness to the gospel and to her friendship with Francis. Inspired by Francis, Clare lived gospel poverty in "her unique feminine way."[4] Friends do not erase each other's uniqueness but rather enhance it, just as friendship is not an absorption into God but a union of two unique realities.

About the same time at Bologna a friendship between Blessed Jordan of Saxony, the successor to Saint Dominic as master general of the Dominicans, and a Dominican nun, Blessed Diana d'Andalo, blossomed like a lovely flower. Unfortunately Diana's letters to Jordan do not survive. Only Jordan's letters to Diana and others to her convent at Bologna are extant. These letters are full of tenderness and wisdom about a journey to God rooted in the experience of Christ. Here are selected lines that Jordan wrote to Diana:

"I do not requite your love fully; of that I am deeply convinced; you love me more than I love you." "Yet I cannot wonder that you are sad when I am far from you since, do what I may, I myself cannot but be sad that you are far from me." "The longer we are separated from one another, the greater becomes our desire to see one another again." "Yet whatever we may write to each other matters little, beloved: within our hearts is the ardour of our love in the Lord whereby you speak to me and I to you continuously in those wordless outpourings of charity which no tongue can express nor letter contain."[5]

These sentiments were written by a friar to a nun both of whom were totally committed to celibacy. Between them was a warm and caring relationship fully integrated into their spiritual lives.

Now to the twentieth century. A beautiful young woman, Raissa Ousmanoff, a Jewish exile from Russia and a university student in Paris, wrote about her first meeting with her husband, Jacques Maritain whom she called "the greatest of my friends." The following words from the first volume of her autobiography, *We Have Been*

---

4. Clare of Assisi, *Early Documents,* ed. and trans. Regis Armstrong (New York: Paulist Press, 1988) 10.

5. *To Heaven with Diana! A Study of Jordan of Saxony and Diana d'Andalo with a Translation of the Letters of Jordan,* trans. Gerald Vann (Chicago: Henry Regnery, 1965) 84, 136, 138.

Friends Together, reveal how important friendship was to Raissa
Maritain.

> I was leaving M. Matruchot's plant physiology class one day in a
> rather downcast frame of mind, when I saw coming toward me a
> young man with a gentle face, a heavy shock of blond hair, a light
> beard and a slightly stoop-shouldered carriage....After class he
> would walk home with me....Our conversations were endless....
> Jacques Maritain had the same profound concerns as I; the same
> questions tormented him, the same desire for truth wholly moved
> him.[6]

Raissa Maritain described her engagement to her friend with
feeling that is still palpable.

> Our engagement took place in the simplest way, without any pro-
> posal. We were alone in my parents' living room. Jacques was sit-
> ting on the rug, close to my chair; it suddenly seemed to me that
> we had always been near each other, and that we would always be
> so. Without thinking, I put out my hand and stroked his hair; he
> looked at me and all was clear to us. The feeling flowed through
> me that always—for my happiness and my salvation (I thought
> precisely that, although then the word "salvation" meant nothing
> to me)—that always my life would be bound up with Jacques'. It
> was one of those tender and peaceful feelings which are like a gift
> flowing from a region higher than ourselves, illuminating the
> future and deepening the present.[7]

Friendship became a key to the intellectual and spiritual lives of
the Maritains. Throughout their lives Raissa and Jacques gathered
around them circles of friends—poets, painters, film-makers, theologians and philosophers. One Sunday a month they invited a circle
of friends to share intellectual conversation and prayer.[8]

Raissa Maritain's autobiography is the story of her friendship

---

6. *We Have Been Friends Together* and *Adventures in Grace: The
Memoirs of Raissa Maritain,* 2 vols., trans. Julie Kernan (Garden City:
Image Books Edition, 1961) I, 41-42.

7. Ibid. 84-85.

8. Jacques Maritain, "Thomist Study Circles and Their Annual
Retreats," *Notebooks,* trans. Joseph W. Evans (Albany: Magi Books, 1984)
133-85.

with her spouse, Jacques, but it is also a story of the friends so important to them throughout their lives. Raissa described the friendship of Jacques with Ernest Psichari who was killed in World War I.

> Jacques was as enthusiastic about Ernest as Ernest was about Jacques....Their very different dispositions were absolutely congenial; their qualities complemented rather than opposed each other. They were alike in an equal capacity for enthusiasm, an equal love for ideas....From the beginning their affection was very deep. According to an invariable trait in his character, Jacques surrounded Ernest with solicitude; when Jacques was ill Ernest was beside himself. On one grave occasion he braved the danger of contagion; nothing could stop him from entering the room where the invalid lay ill of smallpox.[9]

Friendship stories celebrate life's splendid moments. The stories above are but a few of countless tales of friendships that speak of the beauty and power of human friendship. Stories like these keep one from becoming cynical about life and others. Stories about friends, their loyalty to each other and the joy that friends bring each other implant hope in the human spirit.

The Classical Tradition

Ever so briefly we shall sample some wisdom about friendship found in the Greco-Roman world where friendship was highly cherished. This wisdom was passed on to posterity by authors like the Greek philosopher Aristotle[10] and Cicero the Latin orator.[11] Aristotle more than anyone else laid the ground rules for an understanding of friendship in western civilization. For Aristotle the most genuine friendship exists between those who are good and virtuous. Moreover, friendship for Aristotle, as it must be always, exists as part of a larger reality, as an ingredient enriching a larger society. My friend and I are not an island, to paraphrase John Donne; we

---

9. *Adventures in Grace* 101.

10. Aristotle, *Nicomachean Ethics,* trans. H. Rackham, "Loeb Classical Library" (Cambridge: Harvard University Press, 1956) Books 8 and 9.

11. Cicero, *Laelius (De Amicitia, On Friendship),* trans. W. A. Falconer (Loeb: London, 1923).

are connected to a whole.[12] Friendship is not a private relationship. Aristotle says that friends are needed for happiness, and they help each other become virtuous. Virtue and happiness make society a community, not a collection of individuals. True friendship, moreover, exists, says Aristotle, among friends who are truly good people.

Cicero's treatise *On Friendship* had an enormous impact on the middle ages, especially on the development of a monastic notion of friendship in the twelfth century. The monks of this era delighted in and extracted much from Cicero's ideas about friendship. The Latin title of Cicero's essay, *De Amicitia,* says much about friendship in the ancient world. The Latin root word in *amicitia* is *amo*— I love. Friends are those who love one another. This is a love not limited by the modern romantic love which too often focuses on what one receives from another, not on what one gives to the other.

The Greeks had a special word for love as friendship: *philia,* a word that occurs frequently in various forms in the New Testament which would raise friendship to a new level of love, *agape.*

Cicero knew that friendship makes people better citizens. In the ancient world friends took time to engage in conversation. Then as now friends as conversation partners raised the quality of life around them by the quality of their conversation. No one will ever know how much good has been done by the insights friends share with one another.

In the ancient world friendship was a key ideal which flourished in the depths of the human spirit and ennobled human life. Horace wrote of his friend Virgil that he was half his soul,[13] a sentiment expressed frequently ever since. Western culture has inherited from antiquity this noble ideal of friendship. Our era will be enriched by reflection upon this classical tradition, but for all its wisdom this classical tradition from another time and another place must be critiqued carefully. Thus the patriarchal character of ancient society paid scant attention to female friendships.

---

12. Brian Patrick McGuire, *Friendship and Community: The Monastic Experience, 350-1250* (Kalamazoo: Cistercian Publications, 1988). This book by title and argument continually connects friendship with the larger reality of community. See p. 426 as an instance.

13. Horace, *Odes* 3.8.

Friendship in Christianity[14]

A moving moment in the gospels occurred at the last supper when Jesus shared with his followers reflections on friendship.

> This is my commandment, that you love one another as I have loved you. No one has greater love than this, to lay down one's life for one's friends. You are my friends if you do what I command you. I do not call you servants any longer, because the servant does not know what the master is doing; but I have called you friends, because I have made known to you everything that I have heard from my Father (Jn 15:12-15).

These words of Jesus contain inspiration enough for a whole month of Sundays. This gospel text uses a combination of Greek words *philos* (friend) and *agape* (Christ-like love). Does not this precious moment in the formation of Christian disciples add *agape* to the notion of friendship without losing those qualities of friendship cherished in the ancient world?[15]

Love of God and love of neighbor were not abstract ideals for Jesus. For love of his friends Jesus laid down his life. The cross communicates how dearly loved are the friends of Jesus. Moreover, Jesus loved tenderly and compassionately. He looked at the man who wished to follow him and "loved him" (Mk 10:21). The tenderness of his love for his follower known as the "beloved disciple" is the stuff of poetry.[16] Jesus had special affection for some of his female disciples. Jesus "loved Martha and her sister and Lazarus" (Jn 11:5).

No voice in Christian history has spoken more eloquently about friendship than Augustine, the bishop of Hippo. He wrote about a friendship that "had been sweet to me beyond all the sweetness of life." Augustine also called Nebridius "a sweet friend," and he referred to another friend, Alypius, as "my heart's brother."[17] Augustine knew the strength that derived from friends, but typically he was aware of the troublesome influence of less than virtuous companions. Despite his conviction that "human friendship

---

14. See Carolinne White, *Christian Friendship in the Fourth Century* (Cambridge: Cambridge University Press, 1992).

15. See the play on these words for love in John 21:15-18.

16. Cf. "Beloved Disciple," *Harper's Bible Dictionary* 102.

17. Augustine, *The Confessions* 9.3.6; 9.4.7

is...a nest of love and gentleness because of the unity it brings about between many souls," Augustine was convinced that "had I been alone I would not have" stolen those famous pears.[18] Augustine had an uncommon sense of human solidarity, good and bad.

Augustine would have preferred to spend his life among the friends gathered together to search for truth. But Augustine had to alter his expectations when he was called to serve the church as a busy bishop.[19] Augustine still yearned for friendship and created a community out of which he ministered to his diocese. Augustine adapted to his own circumstances the classical tradition of friendship, especially Cicero's version. Augustine was never without friends if he could help it. He realized that friends were united in Christ through the Holy Spirit: "There is no true friendship unless You weld it between souls that cleave together through that charity which is shed in our hearts by the Holy Ghost who is given to us."[20]

Augustine's experience and reflections on friendship have inspired Christians who have learned from him that friendship is not only a marvelous human experience but it is also a special gift from God.

Aelred of Rievaulx and the Cistercians

This chapter has space for only a few comments on the neglected Christian tradition of friendship. But friendship among Cistercian monks of the twelfth century cannot be omitted. These monks cast the whole tradition of friendship into a unique and engaging facet of monastic life.

The Cistercians originated at the wilderness of Citeaux in Burgundy in 1098. This monastery sought simplicity of life but struggled almost to extinction until a young man arrived at the gates of the monastery with thirty relatives and friends as new recruits. Bernard of Clairvaux put the Cistercians on the monastic map for all time. Bernard's eloquence, e.g. his *Sermons on the Song of Songs,* bespoke a new and powerful religious sentiment that has ever since

---

18. *Confessions* 2.5.10; 8.16.

19. Gilbert Meilaender, *Friendship: A Study in Theological Ethics* (Notre Dame: University of Notre Dame Press, 1981) 103.

20. Marie Aquinas McNamara, *Friends and Friendship for Saint Augustine* (Staten Island: Alba House, 1964) 237. The author does not give the source for this quote.

had an impact on religious writing. Bernard urged a younger Cistercian monk from the north of England, Aelred of Rievaulx, to take up his pen to write about love.[21] We owe to that intervention a significant writing career, including what may be the most important Christian text on friendship as holiness, *Spiritual Friendship*.[22] Aelred, whom David Knowles described as a man of "gentleness, radiance of affection and wide sympathy,"[23] composed a treatise on friendship that reveals his own deep commitment to friendship and his keen insights into the meaning and joys of friendship.

Cicero's *On Friendship*, which Aelred read as a boy, had a profound influence on this Cistercian who was the son and the grandson of priests. The scriptures, especially John's gospel, Augustine, and Aelred's experience shaped his simple, direct and yet deeply moving treatise on spiritual friendship. Some modern writers have detected a homosexual orientation behind this text.[24] Whatever the reality may be, it is clear that Aelred's commitment was to chaste and celibate friendship. Aelred wrote: "I decided to write my own book on spiritual friendship and to draw up for myself rules for a chaste and holy love" (SF, Prologue 6).[25]

Aelred's exquisite text, *Spiritual Friendship,* although written for a monastic audience in the twelfth century, has perennial wisdom and inspiration for those who seek to integrate friendship into their spiritual journeys. One of Aelred's dialogue partners in the text, Daniel, felt that he and Gratian, must be content with everyday friendship:

> This friendship is so sublime and perfect that I dare not aspire to it. For me and our friend Gratian that type of friendship suffices which your Augustine describes: namely, to converse and jest together, with good-will to humor one another, to read together, to

21. Aelred of Rievaulx, *The Mirror of Charity*, trans. Elizabeth Connor (Kalamazoo: Cistercian Publications, 1990).

22. Aelred of Rievaulx, *Spiritual Friendship*, trans. Mary Eugenia Laker (Kalamazoo: Cistercian Publications, 1977). Henceforth: SF.

23. David Knowles, *The Monastic Order in England,* 2nd ed. (Cambridge: University Press, 1963) 242.

24. See Brian P. McGuire, *Aelred of Rievaulx: Brother and Lover* (New York: Crossroad, 1994) 142-43, passim.

25. The following essay argues with extensive documentation from the sources against a homosexual interpretation of Aelred's text. Marsha L. Dutton, "Aelred of Rievaulx on Friendship, Chastity and Sex: The Sources," *Cistercian Studies Quarterly* 29 (1994) 121-96.

discuss matters together, together to trifle, and together to be in earnest; to differ at times without ill-humor... (SF 3.85).

Aelred tells his conversation partners that, indeed, this friendship can be the "beginnings...of a holier friendship." Aelred says that this ordinary friendship is a "region close by" "where the friendship of man could be easily translated into a friendship for God himself because of the similarity between both" (SF 3.87). Ivo asks Aelred, "Shall I say of friendship what John, the friend of Jesus, says of charity: 'God is friendship'?" Aelred replies, "That would be unusual, to be sure, nor does it have the sanction of the scriptures. But still what is true of charity, I surely do not hesitate to grant to friendship, since 'he that abides in friendship, abides in God, and God in him'" (SF 1.69-70).

The charming and likable abbot of Rievaulx did not reduce the contemplative quest for God to something superficial. Rather, for him friendship oriented to God brings those united to each other to divine contemplation (SF 2.61). Bernard McGinn has demonstrated how Aelred's teaching on spiritual friendship is intimately connected with the mystical life; in fact, the Cistercian abbot saw spiritual friendship as a journey to the mystical experience of God.[26]

Aelred was not merely throwing holy water on the secular experience of friendship. Rather, he saw the demanding responsibilities of friendship as a stage on the way to union with God. Thus friendship is nature coming to its fullness through grace. Aelred shared his experience of friendship and his reflections on it with the monks he served as abbot. *Spiritual Friendship* is a text that expands current notions of friendship and roots them in a sacramental reality.

Walter Daniel described Aelred's final days. Aelred said farewell to his monks, leaving them some of his favorite things: a psalter, John's gospel, Augustine's *Confessions,* a cherished crucifix and some relics. To his monks Aelred said: "God who knows all things knows that I love you all as myself, and, as earnestly as a mother after her sons, 'I long after you all in the bowels of Jesus Christ.'"[27] Human friendship had prepared Aelred for the journey to everlasting friendship with God.

Aelred of Rievaulx was not the only twelfth century monastic

---

26. Bernard McGinn, *The Growth of Mysticism* (New York: Crossroad, 1994) 309-23.

27. Walter Daniel, *The Life of Aelred of Rievaulx,* trans. F. M. Powicke (Kalamazoo: Cistercian Publications, 1994) 135.

voice to see friendship as a path to God. He was merely the most explicit and memorable advocate of the virtue of friendship. Anselm of Canterbury, who composed prayers for those who requested them, wrote a "Prayer for Friends" in which Anselm addresses Jesus as "Good man, good God, good Lord, good friend."[28]

Friendship with God: Thomas Aquinas

The tradition spoke of Jesus and God as friend. For justification Christians need only recall the words of Jesus to his disciples: "I have called you friends" (Jn 15:15). What is more, the Hebrew scriptures saw both Moses and Abraham as friends of God (Ex 33:11; 2 Chr 20:7; Is 41:8; see also Jas 2:23). The wise were also called friends of God (Wis 7:27). Plato had spoken of the lover given to divine contemplation as a "friend of God,"[29] but the Jewish and especially the Christian tradition saw the relationship with a personal God as an intimacy like that found in human friendship.

The Dominican Thomas Aquinas developed a theology of friendship with God that has received all too little attention.[30] Following the lead of his mentor Aristotle, Friar Thomas perceived friendship as a virtue. But Thomas moved beyond Aristotle's philosophical reflections on friendship. Thomas could do this because of his principle of analogy, that is, friendship in God has a likeness to human friendships. Says Thomas Aquinas: "Charity signifies not only the love of God, but also a certain friendship with him."[31] Elsewhere Thomas wrote that "charity is friendship." Thomas' latter comment is made in the context of his exploration of the virtue of charity.[32]

The divine foundation for love of God and love of neighbor is the charity/love that exists in the triune God. God is friend because love and friendship exist already in the Trinity. The Holy Spirit is love,

---

28. *The Prayers and Meditations of St. Anselm,* trans. Benedicta Ward (Baltimore: Penguin, 1973) 212-15.

29. Bernard McGinn, *The Foundations of Mysticism* (New York: Crossroad, 1991) 27.

30. An exception is Paul J. Wadell, *Friends of God: Virtues and Gifts in Aquinas* (New York: Peter Lang, 1991). A helpful introduction to God as friend does not take into account Aquinas' contribution: Sallie McFague, "God as Friend," *Models of God; Theology for an Ecological, Nuclear Age* (Philadelphia: Fortress Press, 1987) 157-80.

31. *Summa theologiae* 1.2; 65.5.

32. Ibid. 2.2.23.

is friendship between the Father and the Son. So friendship exists
first in God. God has bestowed friendship upon the human community by sending the Holy Spirit as friend.[33] Thomas perceived that
God desires to be a friend to women and men. God's friendship with
the human community initiates a desire for friendship with God.
Thomas Aquinas taught that Christian perfection consists in love,
charity—love of God and love of neighbor. We were created, says
Thomas, for happiness. Friendship with God is happiness, here and
hereafter, just as human friendship is a happiness, a delight, a joy.
The human person was made to take delight in the good. That is
why friends take delight in each other.

Thomas Aquinas has not only perceived that human friendship
is anchored in a divine reality, he has also provided grounds for the
development of an ethic or morality based on friendship. If God is
friend, then there are responsibilities between human persons and
God—faithfulness, conversation, love, service. There are also like
consequences for human friends. Thomas Aquinas wrote of the
"love of friendship," that is, love for the other for the sake of the
other, what some have called disinterested, selfless love. Would not
our moral lives, our moral theory be enriched if we explored more
deeply the wisdom of friendship, human and divine?[34]

Since Thomas Aquinas developed his theology of friendship,
there has been too little attention paid to a theology of friendship
with God. However, mystics and saints have regularly spoken of
God as friend. A constant theme in the writings of Teresa of Avila is
divine friendship. She calls God "true Friend and Spouse,"[35] and
Teresa describes Jesus as "so good a friend."[36] She also wrote that
"mental prayer in my opinion is nothing else than an intimate sharing between friends."[37] John of the Cross has written of growth in
the mystical life as "loving friendship with God."[38]

Not only has there been a lack of theological exploration of
friendship with God, but friendship as a monastic ideal declined

---

33. Wadell, 15ff.

34. See Paul J. Wadell, *Friendship and the Moral Life* (Notre Dame:
University of Notre Dame Press, 1989).

35. *The Way of Perfection,* Vol. 2, *The Collected Works of St. Teresa of
Avila,* 3 vols., trans. Kieran Kavanaugh and Otilio Rodriguez (Washington,
DC: Institute of Carmelite Studies, 1976, 1980, 1985) 9, 4.

36. Ibid. 26.1.

37. *The Book of Her Life* 8.5, Vol. 1, *The Collected Works* 67.

38. *The Dark Night* 2.7.4.

from the beginning of the thirteenth century. A less optimistic out-
look on humanity than the vigorous humanism of the twelfth century made the bonds of human friendship seem less religious and
joyful. The fourteenth century spiritual classic, *The Imitation of
Christ*, is an example of a hugely popular text that spurned human
friendships for the sake of the only true friend.[39] The fourteenth
century movement, "Friends of God," some of whose members were
under suspicion for heresy, may have caused some late medievals to
be less enthusiastic about the theme of friendship.[40]

A less than positive view of human relationships in religious
communities continued from the late middle ages well into the first
half of the twentieth century. The phrase "particular friendship,"
used by the seventeenth century Saint Francis de Sales in his
immensely popular *Introduction to the Devout Life*,[41] added to the
suspicion that friendships can detract from community life or lead
to manifestations of homosexuality. The latter was a fear not often
explicitly articulated but present as a subtext.[42] The cautious attitude toward friendship occasioned by the writings of Francis de
Sales occurred despite the saint's own beneficial friendships,[43] especially his beautiful friendship with the widow Saint Jeanne de
Chantal. To her Francis de Sales wrote

> I have never intended for there to be any connection between us
> that carries any obligation except that of love and true Christian
> friendship, whose binding force Saint Paul calls "the bond of
> perfection."[44]

While various mystics spoke of their friendship with God, there

---

39. McGuire, *Friendship and Community* 424.

40. Alois M. Haas, "Schools of Late Medieval Mysticism," *Christian
Spirituality: High Middle Ages and Reformation*, Vol. 17 of *World
Spirituality*, ed. Jill Raitt (New York: Crossroad, 1987) 158-59.

41. For a treatment of particular friendship in religious communities
just as modern renewal ideas were beginning to take hold, cf. the audio-
cassette by Thomas Merton, *Authentic Friendship* (Kansas City: Credence
Cassettes, n.d.).

42. McGuire, *Friendship and Community* 420-421.

43. For the friendship between Francis and Antonio Favre, see
Elisabeth Stopp, "Saint Francis de Sales: Attitudes to Friendship," *The
Downside Review* 113 (1995) 175-92.

44. Wendy M. Wright, *Bond of Perfection: Jeanne de Chantal & Francis
de Sales* (New York: Paulist, 1985) 103 04.

was little explicit religious commentary on friendship after the middle ages, but Teresa of Avila explored friendship for the young women who came to join her reformed monasteries. She wanted these monasteries to be a community of friends: "All must be friends, all must be loved, all must be held dear, all must be helped."[45] In her *The Way of Perfection* Teresa developed a positive understanding of a loving community despite an awareness of the harm that can occur through imperfect friendships.[46]

Those whom Teresa called "friends and daughters" probably learned more from Teresa's example than from her books. Teresa was warm, quick-witted, outgoing, honest and concerned about the details of others' lives. Teresa had a marvelous capacity for friendship. She had a special affection for a young Carmelite thirty years her junior, Jerome Gracian, in whom she took great delight: "Oh, Jesus, how wonderful it is when two souls understand each other! They never lack anything to say and never grow weary (of saying it)."[47] Friendship was a gift that enabled Teresa and her friends to journey together to God. Since Teresa's time there have been wonderful examples of friendships filled with God's grace. There is not space here to explore these many friendships. For that reason we skip to a future when we hope more and more people will be blessed with good and true friends who energize them on the journey to God, friend par excellence.

Friendship in the Twenty-First Century

The desire for friends and the joy they bring are too deeply ingrained in the human heart for friendship to disappear. However, our culture at times puts the quality of friendship in jeopardy and keeps friendships entirely secular and without spiritual significance. In 1985 Robert Bellah and his associates published their study *Habits of the Heart: Individualism and Commitment in American Life.*[48] This study indicts the individualism that has

---

45. *The Way of Perfection* 4.7, *The Collected Works* 55. See Keith J. Egan, *A Praying Community of Friends* (audio-taped lectures) (Canfield: Alba House, 1988).

46. For Teresa's treatment of friendship in the monastery see *The Way of Perfection,* chapters 4-15.

47. *The Letters of Saint Teresa of Jesus,* 2 Vols., trans. E. Allison Peers (London: Sheed and Ward, 1951, 1980) I, 368.

48. New York: Harper and Row, 1985.

robbed Americans of the ability to form and be faithful to relationships of all kind. This book invites widespread conversation about the precarious nature of friendship in our time.

Traditional friendship in Aristotelian and Ciceronian terms was known and valued in the early American era. Today friendship is seen by many only in a therapeutic light—friends make me feel better. The authors of *Habits of the Heart* have found little evidence of "shared commitment to the good" or of "friendship in terms of common moral commitments." Lost is the notion of friendship as an essential ingredient in community and society:

> Traditionally, it was the virtues indelibly associated with friendship that were central to the "habits of the heart." It is also part of the traditional view that friendship and its virtues are not merely private: they are public, even political, for a civic order, a "city," is above all a network of friends. Without civic friendship, a city will degenerate into a struggle of contending interest groups unmediated by any public solidarity.[49]

The authors of *Habits of the Heart* say that the commitment to friendship by early Americans is not now much in evidence and needs to be retrieved. The book retells the story of the patching up of the broken relationship between John Adams and Thomas Jefferson. When both were on in years, Jefferson wrote to his friend: "We have, willingly, done injury to no man; and have done for our country the good which has fallen in our way....In the meantime be our last as cordial as were our first affections."[50] In the wake of violence that has so scarred our landscape, one hopes that circles of friends will increase and that these circles extend to others the affection they find in friends. The small faith communities that began in Latin America and which are now in evidence in North America are a call for friends to share the wisdom of the scriptures.

Conversations About Friendship

The lonely and dispirited often find themselves friendless. Many complain that there is no time for the leisure and hospitality that friendships require. Busyness at work and in academic life and even at home endangers fragile friendships that would keep work

49. Ibid. 115-16.
50. Ibid. 116.

and study from being dehumanized. Indeed, a willingness to love a friend for her or his sake, what Thomas Aquinas calls the love of friendship, seems less in evidence, less an ideal in these days when popular culture romanticizes love and friendship. This romanticism robs one of the realization that friendship thrives only with other-centeredness and hard work.

The tradition of friendship inherited from antiquity and enriched by Christianity must not be allowed to disappear. How shall we honor this tradition so that it may thrive in our time? Friends are a gift. They are not manufactured. Friendships cannot be contrived. However, one can open oneself up, be disposed to the discovery of friends, be hospitable to guests, remain faithful to the obligations of friendship. Genuine caring for others, attention to their needs, a willingness to listen to them attentively, taking time for them—all of these actions discover spaces in the heart where friends may enter.

Yet friendships are not earned, nor does self-worth depend on a supposed long list of friends, prestigious or not. All life, all love are gift. A freedom of spirit is needed so that friends can be received as a gift rather than as something to be grasped. Friendship requires vulnerability, a willingness to risk love.

Friendships fade or disappear for all kinds of reasons, some of which we cannot control. Friendships require mutuality, leisure for each other, attention to the needs of the other, loyalty, and most of all a love that is other-centered.

Friendship is, however, more than personal, more than a one-on-one relationship. Friendship is a movement toward community that yet maintains the intimacy of friends. A society that does not foster friendships will soon come apart at the seams. Indeed, there has been a history of societies that discover that preferential love can create destructive tensions, e.g. a monastery, a family, a group of friends can experience the stress caused by those friends who do not reach out to others. A sensitivity about the feelings of others is needed, but does not mean that a society must discourage genuine friendships as religious life did at times in the past because of the fear of "particular friendships." Love and friendship do not grow without pain and disappointment. A spirituality of friendship is based on those relationships where friends share the journey to God, a journey where the Spirit of Christ is the source of growth in love for friends and for God. Friendship among disciples of Jesus enables them to respond more fully to the call of Christ, "Come, follow me."

Since friendships thrive where communities honor the tradition of authentic friendship, and since there is a lack of knowledge about this tradition, conversations about this tradition of friendship, about the requirements of friendship, incline us to honor the relational capacities, tendencies and desires of the human heart for friendship. Think of the search for truth that occurred when friends collaborated in the ancient world; think of the delight in the spiritual life that monk-friends offered each other in the twelfth century. If friendship, its joys, its enlargement of the human spirit were better appreciated, we would all be inclined to take time and make the other commitments necessary to foster a society where circles of friends abound. A crucial challenge is to become conversation partners with the great traditions of friendship, to listen to the historical and literary stories of friendship and to discover the deeply religious and spiritual significance of friendship.

Women's Experience of Friendship

Friendship in the ancient world, in Christian circles like Augustine's and among the monks of the twelfth century, was a male domain. We know better. Women have always had a profound capacity for friendship. Writers like Mary Gordon, whose novel *In the Company of Women* explores women's relationships, need to continue this exploration. More historical work like the studies of friendships among medieval women mystics is needed so that stories of women's friendships may be unearthed.[51] Women and men need to listen carefully to the female experience of friendship. Modern culture has constricted male emotional responses beyond the sexual while women have long felt free to express their deepest feelings. Emotional isolation keeps relationships from developing into strong and lasting friendships. Women's experience of friendship has much to teach men about the inner richness that friends bring to one another. Poets, novelists, painters, historians who tell the stories of women's experience of friendship will greatly enrich a tradition that has too often neglected this experience.

---

51. U. Wiethaus, "In Search of Medieval Women's Friendships," *Maps of Flesh and Light: The Religious Experience of Medieval Women Mystics,* ed. Ulrike Wiethaus (Syracuse: Syracuse University Press, 1993) 93-111.

Friends and Lovers

The Song of Songs celebrates the love and friendship between a woman and man. This celebration of human love contains inspiration for anyone who seeks to be more deeply aware of the glory of the love between a woman and a man. The mystics and the celibate community have turned over and over again to these songs to gain some sense of the power and the beauty of divine love received and returned.

The Song of Songs has a very special message for married women and men who are called, indeed, to be friends and lovers. In these songs the young woman says to the young man: "This is my beloved, this is my friend" (5:16). Sexual attraction alone is never enough to keep a marriage strong and growing. However, sexual love combined with the common demands and joys of friendship will make marriage a relationship that weathers the inevitable storms that threaten to undermine marriage commitments. Young lovers are meant to become old lovers.

Conversation before marriage about friendship, serious dialogue about the willingness of partners to put time, energy, prayer and reflection into their friendship—these practices put hope, joy and stability into marriage. Statistics about failing marriages would differ if spouses were committed friends. Spouses who are, indeed, good friends can expect that their love will be like the love celebrated in the Song of Songs.

> For love is strong as death,
> passion fierce as the grave.
> Its flashes are flashes of fire, a raging flame.
> Many waters cannot quench love,
> neither can floods drown it (8:6-7).

Movements during the 1950s and 1960s like the Christian Family Movement and later Marriage Encounter have been a way for spouses to contribute and benefit from circles of friends who cherish the human capacity for love and friendship within marriage. Perhaps there are other ways that will spread the word that marriage is more fun, richer and more fulfilling when partners are good friends with mutual responsibilities to their friendship. Marriage, indeed, is not a cheap grace.

Sacrament of Friendship

This chapter has been a brief exploration of a theme that needs more exploration—the spirituality of friendship. Conflicts in the past among various Christian denominations about the number of the sacraments have led to an emphasis in Catholic circles on its seven official sacraments. As a result there has been a tendency to lose sight of the sacramental principle which says that God manifests God's self in creation and in human relationships. God's grace supports human life and relationships in many forms. Friends who love one another must know that, since God is love, their love participates in God's own life. From the twelfth century on there has been a special recognition of the sacramentality of marriage. Friendship in marriage deepens participation in this sacrament of love. But are not all free and loving friendships sacramental?

Since, as Thomas Aquinas has shown, human friendship is a reflection of the loving relationship that exists in the triune God, and since charity/love/friendship is what Thomas called Christian perfection, then are not right in seeing friendship as a sacramental reality? Are we not right in expecting God to enrich our friendships with those graces that enable friendship to be a revelation of God's life and love?

John of the Cross was so bold as to see mystical growth as leading to an equality with God. Unthinkable, indeed, unless God has gifted the human person with divine friendship. John says that when the soul "possesses perfect love, she is called the bride of the Son of God, which signifies equality with him. In this equality of friendship the possessions of both are held in common."[52]

Then, like Christ the Son of God, the Christian lives willing "to lay down one's life for one's friends," for "no one has greater love than this" (Jn 15:13).

Further Reading

Allen, Diogenes, *Christian Romance, Marriage, Friendship* (Cambridge: Cowley, 1987). This is a treatment of friendship in the context of other loves.

---

52. *The Spiritual Canticle* 28.1, *The Collected Works of St. John of the Cross,* trans. Kieran Kavanaugh and Otilio Rodriguez, rev. ed. (Washington, DC: Institute of Carmelite Studies, 1991) 584.

Fiske, Adele, *Friend and Friendship in the Monastic Tradition,* (Cuernavaca: Civoc Cuaderno, 1970). A look at a tradition rich in its connection between friendship and holiness.

Lewis, C. S., *The Four Loves* (New York: Harcourt Brace Jovanovich, 1960). A modern classic through the famous C. S. Lewis lens.

Ripple, Paula, *Called To Be Friends* (Notre Dame: University of Notre Dame Press, 1980). Treats the Christian call to friendship.

Rouner, Leroy S., ed., *The Changing Face of Friendship* (Notre Dame: University of Notre Dame Press, 1994). Here scholars treat many themes connected with friendship.

Welty, Eudora, and Ronald A. Sharp, eds., *The Norton Book of Friendship* (New York: W. W. Norton, 1991). A rather random collection of readings somehow connected with friendship.

White, Carolinne, *Christian Friendship in the Fourth Century* (Cambridge: Cambridge University Press, 1992). This book examines a critical era for the development of the Christian ideal of friendship.

Exercises

(1) Make an outline of a homily entitled, "Friends and Lovers," for the wedding of your sister, brother or a good friend. Include a selection of quotations from the Song of Songs.

(2) Read Aristotle, Books 8 and 9 of the Nicomachean Ethics. *Make a list of quotations from Aristotle that contain wisdom still applicable to friendship in the modern world.*

(3) Read Cicero On Friendship. *Make a list of quotations from this text that contain wisdom for friendship in our time.*

(4) Think about your best friend. How has your friend enriched your life? What does this friendship mean to you? Has this friendship changed your life?

(5) Compose a prayer to God/Christ. Use imagery that describes God as a friend.

10

Eucharist: Source and Summit of the Christian Life

"Blessed is anyone who will eat bread in the kingdom of God" (Lk 14:15).

*T*he Lord's supper quickly became the central celebration of Christianity and has remained so through the centuries. This book concludes, fittingly, we think, with an exploration of this sacrament which the Second Vatican Council called "the source and summit" of the Christian life[1] and a "foretaste of the heavenly banquet."[2] In fact, all the themes from the Christian spiritual tradition explored in this book are celebrated when the Christian assembly gathers at the table of the Lord.

As faithful disciples, Christians heed the challenge of Jesus at the last supper: "Do this in remembrance of me" (Lk 22:19; 1 Cor 11:24-25). Christian disciples have responded to this desire of Jesus in ways ranging from the Catholic ceremonial tradition to Christian communities who celebrate the Lord's supper more simply and less frequently, e.g. the Mennonites, and some not at all, like the Quakers. It is impossible to treat here the great variety of ways that Christians have celebrated the Lord's supper. Consequently, this chapter concentrates on the Catholic eucharistic tradition. However,

---

1. Vatican II, Dogmatic Constitution on the Church, 11; see also Vatican II's Decree on the Ministry and Life of Priests, 5; John Paul II, "Mystery and Worship of the Holy Eucharist," *Origins* 9 (March 27, 1980) 2, 4; "Eucharist Apex of Church Life," April 8, 1992. "Instruction on the Worship of the Eucharistic Mystery," Sacred Congregation of Rites, May 25, 1967. *Vatican Council II: The Conciliar and Post Conciliar Documents,* ed. Austin Flannery (Washington, DC: Scholarly Resources, 1975) 100.

2. Dogmatic Constitution on the Church, 38.

the many convergences of eucharistic practice and theology render this focus broader than may at first be apparent in the use of Catholic experience and vocabulary.

Citing Paul's statement that "because there is one bread, we who are many are one body" (1 Cor 10:17), Thomas Aquinas calls the eucharist "the sacrament of the church's unity."[3] The eucharist is the celebration of unity despite the divergent interpretations of this sacrament. Though the unity desired by Jesus at the last supper, "that they all may be one" (Jn 17:21), is only a distant dream, the aim of every Christian must be a common gathering at the Lord's table to celebrate the one body of Christ. In the search for ecclesial unity one remembers that the eucharist makes the church present. Christian spirituality must never turn in on itself but search for the unity prayed for by Jesus.

Before sharing one cup and one loaf of bread at the same table, Christians of many kinds need to explore the meaning of the eucharist in the scriptures, in the various traditions and in dialogue with each other. The disunity of Christians, graphically apparent from the differing interpretations of eucharist, is a scandal to be healed by prayer, study, ecumenical dialogue and service to others so that the eucharist may be a genuine expression of this one body of Christ. This search for eucharistic unity is not, however, a search for cultural conformity but for the unity Luke saw in Christians at Jerusalem who were "of one heart and soul" (Acts 4:32).

Much has been accomplished ecumenically since Vatican II, especially through the dialogues between different traditions, like those between Lutherans and Catholics, and between Anglicans and Catholics. However, there is a special need for grassroots ecumenism among local congregations so that communities may learn from each other wisdom about the eucharist, its fruitful celebration and its spirituality.

This chapter asks: How can the eucharist, in the third Christian millennium, be more fully appreciated as the "source and summit" of the Christian life and as a fuller anticipation of the messianic banquet? Centuries ago Thomas Aquinas taught that "the eucharist is the summit of the spiritual life and all the sacraments are ordered to it." Thomas added that "the eucharist is necessary in order to bring it [the spiritual life] to its culmination."[4] As a celebration of

---

3. *Summa theologiae* 3.73.2.
4. Ibid. 3.73.3.

Christian spirituality, the eucharist keeps this spirituality from deteriorating into an individualistic piety.

Moreover, in the context of this book, we ask how the eucharist can be recognized as the central celebration of that Christian spirituality which is a living, inwardly and outwardly, of Christian discipleship under the influence of the Holy Spirit. That the eucharist is the central celebration of this spirituality and, in fact, is "the very heartbeat"[5] of the Christian life was the conviction of the first followers of Jesus and has remained so for most Christians from then till now. Indeed, one cannot imagine the Catholic tradition without the regular celebration of the eucharist. Moreover, Catholic spirituality would go uncelebrated if the eucharist became a rarity.

Learning To Celebrate

But to celebrate the eucharist well we must learn, first of all, how to celebrate, to make festival, to make "sabbath."[6] What does not happen outside of eucharist will not happen at the eucharist: we cannot become instant celebrators, festive people, merely by walking through a church door. We cannot celebrate the eucharist well if we do not celebrate well elsewhere.[7] The Holy Spirit who transforms the bread and the wine into the body and blood of Christ seeks a fitting human milieu in which to manifest the presence of Christ. The human and the ordinary are clay in God's hands. God the artist seizes the ordinary in order to manifest the divine presence. The assembly must develop a "listening heart" (1 Kgs 3:9) and eyes of the soul[8] in order to hear and to see in faith

---

5. Vatican II, Decree on the Ministry and Life of Priests, 5.

6. Leisure, play, celebration, festivity need to be recovered so that humanity may be prepared for encounters with the divine. On leisure see Josef Pieper, *Leisure: The Basis of Culture,* rev. ed. (New York: Herder and Herder, 1964). On festivity and play see Josef Pieper, *In Tune with the World: A Theory of Festivity,* trans. R. and C. Winston (New York: Harcourt, Brace and World, 1965); Hugo Rahner, *Man at Play* (New York: Herder and Herder, 1965).

7. These statements are made with a recognition that neither the holiness and the abilities of the presider nor those of the assembly constitute the validity of the eucharist.

8. John of the Cross, *The Living Flame of Love* 3.71, *The Collected Works of St. John of the Cross,* rev. ed., trans. Kieran Kavanaugh and Otilio Rodriguez (Washington, DC: Institute of Carmelite Studies, 1991) 703.

the presence of Jesus at the eucharistic meal. The Acts of the Apostles (2:42-46) calls this milieu, where bread is broken, the Christian community—in Greek *koinonia*. However, where community is a sham, the eucharist speaks weakly. Only a loving and serving Christian community celebrates authentically.

The devotions, eucharistic and otherwise, that characterized Catholic life before Vatican II disappeared quickly after the council. Novenas, benedictions, Corpus Christi processions, the rosary, and the stations of the cross are no longer as common as they once were. A new focus on the eucharist was one factor in their demise, but devotion to the eucharist as a celebration of the word of God, as a meal, as a sacrifice, must now be promoted. Devotion is essential. Particular devotions may or may not be helpful but should always be rooted in the eucharist. Attendance at the eucharist, even though often passive in the past, nourished Catholics for a long time, but passivity does not fit Vatican II's profile for the celebration of the eucharist. The first document of Vatican II calls for a full and active participation in the liturgy.

> Mother Church earnestly desires that all the faithful be led to that full, conscious and active participation in liturgical celebrations which is demanded by the very nature of the liturgy. Such participation by the Christian people as "a chosen race, a royal priesthood, a holy nation, a purchased people" (1 Pet 2:9; cf. 2:4-5), is their right and duty by reason of their baptism.[9]

The Christian community must now seek to celebrate a eucharist that is shaped by the word of God, by the wisdom of the tradition and by the spiritual sensitivities of those who will live in the twenty-first century. Though the church must continually be reformed, genuine reform comes slowly and painfully. In the late middle ages the church and religious orders tried over and over again to reform themselves. However, creative reforms had to await a Martin Luther, an Ignatius of Loyola, a John Calvin and a Teresa of Avila.[10] Even then some reforms ended in divisions that have yet to be healed.

The theologian Elizabeth Johnson has written about the waves of new insights in our time concerning Jesus Christ.[11] Since the

---

9. Constitution on the Sacred Liturgy, 14, see also 11.

10. H. Outram Evennett, *The Spirit of the Counter-Reformation,* ed. John Bossy (Cambridge: Cambridge University Press, 1968) 25.

11. Elizabeth A. Johnson, *Consider Jesus: Waves of Renewal in Christology* (New York: Crossroad, 1990).

beginnings of the liturgical movement in the nineteenth century, there have been waves of liturgical reform that culminated in Vatican II's Constitution on the Sacred Liturgy. If the eucharist is to be the central celebration of Catholic spirituality, there is a need to reflect on those waves and determine what responses "to the requirements of our times" are necessary.[12]

Catholic spirituality, eucharistic to the core, will not grow, however, through mere repetition of the eucharist. Nor will wishful thinking bring a renewed eucharistic spirituality. That will come only when the Catholic community is attentive to the urgings of the Holy Spirit. Mere formalism is no response to the command of Jesus: "Do this in remembrance of me." Remembrance for the early Christian community was not mere recall. Remembrance included the rich Hebrew sense of being present through ritual to past events as the passover meal is a presence to the liberating and saving exodus.[13] In the Christian tradition, remembrance (the Greek word is *anamnesis*) includes a sacramental presence of the community to the last supper and to the dying and rising of Jesus.

The church is not a museum but a living organism that must grow and adapt to new circumstances. Indeed, the pluralistic and multi-cultural age in which we live calls for varying styles of celebration. Pope John Paul as far back as 1980 recognized this call to diversity when he spoke of a "pluralism of eucharistic worship envisioned by the Second Vatican Council."[14]

However, in this age of diversity when the signs of the times must be discerned with care, eucharistic spirituality must be rooted in the scriptures, in the experience of the early church and in the theological traditions of the eucharist. Here we can reflect on only a few of these themes: active and full participation, the eucharist as meal with the concomitant characteristics of hospitality, forgiveness, and presence, and especially the retrieval of a sense of mystery.

Names for the Eucharist

But, first, we will explore some of the ways the tradition, in its exploration of the mystery of this sacrament, has named this

---

12. Constitution on the Sacred Liturgy, 1.

13. See David Power, *The Eucharistic Mystery: Revitalizing the Tradition* (New York: Crossroad, 1992) chapter 3.

14. John Paul II, "Mystery and Worship of the Holy Eucharist," 12.

"source and summit" of the Christian life. In doing so, we take a page from the new *Catechism of the Catholic Church,* Thomas Aquinas and the Lima Document where names used by Christians for this sacrament demonstrate its richness.[15] No one name can adequately express that mystery of faith[16] which we call eucharist but which was regularly called the mass earlier in the twentieth century by Catholics. The variety of names hints at the inexhaustible depths of this sacrament.

St. Paul referred to this event as the Lord's supper (1 Cor 11:20), a reminder of the eucharist as meal, a reality not so discernible in the post-Tridentine church. Borrowed from a ritual at Jewish meals, the phrase the "breaking of bread" was a way of referring to at least this aspect of the Lord's supper.[17] Once again the theme of food is highlighted. Since Vatican II there has been a return, especially in Catholic circles, to the use of the word "eucharist" which translates the Greek word for thanksgiving. The name "eucharist" appears in the New Testament stories of the multiplication of loaves since these stories were perceived to have eucharistic significance (Mk 6:41; 8:6; Mt 14:19; 15:36).

The Byzantine Church has called the eucharist the divine liturgy. In the eastern church the word for assembly, "synaxis," could refer to the eucharistic celebration. Since Vatican II, synaxis has been applied in the west to the eucharist. In the Latin church the word "mass" was derived from the dismissal formula: *Ite missa est*—Go, the mass has ended. The holy sacrifice of the mass points to the sacramental connection of the eucharist with the redemptive death of Jesus on the cross. Holy communion has been a common name among Anglicans and some Protestant denominations to specify the union that occurs through the reception of the consecrated bread and wine. Among Protestants, worship or morning worship is sometimes used. Sacrament of the altar is another way to refer to this celebration. Most Blessed Sacrament usually indicates the reserved consecrated bread, while *viaticum*, Latin for "with you on the way," describes the eucharist received by those

---

15. *Catechism of the Catholic Church* (Washington, DC: United States Catholic Conference, 1994) 335-36; *Summa theologiae* 3.73.4; Lima Document: *Baptism, Eucharist and Ministry*, "Faith and Order Paper No. 111" (Geneva: World Council of Churches, 1982).

16. See William V. Dych, *The Mystery of Faith: A Christian Creed for Today* (Collegeville: Liturgical Press, 1995).

17. Acts 2:46; 20:7,11; 27:35; Lk 9:16-17; 22:19; 24:28, 35.

approaching death, a reception with a long history in the stories about saints' deaths. Gregory the Great wrote that Saint Benedict "...had his disciples carry him into the chapel, where he received the Body and Blood of our Lord to gain strength for his approaching end."[18]

These are some of the ways that Christians have named this sacrament. Like names for God, the names for the eucharist are indicative of the mystery that we glimpse ever so partially but cannot fathom. These names and others hint at a mystery that modern liturgies sometimes fail to communicate. We are, indeed, challenged in our time to find ways of celebrating that reveal something of the mystery of Christ's presence in the Christian sacraments.

Participation in the Lord's Supper

One of the most noticeable changes in Catholic life after Vatican II is the new format of the Christian liturgy. Prior to Vatican II there was a presider-oriented liturgy in a classical language with the laity in near passive attendance. Now there is an assembly-centered liturgy with a call for full and active participation by all. The Constitution on the Sacred Liturgy is emphatic about this participation.

The Church, therefore, earnestly desires that Christ's faithful, when present at this mystery of faith, should not be there as strangers or silent spectators. On the contrary, through a proper appreciation of the rites and prayers they should participate knowingly, devoutly, and actively.[19]

As the word "liturgy", the work of the people, connotes, the eucharist requires full and active participation of the whole assembly. Can you imagine those at the Last Supper uninvolved or inattentive? Surely Christians who, after the ascension, gathered for the eucharist in their homes were never mere spectators.

After Constantine permitted the Christian church to go public in the year 313, officers of the church had to take full control of the

---

18. Saint Gregory the Great, *Dialogues,* trans. O.J. Zimmerman, "Fathers of the Church," Vol. 39 (New York: Fathers of the Church, 1959) 107-08.

19. Constitution on the Sacred Liturgy, 48; see also paragraphs 11, 14, 21, 30, 41, 112.

eucharistic worship. The lay assembly, removed from the altar, became less and less involved in the rituals of the eucharist. However, recent scholarship makes one cautious about generalizations concerning lay involvement in late medieval liturgy and perhaps at earlier times. Professor Eamon Duffy of the University of Cambridge has shown that the laity in late medieval England found many effective ways of involving themselves in the celebration of the mass. For a long time the presumption was that the English laity were disenfranchised and unhappy with what historians saw as their passive and even disaffected roles.[20] More research is needed into the state of lay involvement in the liturgy during the era prior to the Reformation. No matter what, the issue now is greater involvement by all in the assembly's worship.

Developments since Vatican II have called women and men to many ministries at the eucharist: greeters, cantors, readers, servers, eucharistic ministers, etc. This democratization of the ministries of the eucharist reflects the earliest experience of Christian worship. The eucharist occurred in house churches at a time when the church had not yet assigned all ministerial roles to professional ministers. The current involvement of many people according to their gifts in eucharistic ministry is in accord with Vatican II's spirit, but the call to active participation means that every person is to be as involved as her or his gifts and calling permit. Passive attendance at the eucharist creates a passive church uninvolved in the commitments of discipleship.

Participation is not mere performance of a function at the eucharist. Rather participation at its deepest level is an intimate involvement of the baptized person in the sacramental action of Jesus who is *the* presider at the eucharist. Then the assembly and the human presider offer and celebrate the eucharist together. This participation in the eucharist is an exercise of the common priesthood of all believers, a doctrine reclaimed by Vatican II.

For their part the faithful join in the offering of the Eucharist by virtue of their royal priesthood. They likewise exercise that priesthood by receiving the sacraments, by prayer and thanksgiving, by the witness of a holy life, and by self-denial and active charity.[21]

---

20. Eamon Duffy, *The Stripping of the Altars: Traditional Religion in England, c.1400–c.1580* (New Haven: Yale University, 1992).
21. Dogmatic Constitution on the Church, #10.

The eucharist does not belong to the few; every member of the Christian community is called to be somewhere around the table of the Lord, not far from Jesus. If the eucharist is the central celebration of Christian discipleship, the community must welcome wholeheartedly everyone to that place where she or he may more fully participate in the eucharistic action of Christ. The sacrifice of the mass celebrates the liberation of all people so that they may be free for their journey to intimacy with God.

The kind of participation called for by Vatican II and by the nature of the eucharistic meal is intimate sharing by all in the action of this sacrament which occurs at the table of the word of God and at the table of the bread of God.[22]

The Meals of Jesus

By reflecting on the eucharist as a meal, one can gain a better sense of that intimate participation that marked those whom Jesus at the last supper no longer calls servants but friends (Jn 15:15). It may seem strange to suggest that a focus on meals will help to recover a sense of mystery at the eucharist. Has not and will not the opposite happen? Are not modern meals fast, trivial and bland? The recovery of the importance of the meal is not only a religious challenge, it is a cultural imperative lest we drift further into meaninglessness as people unable to celebrate with food and drink. But at the ritual meal of the eucharist the Holy Spirit transforms an ordinary meal into a sacrament, a great mystery, the mystery of faith. If we do not know how to celebrate love and friendship at our family table and wherever else we share meals, it is nigh impossible to become a festive person who is able to celebrate wholeheartedly the eucharist. Moreover, as we shall see, the meals of Jesus introduce us to transcendent events that occurred at these meals.

Unfortunately there is not space here to explore extensively the meaning of meal sharing, but the bonding, forgiving, sharing of stories and remembering that occur at common meals are crucial human experiences.[23] However, too important to pass up is an

22. John Paul II, "Mystery and Worship of the Holy Eucharist," 10-11.

23. Philippe Rouillard, "From Human Meal to Christian Eucharist," *Living Bread, Saving Cup: Readings on the Eucharist,* ed. R. Kevin Seasoltz (Collegeville: Liturgical Press, 1987) 126-57; Robert J. Karris, "The Theme of Food," *Luke: Artist and Theologian* (New York: Paulist, 1987); Robert Fabing, *Real Food: A Spirituality of the Eucharist* (New York: Paulist, 1994).

opportunity to draw attention to rich resources for the development of a eucharistic spirituality and for deepening of one's participation at the Lord's supper. These resources are the reports of the meals of Jesus. For a long time the last supper was the sole paradigm for the eucharist. Controversies since the ninth century about the nature of the presence of Jesus in the eucharist have forced a concentration on the institution narratives as they are called.[24]

Thomas Aquinas was not shy about speaking of the eucharist as spiritually nourishing food.[25] About the three sacraments of initiation, Thomas wrote: "...in the spiritual life there is baptism which is spiritual birth and confirmation which is spiritual growth. Likewise the eucharist is needed; it is our spiritual food." For Thomas the purpose of the eucharist is "to refresh us spiritually, as bodily nourishment does physically."[26]

The eucharist is a meal—not any meal, but a sacred meal. Eucharistic celebrations should make it apparent that the assembly has come together for a meal, a sacramental meal where transcendent events occur. This meal is not only the transformation of the bread and wine into the body and blood of Christ but a meal where occur forgiveness, real presence, divine and human hospitality and the transformation of the assembly into disciples nourished by the body and blood of Christ.

The last supper of Jesus with his disciples was precisely that— the *last* of numerous meals which Jesus had shared not only with his followers but also with tax collectors and sinners (Lk 5:30). Jesus knew that his adversaries thought ill of his table activities and his table companions: "Look, a glutton and a drunkard, a friend of tax collectors and sinners" (Lk 7:34). Fr. Robert Karris claims "that in Luke's gospel Jesus got himself crucified by the way he ate."[27] Not only sinners were table partners with Jesus but he welcomed the disabled and the marginalized. Jesus told a parable in which a slave was instructed to "go out at once into the streets and lanes of the town and bring in the poor, the crippled, the blind, and the lame" (Lk 14:21). Jewish priests who were blind, lame or crippled could not offer bread in the sanctuary (Lev 21:16-23), but Jesus practiced an extraordinarily open table. He ate not only with

---

24. See Gary Macy, *The Banquet's Wisdom: A Short History of the Theologies of the Lord's Supper* (New York: Paulist, 1992).

25. *Summa theologiae* 3.79.3 and 4.

26. Ibid. 3.73.1.

27. Karris 47.

the poor and disabled but with the sinners for whom he would die on the cross. It is easy to see why the cross and sacrifice quickly became connected with the eucharist. Paul the apostle announced this connection very early in his ministry: "For as often as you eat this bread and drink the cup, you proclaim the Lord's death until he comes" (1 Cor 11:26).

Forgiveness and Compassion

Meal-sharing is a time of revelation. Those who eat together get to know each other well. The gospels record many meals from which we get to know Jesus quite well, meals which culminated in the last supper.[28] The cross of Jesus and his meals are special vantage points for getting to know God revealed in Jesus Christ. Thus we glimpse the forgiveness that Jesus granted at meals when he said to the woman who bathed his feet with her tears and dried them with her hair: "Your sins are forgiven." Then "...those who were at table with him began to say among themselves, 'Who is this who even forgives sins?'" (Lk 7:48-49). Zacchaeus, the short but rich chief tax collector, encountered a forgiving Jesus who was, to the astonishment of bystanders, a "guest of one who was a sinner" (Lk 19:7).

Here as elsewhere Jesus the guest became the host, a reversal of roles that shows how deeply Jesus entered into the dynamics of meal-sharing and hospitality (Lk 19:1-10). According to Thomas Aquinas, participants in the eucharist experience forgiveness of sins as long as they are not attached to a sinfulness that has deadened the spiritual life.[29]

Many meals reveal the compassion of Jesus, e.g. his sympathy for the embarrassed couple at Cana where as a guest Jesus became the host who provided the wine needed to continue the wedding feast (Jn 2:1-11). Would not Jesus have taken full part in these wedding festivities including the dancing that occurred at these feasts? Recall that the parable of the merciful father included music and dancing at the celebration honoring the repentant son (Lk 15:25).

---

28. Eugene LaVerdiere, *Dining in the Kingdom of God: The Origins of Eucharist According to Luke* (Chicago: Liturgy Training Publications, 1994) chapter 1.

29. *Summa theologiae* 3.79.3 and 4.

These and other meals reveal someone whose heart reached out in forgiveness and compassion for those with whom he ate.

Hospitality

We have already mentioned that Jesus, often the guest, became the host at many meals. Hospitality in Jesus' time required the reception of strangers who were all too often suspect and feared. Jesus opened his table to strangers who were, in addition, tax collectors and sinners. Jesus, the young rabbi, accepted those whom others shunned. The gathering rites at the modern eucharist seek to learn from Jesus how to accept not only family and friends but strangers and others whom society neglects and relegates to places out of sight. A caring and courageous Jesus reached out compassionately to those who joined him at the table.

Although Simon the Pharisee denied Jesus the hospitality of footwashing (Lk 7:44), Jesus washed the feet of his disciples at the last supper. This hospitality of footwashing is recalled once a year at the Holy Thursday liturgy. But should there not be the spirit of footwashing at every eucharist? "So if I, your Lord and teacher, have washed your feet, you ought to wash one another's feet" (Jn 13:1-20). Are not disciples of Jesus to be footwashers who, like Mother Teresa, serve the abandoned and forgotten? Eating and drinking at the table of the Lord sends one forth to a service born of love. "I give you a new commandment, that you love one another" (Jn 13:34).

Participation at the eucharist is enhanced by meditation on Jesus as a table companion (one who takes bread with another). His disciples were prepared for the last supper, the cross and the resurrection by listening to his words and by sharing with him food and drink. The disciples were with Jesus at Peter's house when he healed Peter's mother-in-law, and at many other meals including the last supper, and when at daybreak the risen Jesus said to his disciples, "Come and have breakfast" (Jn 21:12).

An appendix at the end of this chapter contains a list of some of the meals of Jesus, and an exercise at the end of this chapter suggests consultation of this appendix as a way of becoming a better table companion with Jesus. Would we not all be better table companions at the eucharist if the spirit of the meals of Jesus permeated our consciousness? Praying with these meals in small groups would have a beneficial impact on the way we participate in the eucharist.

Presence

Unfortunately the topic of the presence of the body and blood of Christ became, through the centuries, so controversial that it has left little opportunity for an appreciation of a broader and richer awareness of divine and human presence at the celebration of the eucharist. These controversies left us with questions that were too narrow. Vatican II took the lead in opening up the notion of eucharistic presence. The council pointed to the presence of Christ in the church, in the word, in the assembly, in the bread and in the wine, and in the presiding minister.[30]

The assembly, gathered in the name of Jesus (Mt 18:20), is a sacrament of the presence of Jesus. The sacramental character of the assembly calls for a transforming awareness that Jesus resides among those who come together to celebrate the eucharist. Empowered with this awareness, those in the assembly listen to Jesus who is present in the proclamation of the word of God and they praise and thank the Father for the presence of Jesus in the bread and wine that has occurred through the activity of the Holy Spirit: "Let your Spirit come upon these gifts to make them holy, so that they may become for us the body and blood of our Lord, Jesus Christ."[31] The unique presence of the body and blood of Jesus in the bread and wine is a great mystery, but this mystery belongs within the whole mystery of a God who is present throughout creation and in the redemptive presence of Jesus at the eucharist.

There can be no *adequate* explanation, even transubstantiation, for the mystery which is the gracious and saving presence of Christ in a variety of ways at the eucharistic action. Jesus himself has chosen to be present in this sacramental action. We can learn something about the quality of that presence by meditating on the various meals of Jesus and especially the meal he shared with his followers the night before he died. Jesus was present at those meals as one whose love transformed those who sat and reclined with him at table.

What has been neglected in eucharistic piety is a sense of the

---

30. Constitution on the Sacred Liturgy, 7.
31. Eucharistic Prayer II.

assembly as being really present to each other as Christian hospitality requires and as the sign or kiss of peace signifies.[32] Generous gathering rites foster a sense that we gather at the eucharist as friends. Neglected also has been a spirituality of active presence of the assembly to the triune God present in special ways at this meal. John of the Cross recommends to contemplatives that they conduct themselves before God with "simple, loving awareness, as when opening one's eyes with loving attention."[33] Loving attention to Jesus present in various ways at the eucharist would make it less likely that the consecrated bread and wine would be viewed as objects, even as sacred objects. Loving attention to one's sisters, brothers and strangers at the eucharist also precludes our viewing them as objects.

Jesus is present in the sacraments as he who died and rose for us. His presence is a personal presence. So must our presence be personal. The eucharist is a thanksgiving celebration of God's love for humankind manifested in creation and redemption. In the early church, meals known as love-feasts occurred with the eucharist but were separated from the eucharist for reasons that Paul and the letter of Jude attest (1 Cor 11; Jude 12). In this climate of presence, forgiveness, hospitality and love the assembly gathers to sing the song of praise that has long been the assembly's special song: "Holy holy holy, Lord God of power and might, heaven and earth are full of your glory."

An appreciation of the presence of Jesus in the eucharist will become more vivid for us who are gathered around the table of the Lord when we are more personally present to each other and when we exercise a warm hospitality and extend to each other mutual forgiveness.

The Retrieval of a Sense of Mystery

About the time of Vatican II, the scholar Christine Mohrmann told an audience at The Catholic University of America that the change from Latin to the vernacular in the liturgy might bring great comprehension but would raise a problem of another kind.

---

32. Thomas J. Reese, "In the Catholic Church, A Kiss Is Never Just a Kiss," *America* 172 (April 15, 1995) 12-19.

33. *The Living Flame of Love* 3.33, *The Collected Works of St. John of the Cross* 686.

Intelligibility would come, she said, at the loss of mystery. Professor Mohrmann's warning has come home to roost. We do not suggest a return to Latin, but we do suggest that the Christian community search its soul for what Peter Berger called a rumor of angels, a way of celebrating transcendent mystery.

First of all, suggestions made earlier in this chapter about the meals of Jesus, hospitality, forgiveness and presence are, in fact, ways of heightening an awareness that these seemingly human actions are, in fact, transcendent realities made so by the action of the Holy Spirit and the presence of Christ. Prayer and preaching can make these transcendent qualities better known to those who gather weekly for the eucharist.

The late Edward Kilmartin, a Jesuit from the Pontifical Oriental Institute in Rome, shared with Father David Power and others like Nathan Mitchell concern about the need for the development of an adequate theology of the eucharist that would help us celebrate more vibrantly the presence of the gracious mystery who is our God.[34] Kilmartin has suggested that we pay more attention to reflection on the way the church has prayed, especially on the eucharistic prayers, the *lex orandi* tradition.[35]

A common search for the mystery of the eucharist requires a more contemplative church that comes to the eucharist in a spirit of active waiting learned through the habit of meditation. Then, gathered at the eucharist, the assembly possesses a sense of awe that realizes that "the darkness shall be the light, and the stillness the dancing."[36]

While scholars like Power, Kilmartin and Mitchell have made suggestions for the retrieval of mystery, Catholic congregations must take responsibility for becoming a more contemplative church where mystery is honored. The eucharist cannot be renewed only from the top or by scholars. A grass-roots spirituality of the eucharist will emerge from a discipleship faithful to its biblical,

---

34. Edward J. Kilmartin, "The Catholic Tradition of Eucharistic Theology: Towards the Third Millennium," *Theological Studies* 55 (1994) 405-57; David N. Power, *The Eucharistic Mystery: Revitalizing the Tradition* (New York: Crossroad, 1992); Nathan Mitchell, "Who Is at the Table? Reclaiming Real Presence," *Commonweal* 122 (27 January 1995) 10-15.

35. Geoffrey Wainwright, *Doxology: The Praise of God in Worship, Doctrine and Life* (New York: Oxford University, 1980) chapters 7 and 8.

36. T. S. Eliot, "East Coker," *Four Quartets, The Complete Poems and Plays* 126.

patristic and liturgical roots. Preaching and teaching on this tradition in adult religious education classes will inspire a eucharistic spirituality open to the manifestation of divine presence. The eucharistic Christian lives and worships in the presence of Jesus.

Eucharist: A Way of Life

The eucharist makes the church present as a community worshiping the triune God. Those who live by faith in Jesus need no justification for participating in this worship. No sense of obligation is needed to bring believers to this celebration where they listen to the word of God, rejoice in the presence of Jesus, accept in love their sisters and brothers as well as strangers, partake of the body and blood of Jesus and are sent forth to carry out the mission of the Holy Spirit. However, eucharistic worship is not an isolated action unrelated to the rest of life. In other words, the eucharist has both a vertical and a horizontal dimension. Not only is the eucharist thankful worship, it is a gathering of the community of the disciples of Jesus. This is a community called to love one another as Jesus loves them (Jn 15:12). Eucharistic worship is a celebration which shapes the community's relationship to God and to one another. Is it not true that we celebrate as well as we live and we live as well as we celebrate? Eucharistic celebrations are for the sake of a eucharistic life in which we worship the Father and, like Jesus, become through the Holy Spirit bread and wine for a hungry and thirsty world. Thomas Aquinas called the eucharist "food for pilgrims."

Members of the assembly come to the eucharist as those who have been baptized into the dying and rising of Jesus (Rom 6:3-4; Col 2:12-13). At the eucharist Christians celebrate their incorporation into Christ so that, associated with Christ in the sacraments of initiation, they are shaped by the grace of Christ that they may grow with the life of Christ. At the eucharistic memorial of the death and resurrection of Jesus, Christians encounter Christ crucified. Like Paul they say: "I have been crucified with Christ; and it is no longer I who live, but it is Christ who lives in me. And the life I now live in the flesh I live by faith in the Son of God, who loved me and gave himself for me" (Gal 2:20).

This action of the grace of Christ in baptism, eucharist and confirmation makes the Christian another Christ who is called to be as Christ was, to live as Christ lived, to minister as Christ ministered:

The Spirit of the Lord is upon me because he has anointed me to bring good news to the poor. He has sent me to proclaim release to the captives and recovery of sight to the blind, to let the oppressed go free, to proclaim the year of the Lord's favor (Lk 4:18-19; see Is 61:1 and 2).

The Lord's supper is a celebration where love is the criterion of participation. Discrimination, selfishness, spiritual preening, injustices of any kind are anathema as we hear from Paul's first letter to the Corinthians. The ethics of the eucharist are the ethics of the cross since each celebration of the Lord's supper proclaims "the Lord's death until he comes" (1 Cor 11:2-34).

Redeemed and graced, the assembly is commissioned to be for others what Christ was for the women and men of his time. The assembly of disciples, having experienced the mysteries of the eucharist and having been nourished by his body and blood, are sent from the eucharist to the world as "ambassadors for Christ" (2 Cor 5:20). The assembly, "conformed to the image of his Son" (Rom 8:29), departs with this command and blessing: "Go in peace to love and to serve the Lord."[37]

Further Reading

Deiss, Lucien, *The Mass,* trans. L. Deiss and M. Driscoll (Collegeville: Liturgical Press, 1989). This is a brief commentary on the texts of the eucharist by a liturgical pioneer.

Foley, Edward, *From Age to Age: How Christians Celebrated the Eucharist,* illus. Robin Faulkner (Chicago: Liturgy Training Publications, 1991). For various historical eras Foley explores the architecture, music, books and vessels of the eucharist.

Hellwig, Monika, *The Eucharist and the Hunger of the World,* 2nd ed. (Kansas City: Sheed and Ward, 1992). Hellwig shows how a commitment to justice is central to a eucharist spirituality.

Nichols, Aidan, *The Holy Eucharist: From the New Testament to Pope*

---

37. One of the three dismissal options in the Roman liturgy of the mass approved for English speaking countries.

John Paul II (Dublin: Veritas, 1991). Nichols presents a history of eucharistic doctrine.

Nouwen, Henri J. M., *With Burning Hearts: A Meditation on the Eucharistic Life,* (Maryknoll: Orbis, 1994). Nouwen's small book offers reflections on a spiritual life rooted in the eucharist.

Exercises

1. *Make a list of what delights you most about celebrations, e.g. Thanksgiving Day, Christmas, birthdays, anniversaries, parties with friends. What is the downside of these celebrations? What can we do to improve the quality of our celebrations? What would make us a more festive people?*

2. *Read carefully the four major eucharistic prayers. They can be found in missalettes. List these prayers in your order of preference. What do you like about each of them? What do these prayers teach you about prayer?*

3. *Pick three or four of the meals of Jesus from the list in the appendix to this chapter. Note what these meals tell you about Jesus as a meal partner. Ask yourself what each meal tells you about participation in the eucharist.*

4. *Sketch a ground plan for a church building that expresses a Vatican II theology of baptism and eucharist. Annotate your sketch with comments that indicate your reasons for various aspects of your architectural plan.*

5. *What would you do to heighten the awareness at the eucharist of the mystery of Christ's presence—in word, in the assembly, in consecrated bread and wine and in the ministers?*

Appendix:
The Meals of Jesus: A Selection[38]

Meals Prior to Death and Resurrection of Jesus:

Lk 5:27-32. A meal at the home of Levi the tax collector.

Lk 7:33-34. "Look, a glutton and a drunkard, a friend of tax collectors and sinners." See Dt 21:18-21; Prv 23:20-21.

Lk 7:36-50. Meal at the home of Simon the Pharisee; forgiveness of a woman sinner.

Lk 10:38-42. Jesus a guest at Martha's home.

Lk 15:1-32. "This fellow welcomes sinners and eats with them." Contains the merciful father's celebration.

Lk 14:1-24: Meal on sabbath at home of a leader of the Pharisees. "Invite the poor, the crippled, the lame, and the blind."

Lk 19:1-10. A meal at the home of Zacchaeus, a rich chief tax collector. "Guest of one who is a sinner."

Mk 1:29-31. Simon Peter's mother-in-law serves Jesus and the disciples.

Jn 2:1-11: The wedding feast at Cana.

Jn 12:1-8. Mary anoints the feet of Jesus at dinner.

Multiplication of Loaves:

Mk 6:30-44; 8:1-10; Mt 26:26-29; Lk 22:14-20; Jn 6:1-14. Note how a eucharistic understanding is written into these events.

The Lord's Supper:

1 Cor 11:23-26; Lk 22:14-20; Mk 14:22-25; Mt 26:26-29. See Jn 6 and Jn 13–17.

Meals with the Risen Jesus:

Lk 24:13-35. Journey to Emmaus. Jesus is known in the breaking of bread.

Lk 24:36-43. Jesus eats broiled fish in the presence of the disciples.

Mk 16:14-15. Jesus appears to the eleven while they are at table.

Jn 21:9-14. On the beach Jesus says to the disciples: "Come and have breakfast."

Acts 10:40-41. "...who ate and drank with him after he rose from the dead."

---

38. Bibles with notes will guide one to parallel passages in other gospels.

Bibliography

Abbott and Gallagher, eds. *The Documents of Vatican II*. New York: America Press, 1966.

Achtenmeier, Paul, ed. *Harper's Bible Dictionary*. San Francisco: Harper and Row, 1985.

Aelred of Rievaulx. *The Mirror of Charity*. Trans. Elizabeth Connor. Kalamazoo: Cistercian Publications, 1990.

——. *Spiritual Friendship*. Trans. Mary Eugenia Laker. Kalamazoo: Cistercian Publications, 1977.

Albert's Way. Ed. Michael Mulhall. Barrington: Province of Most Pure Heart of Mary, 1989.

Allen, Diogenes. *Christian Romance, Marriage, Friendship*. Cambridge: Cowley, 1987.

Anselm, St. *The Prayers and Meditations of St. Anselm*. Trans. Benedicta Ward. Baltimore: Penguin, 1973.

Aristotle. *Nicomachean Ethics*. Trans. H. Rackham. Loeb Classical Library. Cambridge: Harvard University Press, 1956.

Armstrong, Regis, trans. *Francis and Clare: The Complete Works*. New York: Paulist Press, 1982.

Ashley, Benedict. *Spiritual Direction in the Dominican Tradition*. New York: Paulist Press, 1995.

Athanasius. *The Life of Antony and the Letter to Marcellinus*. Trans. Robert C. Gregg. New York: Paulist Press, 1980.

Ayo, Nicholas. *The Lord's Prayer*. Notre Dame: University of Notre Dame Press, 1992.

Bellah, Robert et al. *Habits of the Heart: Individualism and Commitment in American Life*. New York: Harper and Row, 1985.

Benedict, St. *RB 1980: The Rule of St. Benedict; In Latin and English with Notes*. Ed. Timothy Fry et al. Collegeville: Liturgical Press, 1981.

Bernard of Clairvaux, *On the Song of Songs*. 4 vols. Trans. Kilian

Walsh and Irene Edmonds. Kalamazoo: Cistercian Publications, 1971-1980.

Bonaventure, St. *The Soul's Journey into God, The Tree of Life, The Life of St. Francis.* Trans. Ewert Cousins. New York: Paulist Press, 1978.

Bonhoeffer, Dietrich. *The Cost of Discipleship.* Rev. ed. New York: Macmillan, 1963.

———. *Life Together.* London: SCM Press, 1954.

Brown, Peter. *The Body and Society: Men, Women and Sexual Renunciation in Early Christianity.* New York: Columbia University Press, 1988.

Brown, R.E., J.A. Fitzmeyer and R.E. Murphy, eds. *The New Jerome Biblical Commentary.* Englewood Cliffs: Prentice-Hall, 1990.

Burton-Christie, Douglas. *The Word in the Desert: Scripture and the Quest for Holiness in Early Christian Monasticism.* New York: Oxford University Press, 1993.

Bynum, Caroline W. *Holy Feast and Holy Fast: The Significance of Food to Medieval Women.* Berkeley: University of California Press, 1987.

Casey, Michael. *The Undivided Heart.* Petersham: St. Bede's Publications, 1994.

Cashen, R.A. *Solitude in the Thought of Thomas Merton.* Kalamazoo: Cistercian Publications, 1981.

Cassian, John. *Conferences.* Trans. Colm Luibheid. New York: Paulist Press, 1985.

Castelli, Jim, ed. *How I Pray.* New York: Ballantine, 1994.

Castle, Tony. The New Book of *Christian Prayers.* New York: Crossroad, 1986.

The Catechism of the Catholic Church. Vatican City: Libreria Editrice Vaticana, 1994.

Certeau, Michel de. *The Mystic Fable.* Vol. 1. Chicago: University of Chicago Press, 1992.

Chadwick, Owen, ed. and trans. *Western Asceticism: Selected Translations.* Philadelphia: Westminster Press, 1958.

Cicero. *Laelius (De Amicitia, On Friendship).* Trans. W.A. Falconer. Loeb Classical Library. London: Witteinemann, 1923.

Clare of Assisi, St. *Early Documents.* Ed. and trans. Regis Armstrong. New York: Paulist Press, 1988.

The Cloud of Unknowing and the Book of Privy Counselling. Ed. William Johnston. Garden City: Doubleday, 1973.

Congar, Yves. *The Word and the Spirit.* New York: Harper and Row, 1986.

Conn, Joann Wolski. *Spirituality and Christian Maturity.* New York: Paulist Press, 1989.

Conn, Walter E. *Christian Conversion.* New York: Paulist Press, 1986.

Cousins, Ewert, ed. *World Spirituality: An Encyclopedic History of the Religious Quest.* New York: Crossroad, 1985.

Cunningham, Lawrence S. *The Catholic Heritage.* New York: Crossroad, 1983.

———. *Catholic Prayer.* New York: Crossroad, 1989.

———, ed. *Thomas Merton: Spiritual Master.* New York: Paulist Press, 1992.

Daniel, Walter. *The Life of Aelred of Rievaulx.* Trans. F.M. Powicke. Kalamazoo: Cistercian Publications, 1994.

Deville, Raymond. *The French School of Spirituality.* Pittsburgh: Duquesne University Press, 1994.

Downey, Michael, ed. *The New Dictionary of Catholic Spirituality.* Collegeville: Liturgical Press, 1993.

Dreyer, Elizabeth A. *Earth Crammed With Heaven: A Spirituality of Everyday Life.* Mahwah: Paulist, 1994.

Dulles, Avery. *A Church To Believe In: Discipleship and the Dynamics of Freedom.* New York: Crossroad, 1982.

Dunne, John S. *The Way of All the Earth: Experiments in Truth and Religion.* New York: Macmillan, 1972.

Dupré, Louis and James Wiseman. *Light from Light: An Anthology of Christian Mysticism.* New York: Paulist Press, 1988.

Dupré, Louis and Don E. Saliers, eds. *World Spirituality.* Vol. 18. New York: Crossroad, 1989.

Early Christian Writings: The Apostolic Fathers. Trans. Maxwell Staniforth. Baltimore: Penguin, 1968.

Eckhart, Meister. *Meister Eckhart: The Essential Sermons.* Ed. Edmund Colledge and Bernard McGinn. New York: Paulist Press, 1981.

Egan, Harvey D. *Christian Mysticism: The Future of a Tradition.* New York: Pueblo, 1984.

Egan, Keith J. *A Praying Community of Friends.* Audio taped lectures. Canfield: Alba House, 1988.

———. *Solitude and Community: The Paradox of Life and Prayer.* 7 audio-cassette tapes. Kansas City, MO: Credence Cassettes, 1981.

———. *What Is Prayer?* Denville: Dimension Books, 1974.

Elgin, Duane. *Voluntary Simplicity.* New York: Bantam, 1982.

Eliade, Mircea. *The Sacred and the Profane.* New York: Harper Torchbook, 1961.

Eliot, T.S. *The Complete Poems and Plays, 1909-1950.* New York: Harcourt, Brace and World, 1962.

Ellacuria, Ignacio and Jon Sobrino, eds. *Mysterium Liberationis: Fundamental Concepts of Liberation Theology.* Maryknoll: Orbis, 1993.

Finley, James. *The Awakening Call.* Notre Dame: Ave Maria Press, 1984.

Fiske, Adele. *Friend and Friendship in the Monastic Tradition.* Cuernavaca: Civoc Cuaderno, 1970.

Foster, Richard J. *Prayer: Finding the Heart's True Home.* San Francisco: HarperSanFrancisco, 1992.

Francis of Assisi, St. *St. Francis of Assisi: Writings and Early Biographies: English Omnibus of the Sources for the Life of St. Francis.* Ed. Marion Habig; 3rd rev. ed. Chicago: Franciscan Herald Press, 1973.

Francis de Sales, St. *Introduction to the Devout Life.* Trans. John Ryan. New York: Harper Torchbooks, 1966.

Galilea, Segundo. *The Future of Our Past: The Spanish Mystics Speak to Contemporary Spirituality.* Notre Dame: Ave Maria Press, 1985.

Gallagher, Michael Paul. *Letters on Prayer.* London: Darton, Longman and Todd, 1994.

Gould, Graham. *The Desert Fathers on Monastic Community.* Oxford. Clarendon Press, 1993.

Gregory the Great, St. *Dialogues.* Trans. Odo J. Zimmerman. New York: Fathers of the Church, 1959.

Gregory of Nyssa. *From Glory to Glory: Texts from Gregory of Nyssa's Mystical Writings.* Introduction by Jean Daniélou. Trans. H. Musurillo. New York: Charles Scribner's Sons, 1961.

———. *The Life of Moses.* Trans. Malherbe/Ferguson. New York: Paulist Press, 1978.

Guigo II. *The Ladder of Monks: A Letter on the Contemplative Life and Twelve Meditations.* Trans. Edmund Colledge and James Walsh. Kalamazoo: Cistercian Publications, 1978.

Gutiérrez, Gustavo. *We Drink from Our Own Wells.* Maryknoll: Orbis, 1984.

Hart, Patrick, ed. *The Monastic Journey.* Garden City: Doubleday Image, 1978.

Haussherr, I. *The Name of Jesus.* Kalamazoo: Cistercian Publications, 1978.

Holladay, William. *The Psalms Through Three Thousand Years.* Minneapolis: Augsburg/Fortress, 1993.

Ignatius of Loyola. *The Spiritual Exercises and Selected Works.* Ed. George E. Ganss. New York: Paulist Press, 1991.

John of the Cross, St. *The Collected Works of St. John of the Cross.* Rev. ed. Trans. Kieran Kavanaugh and Otilio Rodriguez. Washington, DC: Institute of Carmelite Studies, 1991.

John Paul II. *Crossing the Threshold of Hope.* New York: Knopf, 1994.

Johnson, Luke Timothy. *Faith's Freedom: A Classic Spirituality for Contemporary Christians.* Minneapolis: Fortress/Augsburg, 1990.

Jones, C., G. Wainwright, and E. Yarnold, eds. *The Study of Liturgy.* Rev. ed. New York: Oxford University Press, 1992.

———. *The Study of Spirituality.* New York: Oxford University Press, 1986.

Jordan of Saxony. *To Heaven with Diana! A Study of Jordan of Saxony and Diana d'Andalo with a Translation of the Letters of Jordan.* Trans. Gerald Vann. Chicago: Henry Regnery, 1965.

Julian of Norwich. *Showings.* New York: Paulist Press, 1978.

Katz, Steven T., ed. *Mysticism and Religious Traditions.* New York: Oxford University Press, 1983.

Keating, Thomas. *Intimacy with God.* New York: Crossroad, 1994.

Kelty, Matthew. *Flute Solo: Reflections of a Trappist Hermit.* Garden City: Doubleday Image, 1980.

Knowles, David. *The Monastic Order in England.* 2nd ed. Cambridge: University Press, 1963.

Kurtz, Ernest and Katherine Ketcham. *The Spirituality of Imperfection.* New York: Bantam, 1992.

LaCugna, Catherine Mowry, ed. *Freeing Theology: The Essentials of Theology in Feminist Perspective.* San Francisco: Harper/Collins, 1993.

Lathrop, Gordon H. *Holy Things: A Liturgical Theology.* Minneapolis: Fortress, 1993.

Lawrence of the Resurrection. *Brother Lawrence of the Resurrection: On the Practice of the Presence of God.* Trans. S. Sciurba. Washington, DC: Institute of Carmelite Studies, 1994.

Leclercq, Jean. *The Love of Learning and the Desire for God.* 2nd ed. Trans. Catharine Misrahi. New York: Fordham University Press, 1974.

————, François Vandenbroucke and Louis Bouyer. *The Spirituality of the Middle Ages.* New York: Seabury, 1968.

Leech, Kenneth. *Soul Friend.* San Francisco: Harper and Row, 1977.

Lewis, C. S. *The Four Loves.* New York: Harcourt Brace Jovanovich, 1960.

Lossky, Vladimir. *The Mystical Theology of the Eastern Church.* London: James Clarke, 1957, 1968.

Louth, Andrew. *Denys the Areopagite.* Wilton: Morehouse-Barlow, 1989.

————. *The Origins of the Christian Mystical Tradition: From Plato to Denys.* Oxford: Clarendon, 1981.

————. *The Wilderness of God.* London: Darton, Longmann and Todd, 1992.

Macquarrie, John. *Paths in Spirituality.* 2nd ed. Harrisburg: Morehouse, 1992.

Main, John. *The Word into Silence.* New York: Paulist Press, 1980.

Maritain, Jacques. *Notebooks.* Trans. Joseph W. Evans. Albany: Magi Books, 1984.

Maritain, Raissa. *We Have Been Friends Together and Adventures in Grace: The Memoirs of Raissa Maritain.* 2 vols. Trans. Julie Kernan. Garden City: Image Books, 1961.

Martini, Carlo. *The Joy of the Gospel.* Collegeville: Liturgical Press, 1994.

Martz, Louis L. *The Meditative Poem.* Garden City: Doubleday, 1963.

————. *The Poetry of Meditation.* Garden City: Doubleday, 1954, 1963.

McFague, Sally. *Models of God: Theology for an Ecological, Nuclear Age.* Philadelphia: Fortress Press, 1987.

McGinn, Bernard. *The Presence of God: A History of Western Christian Mysticism.* Vol. I: *The Foundations of Mysticism.* Vol. II: *The Growth of Mysticism.* New York: Crossroad, 1991, 1994.

————, ed. *Meister Eckhart and the Beguine Mystics: Hadewijch of Brabant, Mechtild of Magdeburg, and Marguerite Porete.* New York: Continuum, 1994.

McGuire, Brian Patrick. *Aelred of Rievaulx: Brother and Lover.* New York: Crossroad, 1994.

————. *Friendship and Community: The Monastic Experience, 350-1250.* Kalamazoo: Cistercian Publications, 1988.

McNamara, Marie Aquinas. *Friends and Friendship for Saint Augustine.* Staten Island: Alba House, 1964.

Meilaender, Gilbert. *Friendship: A Study in Theological Ethics.* Notre Dame: University of Notre Dame Press, 1981.

Merton, Thomas. *Authentic Friendship.* Audio cassette. Kansas City: Credence Cassettes, n.d.

———. *The Collected Poems of Thomas Merton.* New York: New Directions, 1977.

———. *Conjectures of a Guilty Bystander.* Garden City: Doubleday Image, 1968.

———. *Disputed Questions.* New York: Farrar, Strauss and Cudahy, 1960.

———. *Honorable Reader: Reflections on My Work.* Ed. by Robert E. Daggy. New York: Crossroad, 1989.

———. *New Seeds of Contemplation.* New York: New Directions, 1962.

———. *The Sign of Jonas.* New York: Harcourt Brace, 1953.

———. *Thoughts in Solitude.* Garden City: Image Doubleday, 1958.

Metz, Johannes B. *Followers of Christ.* New York: Paulist Press, 1978.

Miles, Margaret. *Fullness of Life: Historical Foundations for a New Asceticism.* Philadelphia: Westminster, 1981.

Mulholland, M. Robert. *Invitation to a Journey: A Road Map for Spiritual Formation.* Downers Grove: IVP, 1993.

Norris, Kathleen. *Dakota: A Spiritual Geography.* New York: Ticknor and Fields, 1993.

Origen. *An Exhortation to Martyrdom, Prayer, First Principles: Book IV, Prologue to the Commentary on the Song of Songs, Homily XXVII on Numbers.* Trans. Rowan Greer. New York: Paulist Press, 1979.

———. *The Song of Songs, Commentary and Homilies.* Trans. R.P. Lawson. Ancient Christian Writers Series. New York: Newman/Paulist, 1957.

Pennington, Basil. *Centering Prayer.* New York: Doubleday, 1980.

Petroff, Elizabeth, ed. *Body and Soul: Essays on Medieval Women and Mysticism.* New York: Oxford University Press, 1994.

———. *Medieval Women's Visionary Literature.* New York: Oxford University Press, 1986.

Pope, Marvin. *Song of Songs: A New Translation with Introduction and Commentary.* Anchor Bible Series. Garden City: Doubleday, 1977.

Principe, Walter. *Thomas Aquinas' Spirituality.* Toronto: Pontifical Institute of Medieval Studies, 1984.

Pseudo-Dionysius. *Pseudo-Dionysius: The Complete Works*. Trans. Colm Luibheid. New York: Paulist Press, 1987.

Rahner, Karl. *Theological Investigations*. Vol. VII. Trans. David Bourke. New York: Herder and Herder, 1971.

Raitt, Jill, ed. *World Spirituality*. Vol. 17. New York: Crossroad, 1987.

Richard of St. Victor. *The Twelve Patriarchs, The Mystical Ark, Book Three of the Trinity*. Trans. Grover Zinn. New York: Paulist Press, 1979.

Ripple, Paula. *Called To Be Friends*. Notre Dame: Notre Dame University Press, 1980.

Rouner, Leroy S., ed. *The Changing Face of Friendship*. Notre Dame: University of Notre Dame Press, 1994.

The Sayings of the Desert Fathers: The Alphabetical Collection. Trans. Benedicta Ward. Kalamazoo: Cistercian Publications, 1975.

Schimmel, Annemarie. *Mystical Dimensions of Islam*. Chapel Hill: University of North Carolina Press, 1975.

Schneiders, Sandra M. *The Revelatory Text: Interpreting the New Testament as Sacred Scripture*. San Francisco: HarperCollins, 1991.

Segovia, Fernando. *Discipleship in the New Testament*. Philadelphia: Fortress, 1985.

Shank, L.T. and J.A. Nichols, eds. *Peaceweavers*. Vol. 2 of *Medieval Religious Women*. Kalamazoo: Cistercian Publications, 1987.

Shannon, William. *Seeking the Face of God*. New York: Crossroad, 1990.

———. *Silence on Fire: The Prayer of Awareness*. New York: Crossroad, 1994.

Sheldrake, Philip. *Befriending Our Desires*. Notre Dame: Ave Maria Press, 1994.

———. *Spirituality and History: Questions of Interpretation and Method*. New York: Crossroad, 1992.

Spidlik, Tomas. *The Spirituality of the Christian East*. Trans. A.P. Gythiel. Kalamazoo: Cistercian Publications, 1986.

Stanley, David. *Jesus in Gethsemane*. New York: Paulist Press, 1980.

Teresa of Avila, St. *The Collected Works of St. Teresa of Avila*. 3 vols. Trans. Kieran Kavanaugh and Otilio Rodriguez. Washington DC: Institute of Carmelite Studies, 1976, 1980, 1985.

———. *The Letters of Saint Teresa of Jesus*. 2 vols. Trans. E. Allison Peers. London: Sheed and Ward, 1951, 1980.

Thompson, William M. *The Jesus Debate: A Survey and Synthesis.* Mahwah: Paulist, 1985.

Tracy, David. *On Naming the Present.* Maryknoll: Orbis, 1994.

Tugwell, Simon. *Early Dominicans: Selected Writings.* New York: Paulist, 1982.

Underhill, Evelyn. *Mysticism.* New York: World Publishing, 1955.

Vicaire, M.-H. *Saint Dominic and His Times.* New York: McGraw-Hill, 1964.

Wadell, Paul J. *Friends of God: Virtues and Gifts in Aquinas.* New York: Peter Lang, 1991.

———. *Friendship and the Moral Life.* Notre Dame: University of Notre Dame Press, 1989.

Warren, Ann K. *Anchorites and Their Patrons in Medieval England.* Berkeley: University of California Press, 1985.

Welty, Eudora and Ronald A. Sharp, eds. *The Norton Book of Friendship.* New York: W. W. Norton, 1991.

White, Carolinne. *Christian Friendship in the Fourth Century.* Cambridge: Cambridge University Press, 1992.

Wiethaus, Ulrike, ed. *Maps of Flesh and Light: The Religious Experience of Medieval Women Mystics.* Syracuse: Syracuse University Press, 1993.

Williams, Rowan. *Teresa of Avila.* Harrisburg: Morehouse, 1991.

Wimmer, J. *Fasting in the New Testament: A Study In Biblical Theology.* Mahwah: Paulist Press, 1982.

The Wisdom of the Desert: Sayings of the Desert Fathers of the Fourth Century. Trans. Thomas Merton. New York: New Directions, 1960.

The Wisdom of the Desert Fathers: The 'Apothegmata Patrum' (The Anonymous Series). Trans. Benedicta Ward. Oxford: SLG Press, 1975.

Wittgenstein, Ludwig. *Notebooks 1914-1916.* New York: Oxford University Press, 1961.

World Council of Churches, ed. *The World at Prayer.* Mystic: Twenty-Third Publications, 1990.

Wright, John. *A Theology of Christian Prayer.* 2nd ed. New York: Pueblo, 1988.

Wright, Wendy M. *Bond of Perfection: Jeanne de Chantal and Francis de Sales.* New York: Paulist, 1985.

Young, Frances. *Virtuoso Theology: The Bible and Interpretation.* Cleveland: Pilgrim, 1993.

Index